THE EARLY YEARS
Volume I

Now, We Begin

Jeshua

Copyright © 2019 by Audio Enlightenment Press All rights reserved. No part of this publication may be reproduced, distributed, or transmitted in any form or by any means, including photocopying, recording, or other electronic or mechanical methods, without the prior written permission of the publisher, except in the case of brief quotations embodied in critical reviews and certain other non-commercial uses permitted by copyright law. Printed in the United States of America

0 1 2 3 4 5 6 7 8 9

First Printing, December 2019
ISBN 978-1-941489-46-8

WayofMastery.com

WayofMasteryBooks.com

Kindle/ePub / Audiobooks
Available on WayofMasteryBooks.com

First "AudioEnlightenmentPress.Com" Printing
December 2019

CONTENTS

Foreword .... *vii*

Awakening 11

Choose to See 61

Death Earth Changes 87

Decide to be Christ 113

Grace as Reality 137

Healing 185

Heaven on Earth 227

Ignorance is Bliss 259

Joy I 277

Joy II 307

Foreword

The book you hold in your hand is a transcription of channelings given by Jeshua to public groups from the early years of my work with Him. These teachings are an extensive collection of Jeshua's wisdom, a vital part of *The Way of Mastery Pathway*, and are available here for the first time in book form.

As recounted in *The Jeshua Letters*, after my more personal initial communion with Jeshua, a new period of my studentship and work with Him shifted to a more public stage.

From 1988, until the time He began the three year course of *The Way of Mastery: The Christ Mind Trilogy* in 1994, He asked that I remain surrendered to Him. This included stepping into this more public role of channeling for groups, something I was very uncomfortable with to start with!

Regardless, however, as word got out, groups would increasingly gather at my home in Tacoma, Washington, and invitations, taking me farther and farther afield, came in as well. All this requiring that I surrender further and further to a process I did not understand at all!

This began with a first group gathering, in which He lifted me out of my body (or what I have come to see as 'the body'), and then entered into it to communicate with those in attendance.

I refer to this stage as the beginning of the 'channeling' phase of my work with Him, although it important for the reader to understand what is meant by that phrase. Here is what would always happen: I would close my eyes and initiate a simple prayer He had given me to do, and I would feel myself dropping into a deeply meditative space. Then, a peculiar vibration would begin, increasing, and I would be transported out, and above the body; I could see it below, along with the crowd gathered, as well as a circle of light beings fully encircling the group.

Things would accelerate, and I would experience a rapid movement through multi-colored light. I could witness the crowd, and then the house in which the crowd sat, and then further, wider, "telescoping" out until I could see planet Earth herself, and then rapidly even the physical universe itself would vanish, even as the pulsing, vibrating colored light increased!

Then, it would stop, and I would be aware of being with Jeshua, now together with Him in a field of Light. He would teach me while I was there with Him, and yet…while all this was occurring, He was also moving into, and teaching through, 'my body' to the group gathered together!

At some point, He would tell me, 'It is finished now'. I would begin to feel a kind of vibrational change, and the reverse of the journey ensued until I 'zoomed' downward and landed - often with a kind of shock - in the body. It would often take as much as 30 minutes for me to be able to move a finger, or begin to make any sound as I slowly regained adaptation to the body.

After, it would be so charged with energy that I often would be up for hours, yet in an altered state. Everything shimmered in light, and often objects like buildings, trees, telephone poles, and more, were transparent. I could see right through them! After, it would be so charged with energy that I often would be up for hours, yet in an altered state. Everything shimmered in light, and often objects like buildings, trees, telephone poles, and more, were transparent. I could see right through them!

Foreword

One night, I was very sick with a fever and strep throat, and was 'so sure' the evening should be cancelled. He assured me there would be no problem, and – to everyone's shock – as I 'left' and Jeshua entered, I was told later that suddenly there was no trace at all of my sickness!!

Indeed, after returning, I experienced the body radiating in clarity and perfect health, only then to gradually feel it 'sink' as we all know of as the strep throat returned! When I asked Him what had happened, he replied:

'I would suggest that to be a very good question for you to dwell in. Why has what you call 'sickness' returned?'

It is the type of question He lovingly asks, yet it is apparent He is bringing attention and contrast as to why one might use the body for such a thing as sickness, which, apparently, His use of the body did not include!

The Way of Mastery: The Early Years (volumes I & II) transcriptions of these gatherings, originally recorded live, capture what Jeshua taught us all in these beautiful gatherings. The wisdom, guidance, and sheer brilliance of them is astounding; there is so much in these pages, dear reader, that will help you grow in understanding, support you to truly heal into peace, and more!

You might like to know this as well. Jeshua shared that while this mystical alchemy I was undergoing was part of my studentship, it was also His learning curve in acclimating to 'my' body, as well as merging with and learning to utilize the language structure of its 'brain-mind.'

Indeed, the first phases of this period would find Him often communicating in a slow, monotone voice, with no movement of the body at all. Gradually, over time, He could animate it, and seemed to enjoy using my American idioms that He has accessed through this process as well!

Our interactions were varied and amusing. I would often feel His presence as I, for example, watched a bit of television, and he would make comments of the shows and even commercials. He said He was learning of my world through the part of my soul fixated, and operating through, the body, that tiny thing which I was still mistakenly thinking to be 'me'!

The Early Years are filled with ancient wisdom, timeless Love, and even prophecy. In opening to this wonderful trove of material from Jeshua, may you enjoy these jewels that He has given us all!

Blessings to you,
Jayem

December, 2019

Awakening

Now, we begin.

Indeed, once again, greetings unto you, beloved and holy children of Light divine. In Truth, once again I come forth to shower my blessings upon you; and yet I can do nothing but shower those blessings upon you which *you* would choose to receive. Therefore, my giving them to you is *your* giving to yourself. And I do not say that lightly though, indeed, it is given in Light.

For in Truth that which I have given unto you is your own giving to yourself. It must mean that everything I have ever represented to the consciousness of mankind is in you now. And that which was once called the incarnation or the Word made flesh, when it is said that God came and dwelt among us, that must have been your gift to yourself.

How can that be? For you believe that you have perhaps been born in this body for a short time and, if you are lucky, have a good time and then the body will degenerate and you will experience something called death. And the one that was known as Jeshua ben Joseph is said to have been here some two thousand years ago.

How could that incarnation have been a gift to myself?

Quite simply, you are not the body and you are not the personality. What you are transcends all space and all time, and all lives that have ever been lived arise within *you*. And in this drama, this scheme of space and time, even as you have all together as one mind chosen the perception that you are separate from God and therefore separate from one another — so too, as you have been the creator of your world in error, you have been the creator of the form of salvation. And every master and every teacher that has come and given you grand words or brought healing to you, or inspired the heart to look beyond its limitations, each and every one of them has but come as a reflection created by the soul you are, to mirror back to the conscious mind the Truth that necessarily lies within you. And that Truth is not difficult to find. It is not far from you. It is not far from you. Indeed, the Kingdom of Heaven can be no further than the distance of a single choice.

How then to rediscover that Truth? To touch that place that some of you believe that I mirrored so perfectly? How could you see that perfection if you did not already know that that perfection is in you?

How then to rediscover that Truth? Not by striving. Not by seeking. Not by mastering a plethora of techniques. But by wanting above all things—*by wanting above all things*— to become, once again, the Thought of perfect Love in form. To be willing to release every perception you have cherished because once upon a time in your long journey you thought it would make you safe or bring you some greater good. To be willing to give each day back to God. To be willing to become innocent. To set aside and imagine what it would be like if in each day you were to set aside every and each perception you held about what reality is, about where you came from, about what your purpose and function is, about what the brother or sister in front of you means.

To abide in an innocence and a faith that trusts what appears to be unseen, and be willing to allow that unseen love to guide your moment to moment, to teach you anew until each and every perception that has been created in error has been released as a veil from before your mind, before your heart. And then you will not see what you have created. You will see

Awakening

what you have always been. And you will know that there is no such thing as separation, and time and space cannot be a barrier between minds that are joined in love.

To be the Thought of Love in form is to choose to incarnate Christ. Not to wait for another to do it. Not to hope that it has already been done two thousand years ago so you can skip around the corners, but rather to choose to allow your life, what you call "my life" to be transformed—gently perhaps, a moment at a time; and at times not so gently—you call those major breakthroughs. The only reason it feels so major is the thing that you are releasing is something you have been holding on to for so long that you couldn't comprehend being without it. And yet, it has only been a perception— something so flimsy, so thin that it holds no power and does not distort the Light that comes to your soul. But you have looked upon it as something to be cherished and treasured and have made it part of yourself, and have believed that it holds a power to keep you separate from God, or that you have needed it to remain safe in an unsafe world. And that is most interesting because the perception that you abide in an unsafe world is just that—a perception—and it, too, must be released.

Therefore, precious and holy friends—and I do say friends, you who were created with me before time is—you are eternal and unbounded, and within you and before you and all around you lies that wisdom that is available to you in every moment and with every decision you believe you must make. But what seems to be so difficult is the habit of the mind that has believed itself to have been separate from God and must make its own way. It must be the grand maker and doer. It must cling to certain perceptions about what life is and how it ought to be lived. That little habit cannot believe that it could be so simple; and yet it is. And there is no one in this room who in this moment cannot be crucified, dead and buried in the mind, resurrected and ascended to join in perfect union with the Mind of God. It is available to you now.

And all that is ever asked of you is that you make the simple choice to be at peace. To relinquish, to let go of your striving, your grasping, your anxieties, your fears, your doubts. And therefore to begin—and I mean begin every day, until it becomes the beginning of every moment—to begin in the recognition that in reality,

> *I and my Father are one, now.*

Not in the future. Not in a distant past that I somehow managed to throw away by accident with the garbage. But now, right here and right now.

There is nowhere to go and nothing to achieve save to use the power given unto you to acknowledge:

> *I and my Father are one. And I walk in a safe world. And as I walk, that One walks with me, and I walk only in Love, and each step I take takes me into the extension of Love. And I choose to*
>
> *think only loving thoughts. And when my mind is given to memories, I choose only loving memories and I release the rest because everything that has not been loving has been born of illusions of fear.*

Can you imagine what it would be like to live one day in which each step you take, you feel it? And each thought you think, you witness it and you are with it? No more idle thoughts just running about in the mind—but you direct them wholly from that place in you that is Love. What would it be like to begin from this moment and to allow yourself to recognize that no matter what the circumstances seem to be around you, you

Awakening

hold the power to be the presence of the peace of God? What would it be like to live one day, just one day, in which everyone you thought of, everyone you looked upon, you embrace totally with the Love of Christ and did not let a single perception of your own making boomerang on you, to create in you the illusion of the belief that another could hold the power to change your countenance? What would that be like?

And if you can accomplish one day in that manner, rest assured that when you rest your head on the pillow that night, it will be Christ that is going to sleep. One day without a negative or fearful thought. And then indeed you touch that which is eternal, that which has been within you since before time is, has never been tainted, cannot be taken from you. You touch reality.

Now, there have been many that have begun the spiritual path, many that would even seek to follow me — though I would prefer that they follow themselves — and when they begin to discover that awakening isn't going to bring great brass bands to play for you, your neighbors might not even notice it, you may not wake up with winning lottery numbers in your head, you may not even transcend what is perceived as illness in the physical body, that just perhaps it is not quite what you thought the journey would be... Many throw in the towel and say,

> *Well there's nothing to all of that. I might as well go back to the way I was. Perhaps the thrill is yet around the corner.*

When that takes place, remember it is the voice of the ego that does not want you to awaken, for when you choose to awaken, its purpose has been completed and you will put it away as a child puts away an old toy now outgrown.

Awakening is a simple affair. Being awake is a simple affair.

First understand that you *are* awake now — *you are awake, now* — and there is no one in this room but Christ. Yes, there seems to be the appearance of many bodies, but underneath them and just behind them there lies a Love, a Love that is available to you whenever you choose. A Love that throws open the shutters of the heart so wide that you feel your arms could embrace the whole of creation, and you smile no matter who you think about or look upon. You cannot help but smile because you have chosen to be awakened from the dream of the dreamer himself, or herself. You have chosen to just relinquish the grand drama that would lead you to feel that if you hold onto anxiety that it gives life some purpose.

Eventually you will give up the grandiose notion that you must do great things in this world in order to be happy, and you will become happiness itself. And when you become happiness itself, rest assured that grand things will be done through you. Because you are like a Light that just dances in this plane and wherever you are — and I mean this as deeply and profoundly as I can — wherever you are, miracles are taking place in the minds and hearts of those who encounter you. You may not see them visibly but rest assured they are occurring.

Because when you choose to be that Happiness with a capital "H" — not an egoistic happiness but just Happiness, the love from which creation has come forth — right where you are, every mind that encounters you witnesses that Light. How it chooses to react to it is its own choice, but the Light is seen, and when Light has been seen it seeps in and begins to work its miracles. And it may be next week, it might be next year, it could be next lifetime, but that mind will begin to be attracted to the Light it experienced through you. And that is why I have often said to you — and please, please take it deep within your heart: There is no such thing as separation, and the thoughts you choose to hold within yourself affect the whole of creation.

Awakening

Are you then your brother's keeper? Yes. Not out of moral sanction, moral duty. You are your brother's keeper for the simple Truth that you are your brother. And the thought you choose to hold will allow your brother redemption or damnation—to use those kinds of terms—to experience a movement toward freedom or to feel held back. That is the responsibility you have and it's not a burden. It can be done very lightly since you are the presence of Light itself.

Does all of that begin to make sense to you?

Good. Then we are just going to sit here and bring a lot of Light to this world. Are you ready to do that?

Yes.

Remember that right here, right now, though you hear a voice

that seems to come through something called a body, a bag of dust, and that indeed a mind that was associated with one known as Jeshua ben Joseph seems to be directing those words, remember what I said when we began: you are only hearing and seeing a reflection of the Truth you are. Which means you are talking with yourself, right now. And there is only one Mind here if you choose to acknowledge only Christ. Therefore, allow the eyes to close for just a moment. Imagine that by so doing you are turning away from the roar and the din of the world, choosing to relinquish how you may have perceived this day. And with the eyes closed, allow the angel of the breath to move through the cells of the body like a gentle stream of golden light, unlimited forever, given to you freely and eternally, as though you could ride on the crest of that golden Light, that breath. For is it not written that God breathed into man the breath of life? That is how close you are right now to the One Who has created all of us. And with each inbreath you are receiving life eternal and with each outbreath allow that golden Light to be extended beyond the form that you think you are, like rays from the sun that reach out to every corner of the universe.

Allow images perhaps to come into your perception of ancient friends, family members, children, lovers, enemies. Imagine that you could allow the whole of mankind to come into your inner view and still the rays of your Light shine all around them, envelop them and penetrate them. See them becoming that Light itself. But do not strive at this, allow it. Feel the beauty and the simplicity and the joy of embracing the whole of creation with the love that you are. That love is eternal and unbounded and there is not a single obstacle that can impede the extension of your love.

Witness within yourself, creation becoming that Light. See other minds awakening and remembering. And think not it is your imagination for you cannot imagine what you have not experienced somewhere along the way. Begin to feel that joy ever deeper and deeper as you see creation awaken to the Light of its only reality. Feel that joy as though it can begin to lift you out of your chair. Feel gratitude and beauty. Say "yes" to that Light. Indeed.

And if yet you think there is a single shadow left within you, right now turn it over to that Light. Just turn it over. If it's a fear, a doubt, an old hurt, turn it over. It can no longer serve you to hold it. Every chain that has been upon you melted and dissolved. Light of very Light. Truth of all Truths. And the Light grows brighter and brighter and brighter, more and more radiant.

And every solar system is enveloped in your love, and it is expanding to touch even other dimensions that are not physical at all. Embrace them. Embrace all beings upon them. Imagine that you could embrace every master that has ever been. For some of you that communicate with masters on other planes, embrace *them* with the Love you are and see that they have arisen within *your* beauty and *your* Truth.

And look now upon all dimensions and all worlds and all time frames that have ever been and every brother or sister you have ever known — and you have known all of them — and feel the meaning of these words as yours:

> *I am one with all of life. I am one with my Creator and I embrace every aspect of creation as myself. For I have learned the only lesson I have ever needed to learn: that there is nothing outside of me.*

And then in your own way, abiding in that Light, simply feel the energy of eternal gratitude . . . eternal gratitude:

> *I am that Light. I am that Light. As it was in the beginning, is now, and forever shall be. And being that Light, I choose freely — freely — to begin to take on the appearance of a single personality, a single mind. And I will don the cloak of what seems to be but one body and I will choose this time frame on a planet known as Earth, and I am the Light that becomes that form that I would call "myself." But from this moment forward I will utilize that vehicle for no other purpose than to extend the infinite Love that I am, and to give it to this world.*

Coming down then, beginning to feel the flesh of the body. Delight in it. It is not your prison. It holds no power over you. It is a vehicle through which Christ can communicate. And begin now, as though for the first time, to allow the eyes to open. And as they do, look around you. Who do you see that you do not know and love? Welcome to this moment of a rather interesting drama called "space and time." And you, the Word of God, have just chosen incarnation. I would call it rebirth, and that rebirth will continue to be the foundation of everything you do unless and until you choose to reach back into an illusion and bring back to yourself a perception of lack, of limitation, of fear, of guilt. It is not just an exercise that bides your time. It is your own reality remembered.

What do you think, Firewalker? How does it feel to be incarnated as the Word made flesh?

It feels like it is the only game in town.

Have you tried others? Anyone here tried out a few games that didn't quite work out well?

Freedom, indeed, can be expressed whenever you remember that you are not the doer or the maker of your experience and you don't need to be — and thank God for that. But you can be that one who learns to live without effort and without planning, as your world would see planning, if you become one who begins each day remembering who you are, opening like a flower to the Light that is in you and allowing that Light to be your teacher and your guide. It really doesn't matter what words you use. It's the feeling and the knowingness that matters.

In my language that identifies me relative to the time that I walked among you, I would simply say:

> *Holy Father, what would You have this day be for? I am Your child and therefore I am Your servant, for I know that where I walk, you walk with me and nothing is impossible to me. For of myself I could never do anything, but You, Holy Father, through me, can do all things. All I need to do is to be out of Your way. And each time I choose to be the presence of Love, I have given up*

Awakening

the illusion of separation and You can live through me. This world can bring nothing to me of value. Not a single thing. Not an object. Not a bank account. There is nothing here that holds any true value for me.

Therefore, there is nothing that I can draw to myself, but there is everything that I can give to this world, for I have tasted of the only thing that holds value: Love. Just Love. Just Love. Just Love. Love is all things. Love embraces all things, allows all things, trusts all things, celebrates all things; and continually gives itself away.

And the arisen Christ lives each day, though in the appearance of a body — or so it would appear to others — knowing that there is not one thing this world can do to tempt you. There is nothing in it that can bring you happiness or fulfillment because you as the arisen Christ have realized it is only in the giving and extension of the infinite Love you are that you can receive what you have prayed for.

So that makes it, you see, very, very simple. You don't need fourteen hours a day of burning a certain kind of incense. You don't need seventy-two years to wait for the tape to change. You don't have to wait for seventy-two years in terms of learning some foreign language filled with an infinite number of chants. You don't have to learn how to direct energy into your body. *There is nothing you have to do to be who you are.* Nothing. Not one single thing you have to do.

None of it will bring love to you but, rather miraculously, when you simply decide to do nothing but give your love away — to be only love no matter what other minds may choose to be or what game they may choose to play — you will find that what you have been seeking to get from the world all this time is yours now. And then indeed miracles will begin and life can begin to shift and change, because what you experience can only be the result of what you insist on perceiving and believing in.

If you believe there is lack as you perceive it in your life, it must and can only be because somewhere previously you believed that lack could exist. Or perhaps worse, that it must exist for you.

> *How could I be unlimited?*

And when you begin to acknowledge the Truth of who you are, that alone is when you create a new vibration that changes everything.

Does that make sense to you?

If you seek to grow and believe that you are in lack, and you've got to work and strive to learn all the techniques so you can become plentiful and abundant, have you ever noticed that it seems to take forever?

But Jeshua, that's what almost all of us learned from our parents. So you could say, almost from infancy onward we were taught that. Yes, and I know that you've just been a victim of others. Hmm? Beloved friend, it doesn't matter. Understand this well: every time you use the word "but" what you are really saying is,

> *I choose to resist my unlimitedness now and I will find some way to explain why where I am must continue.*

Does that make sense to you? Do not blame your parents. Do not blame your great- great-grandparents. Do not blame your government. There isn't anybody to blame. There is just

Awakening

everybody to love.

I didn't really feel as I was blaming anyone when I said that. My meaning was only: no wonder it comes as such a surprise to us that our thoughts create our abundance. It's not surprising that it is a big surprise to a lot of people.

Reality seems shocking when you begin to see it.

Right.

But, precious friend, look and understand what I am talking about here: the power of the mind right now. As soon as the thought entered the mind,

> *But we've been taught this,*

you have turned your attention to a perception that somehow others have affected where you are now. And what I am trying to share with you is that *there is no one at any time who has not chosen moment by moment which perceptions they will take and make their own.*

If it were true that you are formed, let's say, by your parents, by your educational systems, it would mean that people who have similar experiences — let us say being born into a ghetto and nine hundred and ninety-nine out of a thousand of them become addicted to drugs and one becomes a world leader, a teacher, a doctor — if it were true that all were affected by their environment, there would not be a doctor that would arise out of that thousand. Each brings about their experience by the choice that is made in the mind in each and every moment.

> *The greatest lesson that you must learn is that you are free now. The power is now — not tomorrow — to insist on choosing to live*

only in unlimitedness, only in vision, and only in the present and not in the past. It is the only time healing can come. The only time.

Therefore, precious friend, as you are learning, learn well: there can never be such a thing as an idle thought. Never. You are choosing to indulge in an illusion that has limited you before and will continue as long as you choose to hold it within your mind.

That is why I have said to you that vigilance is so critical. Vigilance. What am I choosing to think, now? Some of you indeed would laugh and chuckle because perhaps you have cursed at the person that runs the stop light in front of you. There is no such thing as an idle thought, and though you may think you are doing it in jest, your body is responding to your judgment and all the chemistry in it has changed immediately to respond to negative thought. And the thought you think is not separate from all other minds. It is so critical to play at choosing only loving and unlimited thoughts and to learn how to abide in (what we will call here) that frequency, constantly.

That is the only way you can awaken the Light that you may perceive as yet dormant within you: to practice in every moment to be that Light. It's the only way anything changes, you see. It's the only way Heaven can return to Earth: for you to choose, with me, to think only thoughts that are unlimited.

Does that make sense to you?

And, you see, that's the great power. That's the gift given unto you — that no matter what has happened in the past, no matter what thoughts you have held, no matter what actions you have done, no matter what anybody's done, what your Father extends to you in every moment is the freedom to think anew, now. Right now. And though you might not see it, every time you have had a negative thought, if you would look back at perhaps a two or three year period or a lifetime, whatever you want to look back upon, and see it as a time of heartache or struggling or loss or what have you, it doesn't matter, all you are doing is looking at a movie that you have brought with you. The experience has already been dissolved in Light.

That is called Love. You could say that your Father is like a grand street sweeper, and though your horses seem to leave a little muck and mire in the street, He comes right behind you and sweeps away all of its effects and waits only for you to understand that there isn't anything to feel guilt over, nothing to bring a heaviness upon your countenance, because the past has already been washed away — it no longer exists.

And when mankind chooses to stop writing history books, it will begin to understand that the future is present now, dependent only on what thoughts are chosen now.

> *Well, we've got to keep our armaments up, because, you see, there have been wars. You hurt me once. I remember. It may have been last week. It may have been ten thousand years ago, but I remember and I am not about ready to forgive you.*

And then you can't understand why there is something in you that doesn't feel forgiven.

You are your brother; and with what measure that you mete unto them, so, too, shall it be meted unto you. That's how it works. Does it mean that if you judge another, somebody is going to come along with something called karma and hit you over the head? You have already done it to yourself. And when you hit yourself over the head, you then prove to yourself, *I must only deserve being hit over the head.* Yes, it's a tough world.

Do you begin to see how it all weaves together? It's so important. Give your forgiveness to the world wholly and as quickly as you can. Let everybody off the hook—you know, all of those beings that you have hung on the hook in your basement?

Good, you are going to stay right there and I am going to remember.

Let them all go. Release them from their cross. Let them go. For as you release your brother, you have released yourself. There is no other way.

When fear seems to come up to prevent you from doing something, remember it's not even your thought. It's an echo of a past that has already been dissolved. And if there is a phone call you have been waiting to make, if there is a presentation you have been wanting to do, if there is an old friend that you have just been missing, if there is a job you want to apply for, by all means go and do it. It's just a drama. That's all it is. You've been playing a game and you took it seriously, and part of the game has been the creation of guilt and pain and suffering and limitation and lack. And right here, right now, you can choose to put a new game piece on the board. You can choose to live unlimitedness and you don't even have to know how to do it. That's the great thing. Does not a loving parent take their child and say,

Here, I will show you how to cross the street.

Your Father will show you how to cross this universe. You don't have to know how to do it. All you need to do is give Him your willingness, no matter what. It is called throwing in the towel of separation and understanding that your will is your Father's will.

Awakening

For there are many of you in this room who have felt the desire for abundance—what we will call here material abundance—and yet, you have blocked it at every turn because somewhere you have perceived that it is not really good to desire material abundance. That is just a thought in your head. Throw it out the window.

Heaven waits. Heaven itself waits on your acceptance, and your brother waits on your acceptance for him of the Heaven that lies within you both. Heaven waits on your acceptance. What if indeed you are the one? What if you are the one that holds the key? You are what they would call the one hundredth monkey? And if *you* choose to adopt that new perception, then suddenly in the twinkling of an eye the whole of mankind will sit up and go,

My goodness gracious, there's no one here but Christ.

What if you were that one? Please join me in not waiting any longer for somebody else to do it. That is the whole essence of the Second Coming of Christ—your choice to turn the key to the Kingdom of Heaven that dwells within you, and to understand you don't have to know how to walk around as a living Christ. All you need is to be willing to ask before every decision and you will have the guidance that you require. And some of you indeed can join me now and can see that as I speak those words—I do not so much see bodies, by the way, I don't find them to be very interesting—but those words met a certain resistance in some because it means giving up the game. It means assuming complete responsibility for every feeling you have; and realizing completely that there is no one outside of you who can affect you unless you allow it. When your Light so shines before men, before mankind, that its radiance cannot be limited, you will then know and understand—to use some Biblical words, since some people seem to like them still—that though you walk through the valley of the shadow of death, you need fear no evil. The rod and the staff of the Love of God is in you, within you, and around you—always. And there is no one there in that valley save yourself, the face of a brother or sister who asks *you* to help them awaken from the dream.

Now, how do you do that? Well, of course, you slap them around a few times and tell them to wake up. No, you don't fix anybody. You can't fix anybody. It's impossible. All you can do is be what you would choose to teach them. That's it.

And allow them to choose to see the Christ in you. For to do so will mean that they must have begun to recognize that Christ in them, too, because only Christ can recognize Christ.

That means that the only thing you are asked to do in this dimension is to live as though you are not an ego; and to live as though you are Christ.

I can't make it any simpler, and only you can make it difficult. Sorry about that. What do you think? Is all of this making sense?

Yes.

Well, then how do you choose to live right now? This moment? Who are you? Nobody knows yet?

Oh, but if I say it out loud I feel a little self-conscious.

The arisen Christ.

Hmm. How do you know that?

I know it because I choose to live my life that way.

Awakening

Ahh. Well, one out of a room isn't so bad.

[Laughter]

Who are you? Stop whispering. Let's go! Who is sitting next to you? What do you want to create on this Earth?

Heaven on Earth.

Well then, don't wait for somebody else to put the spade in the ground. What would it be like to live each day . . . when you walk into your grocery store, you are just beaming with the radiance of Christ and somebody thinks a negative thought and you reach over and you put your hands on their shoulders and you say,

> *Oh, my precious friend. Oh, no. Please, no.*

[Laughter]

The men in the white jackets are ready to take you away.

They won't come and take you away unless you fear it.

What if you looked that one in the eye and say,

> *I know you, even if you don't know yourself.*

Tell them that they are doing what is called playing out or watching a re-run, and there is a new show in town. Ask them if they perhaps have failed to go to their mailbox? The invitations have been sent and the party is beginning. The party is beginning and everybody is invited.

That's what it's all about. It's all it's ever been about. You are the one who has been here throughout all of time and all of space, and you have danced with one another in a million different ways. If you can think of a role, you've played it. Whether it be a role that could be said to be wearing a white hat or a black hat, if you can think it, you've played it. Oh, isn't that embarrassing?

So who are you going to judge? Somehow, in some way, because of the love I see in you, you could say I am like one who looks upon this world and sees parched land; and then I look at each of you and I see this infinite reservoir of the most nurturing waters that one could ever comprehend, without end and without a bottom. Sparkling clear. Radiant Light. Such a perfect water. And all I ever really try to do is to find a way to let you let me open the door and take a glass of it out, so that we together can pour it upon this world. One glass of your love is all it takes. Hmm.

And in everything that I have ever said to you — whether it be this odd form, or the other two thousand and three that I am currently doing similar work with, or through any of the hands of an infinite number of healers that I also communicate and work with, whether it was a single word or act that I ever did through my Father's grace when I walked among you — nothing I have ever said or done has ever been designed for any other purpose except to help you open the floodgates to the Love of Christ that lives within you.

So the cat is out of the bag. And as I have said to some of you: if you want to wait, I can outwait you. So, does the world need saving? No, the world is an illusion; how are you going to save it? All you are asked to do is not to fix anything, whether it be on a macrocosmic scale or the microcosmic scale as you would perceive it called your life. Stop trying to fix what may have occurred in the past. Simply begin now to think with different thoughts. Not to say,

> *I wish I could be unlimited. If only I could get rid of this, whatever it might be.*

Sometimes it's a person. Or a ghost.

Yes. But indeed begin now to put the fullness of your attention on being the unlimitedness of the Love of Christ through Whom anything and everything can be accomplished. And remember, it's easy because *you* don't have to do it. You only have to allow it.

So [addressing someone present in the room], within thirty days I would like you to deliver a speech in front of at least two hundred people about the Kingdom of Heaven. Now, if you don't accomplish that, it will mean at least ten thousand more lifetimes.

Ohhhhh. I know you don't mean that.

You do, huh?

Think about it though. Begin to imagine and visualize yourself giving that talk. Feel it until it is as real as it seems to be now that you are sitting on the floor. Okay? It's your meditation for the next thirty days.

And listen to the words you speak. Feel the effect of the words and realize it is the Holy Spirit speaking through you and open to it. Hear your words and watch and feel that experience as though you are indeed witnessing it, and yet feeling it at the same time. Okay?

Don't worry, because if you think you get stuck, I'll hang a few ... cue cards I believe they are called.
[Laughter] Oh, great.

Hmm. How are we all doing?

Great.

Hmm. Life is really very, very simple. Lament nothing that comes to you. For all that can come to you is either the result of a thought you *used* to think, in which case you are watching it pass you by because you are no longer thinking that way, or you begin to witness the miracles which are the effects of the thoughts you've begun to learn to think. Does that make sense? Those are the only two possibilities.

Think with unlimitedness and miracles will come to be your way of life, and you'll just be shaking your head with a smile on your face:

I used to think I was limited. Well, it was a funny movie.

Now, please do not think that to be unlimited means that you are going to have what you call forty-seven Rolls Royces in the garage. Of course, that's not quite what I am talking about. You can abide with five dollars in the pocket and be totally at peace and know that the path you are walking is absolutely perfect; and you can love every moment of it, and you are as abundant as the richest man that ever lived. But be honest with yourself. If you'd rather have ten instead of five, admit it and begin to do something about it by beginning to allow yourself the feeling of living in unlimitedness, referred to you in the former measurement of golden coins. That's all you are doing. It is just an energy, after all. It's really no different than what makes your heart beat. *It's just an energy.*

Awakening

Those of you that have ever taken a glass of water to your lips — and in any day of your life is there anybody here that has ever done that? Receiving abundance is really like drinking water. You make the choice to allow it to enter into the sphere of your experience. You may not know how and that doesn't matter. All you need to do is be willing — to imagine, to visualize, to feel that abundance, and to ask the Father to set all things in motion so that it is created around you and through you. And then miracles happen. Perhaps a phone call from an old friend. It could happen in a million ways, but it will be there for you. Isn't that right?

Mmmm.

So. What would it be like? What would it be like if you chose to step to the front of the crowd and be the leader that shows everyone else how to live in the unlimitedness of Christ? What if you got so crazy that you abandoned all of your fears, or at least chose to walk through them? Or so crazy that you are willing to stand in front of a crowd of two hundred people and say,

> *Well yes, I'm an expert on the Kingdom of Heaven. Here, I can show you how to create abundance. (Father, how do you do this?)*

Why not?

How can you know what your Father's will is for you? When you are truly willing to be honest about what seems to be the burning desire in your heart. And if you look at that desire and it is not caught up with the manipulation or hurting of anybody, not the taking of anything because you think you need it, but just a burning desire that seems to have been with you no matter how often you tried to ignore it, it's a safe bet that you might as well go for it. And if you do, many miracles will come. Many miracles.

And what you thought was your heart's desire will have been realized to be only a stepping-stone that the Holy Spirit has placed before you, because your Holy Spirit knows what's in your heart, you see, and creates then that desire because you will be attracted to it. And as you step upon it, like a flower it opens up, and you realize that it really meant something else, and you've become something else. Perhaps in your pursuit of abundance you discover that you are asked to be a teacher of God.

Does all of that make sense to you?

Allow yourself to step lightly and with joy upon the stepping-stones that are placed before you. Not one thing arises in your day by accident. It only waits for you to turn your attention to it and embrace it and say,

Well, if this is here, there is a purpose for it.

And in that moment you hold the power to discern its purpose if you are willing to embrace it with your love. Learn from it. Step upon it and go on. And everything serves, everything serves what could be called here, your becoming. For as you have lived in time and have created the dramas that would draw you into the perception of separation from God, so too now, as the arisen Christ, you allow time to be used as the device through which you witness the flowering of the Light and Love you are.

You walk through a magical kingdom. There is nothing realistic about this world. Nothing. Someday you will understand that even the body is not realistic. You walk through a magical kingdom.

Awakening

Everything is being formulated for you out of the thoughts and perceptions you have held, and *when you choose only God, please rest assured that everything quickens and a new power comes to form everything.* And every experience that comes to you is given to you as a stepping-stone, as a touchstone if you will, that leads you ever more into the fullness of the Christ you are. Hmm.

Contemplate what that must mean and see how it asks you to change your perceptions about what you experience. Now, the grand thing is this: if you forget, all you have to do is remember and the game goes on.

And the last thing that I want to say to you before we allow the bodies to have a bit of a break, the last thing I'll say is this: it is absolutely impossible to regress on this journey once you choose to begin it.

So the next time you go,

> *Ohhh, God, I'm really gonnnne...*

—Nonsense. Pinch yourself and wake up and walk on. You can't go backwards, you see, because the past has been washed away from you. There is nowhere back there to step. So even if you experience doing something again—you call it the pattern that goes around in a circle and you can't seem to break it—you are not stepping backwards.

You are fully choosing in the present to create that experience. It is not coming up from behind you to bite you in the butt.

[Laughter]

Take a nice deep breath—the breath of God—and exhale and let your Light radiate out in all directions. And then remind yourself that after all is said and done, *you* are the Light of the world. How about that! And even now many of you have felt in the last twenty-nine and a half seconds the descent of like a blanket of peace, and though this may seem a little fantastic to some of you, to others it won't—I never come and do this work alone. I have some friends, just as you are my friends, but these don't have a body; and they come with me whenever this work is done. And that blanket— how many of you felt it? —is bestowed upon you by what you would perceive as several masters, though I am not so sure we like the term. Think of them as friends that love you deeply; and know that you are not separate from where they are. And that peace is available to you with one breath, any time you choose to receive it. Know you the term, some of you, The Ascended Masters? Perhaps The Great White Brotherhood? Think not that they are unavailable to you. Think not that this my beloved brother has what you call a red phone on the desk. Hmm. There is no one special. And that love and that peace, that opportunity, descends on each equally. What creates the appearances of differences is the willingness to receive it and to enact it.

That's all. That's the only difference.

Remember, and breathe that peace. Just play at it. You might even want to gather with one or two in the corner and just take a nice deep breath together and feel that blanket of peace. It's there for you. And, as you say in your world, practice makes perfect. Peace be unto you, and thank you for me allowing these few moments to create a mirror for you of the Truth that lies within you.

Amen.
[Break]

I want very much for each and every one of you to truly, to truly embrace this simple fact—and I speak unto you now, each individually, if you will. I give thanks to my Father for *your* presence. I bow down before your Light and your Love and your beauty. I cannot possibly find words in any language that can possibly express to you the gratitude and the love that I feel, the joy I feel, when I look upon you.

It isn't what you do. It isn't what you say. It's who you are. And throughout all of eternity I have and will remain in awe at the stupendous Light that you are. Thank you from the depth of my being. Thank you for the Light that you bring to creation.

It's a rather joyous state, you see, to be in a place where constantly, with everyone that comes into your experience, the feeling that I just expressed to you is there—is there always. And yet, it is not a feeling that is peculiar to just me. It simply comes of itself unto any mind or any heart that is truly willing to relinquish the perceptions that have served to do nothing but veil the presence of the peace of God within you.

And what I have just shared with you in words you could just as well share with anybody you saw on your street. Not just as an exercise, but as a Truth, a reality. What is called existence, which is really the practice of awareness, is rather incredible when every moment is lit by the fire of gratitude for the radiance of the being who is before you — even if they are giving you what you call a ticket for moving your automobile too quickly. Indeed.

And as you give, you receive. So if you feel at any time there is maybe a little bit of a drying up of the river of love, find someone to give your love to. Find a way. The situation may not call for the words that I just used as I spoke to each of you individually, but find a way to give the fullness of your love to them. And that fast [snaps fingers], you will see how quickly you can change your own countenance, because as you teach, you learn. And as you give, you receive.

Therein lies the whole of the laws of creation. That is why, you see, our Father receives so much—because He gives so totally of Himself unto the infinite reaches of all that creation is. And therefore, God being but Love, never experiences anything but the unlimited radiance of Love. For He that gives all, receives all. It does seem rather simple, doesn't it?

Hmm. Well, enough of all of that. I just wanted to express my love to you.

We love you, too, Jeshua.

And it is received without a trace of resistance.

[Laughter]

Look well then, for if you perceive a difference between yourself and me, could it be that perhaps there is something in you that feels it should resist, at least a little bit, the overwhelming Love that is the presence of God? Resistance is what makes this world. That's a rather good line. Hmm.

So, some of you that have been around for the past year, have you not noticed that in many ways the form of language has changed?

Yes.

And there are reasons for that. What needed to be said in terms of correcting certain Biblical perceptions has been established, and even though what seems to be different bodies and minds are here to some degree than when we started, the message is

Awakening

being received by all. So that as we moved along, certain walls have been melted, even in those that have come for but the first time. Does that make sense to you?

Yes.

Now, if that is true—and I assure you that it is—it means that every time *you*, in the course of your own life, your own experience, every time *you* choose to be the presence of Love and to teach only love, rest assured you are extending it unto the whole of creation and uplifting it. You could say that you are like one who stands before what seems to be a very long and very high and very thick wall, and your Father has come to you and said,

> *Take down the barrier between creation and Myself. Here is your chisel and here is your hammer.*

And you have put it up against that wall and one thought has been,

> *Oh, my goodness gracious. How will I ever tear this wall down? It's a hundred miles thick, four thousand miles high, and who knows how long?*

And yet when you place the chisel on the wall and tap it lightly with one loving thought, the vibration is felt throughout the whole of that wall. And as you choose to be the presence of Love, you are chipping away at the wall that surrounds the heart of someone on the other side of this planet.

How valuable are your loving thoughts? Hmm. It is that which cannot have a price tag on it. How powerful are your negative? thoughts? Hmm. Those of you that would envision a world transformed, a planet radiant with Light in which all of mankind lives as a brotherhood—or perhaps it's time you start saying as a sisterhood; but if you understand who you are, masculine and feminine terms really don't matter much, they are just forms of language—for those of you that would envision such a world, and there are many in this room that don't just think about it, the vision is pressing upon your heart. Almost so that there is a quickening. Do you know that feeling? As if Light is descending down into the core of your heart so that at times it feels as if it is going to burst? Do you know the feeling?

Be you therefore the one willing to tap the chisel with every single loving thought that you would hold, and choose only loving thoughts. Step back just a little bit and abide in what you could call, some would call, cosmic consciousness. That's an interesting term. It only means that you are aware that separation does not exist. Nowhere. And each loving thought affects the whole, and you can learn, you can literally learn, how to do whatever you do in your life and at the very same moment— which is truly outside of time—to hold the whole of creation in your awareness. And whether you are laying your hands on another's body, whether you momentarily seem to be blending with the mind of one individual amongst many to speak to a small room of people—friends —you can know that in that moment you are addressing or laying your hands on or giving a smile to the whole of creation, and you can literally feel the Truth of that and know it. Not just as a hope, not just as a dream, but as a living reality. And as you practice that, something very miraculous happens. For when you are in relationship—and whether it be with your lover, your mate or the gas station attendant, it doesn't really matter—when you are in relationship and you look into their eyes, you literally see the whole of creation before you and you embrace them with the Love that you are.

That is how vast you are. And that experience, that reality, is

Awakening

really open to you in every moment. It requires only your choice to allow what you have thought to be the mundane and ordinary moments to be translated by the Holy Spirit into the means through which Christ enlightens creation.

That is the power given unto each and every one of us before time began. That's how powerful you are. And all it requires is seventy-two lifetimes in the monastery.

[Laughter]

You have already done that. And that didn't work.

All that is required is that you, in the quiet and the peace of your own heart and mind, make a simple decision:

> *I will be the presence of Love. I am the one sent of my Father to share the joy of unconditional Love in each moment and with every breath.*

That choice not only can transform your entire being, it will trans form this illusory world into that which shall reflect the Kingdom of Heaven on Earth. That choice is the Second Coming of Christ. That is why I said earlier that Heaven waits on you. Ahhh. Thank God it's no longer *my* responsibility.

[Laughter]

What do you think? Perhaps one of these evenings as we begin and everyone is sitting in silence, and hopefully you are not expecting or looking forward, hopefully just abiding in that place . . . perhaps I won't say anything at all and we will just be Christ. But be you therefore vigilant for you will not know the hour or the day in which I might choose to do that. And in that hour would you become impatient? Would you let the mind create thoughts,

I wonder what is going on? It's been forty-five minutes. Has Jeshua left?

Ah, the one that you would call Jon Marc, who I prefer to call Jon (but that's another story)

Oh, the poor thing. He will be so embarrassed.

[Laughter]

Or would you allow yourself to realize there is nowhere to go, nothing to achieve, that I cannot be separate from wherever you choose to abide together in love? For where two or more are gathered in my name, guess what happens? It might be fun. It would be great transcribing.

[Laughter] You want twenty dollars for that booklet, right? It would be worth a thousand. So, how are we all doing? Good. Great. Fine.

Are you happy to be here together?
Yes. Very happy.

You could be out doing what they call celebrating theindependence.

We are.

Frankly, I haven't seen a whole lot of what you call independence in your culture. Inter-dependence in a way that really isn't all too healthy. But that's going to change. Do you know why it is going to change? Because we, the Ascended Masters, are going to make it happen.

Ha!

And on your next Fourth of July I am going to descend in a chariot of fire and land on your White House lawn and take over the government.

I'd vote for you.

Would it be okay if I run on what you call the Independent Ticket?

[Laughter]

The whole point of that, of course, is that there is no group of masters that does not already include *you*. Let no one tell you that there is some group called Ascended Masters that are so far over your head, literally and otherwise, that it will take you lifetimes to go through many initiations to become as grand as they are. It is time to let go of the myth of progression because it is a myth born in time and therefore a language or model that has simply been used because that's all you could hear. You are already in the club . . you are already in the club . . . and I want to let you in on a little secret: those of us to whom many of you have given labels or allowed others to give labels to us called Ascended Masters have just been waiting patiently for you to realize that where you sit in any moment to ask for help from us is inside the clubhouse. You're already there. Does that make sense to you?

You are—and listen carefully—you are *already* an ascended master. It's already been finished. Your resistance to it comes only from the belief that that's not true. You've misperceived that the journey is already finished, and the joke's on you. You are already that Light. It doesn't matter what shape or form your body is in. It doesn't matter what age you are. You are an ascended master. You already awakened. The game is over; you are just watching a re-run. I know that seems almost simplistic, but anyone who chooses, even in this moment, to accept that fully, realizes that I am not kidding. There is nowhere you are going. Nowhere at all. You are already back home where the long, long journey that's never been, began.

I and my Father are one, and there is nothing to do except allow that love that you are to be given away in any number of infinite forms. If you want more forms and more ways in which to give it away, just ask your Father; He will provide them to you.

Oh, but if only I could become a great artist, then I'd be happy.

Be happy and you *are* a great artist. What could take a more delicate touch, a more creative stroke, than to master the art of being the presence of happiness itself? Hmm. Yes!

Well, so here we are together in this experience called creation.

What on Earth shall we do with it? Anyone have any ideas?

First, let's clean it up and make everybody happy.
Let's play while we are doing it.

Let's give away God's love to one another.

Well. Indeed, play well and laugh well while you are repainting the canvas. That's all you are doing: repainting the canvas. In your own life you can repaint the canvas any time you want to

Awakening

start.

I don't like that color. Hmm. A little boring.

So, change it.

Indeed, play—and play well. And yes, of course—play fair.

So, in all of that I've had my piece this evening. Actually I have my peace always, but...

There is really not much else to be said. But if you have questions, we can entertain them. Now, I don't mean to make light of a question that someone feels they have that is a serious matter to them. And yet, all we can do is entertain questions until the soul itself finally comes to the point of being willing to acknowledge that it *is* the answer it seeks.

I regret to inform you that I have never answered a single question in a way that has made any difference whatsoever. It is the willingness of the soul to accept what it already knows, since all I do is read the book in your heart—and I just know how to read well. And when you receive it and go,

Ah, yes,

that's when change occurs. Does all of that make sense to you? Yes.

You have been taught that I was created to be the savior of the world. Hmm. Actually, my Father said,

Do you know, Jeshua ben Joseph, I hope you don't mind, but I am just going to make you into a mirror. Go around and let people see their reflection. I know it sounds a little boring. It's not too

royal or grand. But that's what I want you to do.

So I said,

Fine. Make me a mirror.

And He did. And I said,

Whoa, look at that.

That fast I became a mirror with nothing to do except reflect. And it's not a very boring way to exist.

So, do you have any questions? Or better yet, do you have any statements?

Jeshua, I have a question since nobody is jumping up to say something here.

In what we perceive as time and in what we perceive as having lived many lifetimes, what the soul learns in a lifetime does not seem to be carried forward into the next lifetime on a conscious level. Does that make sense? I really want to know if our souls, as we go through lifetimes, if our souls remember the Truths that we learned in each lifetime; and if we do, does it impact our consciousness in that next lifetime or many lifetimes?

Now, we are going to give you an answer in two different ways. First: what the Son decrees, is. What does that mean? You are the one. You *are* the one. And what you decree, that is, what you select to perceive and believe, will be your experience. That means that if you hold the perception of a model that souls go through many, many lifetimes and learn lessons that are added to their luggage, and they carry them with them so that they are progressively becoming wiser, then that will be your experience; and you will believe it because you will have wanted to choose the experience of a progression through time. So far, so good?

Yes.

Therefore, if you ask me, given this model, does this follow? What I will say to you is: do you want it to follow — that the soul gains knowledge that is carried?

Well, now I am confused. I thought I understood you to say many times in our evenings that we have gone through countless lifetimes because we never get it straight.

That is absolutely true, but that does not deny the fact that you are the one choosing on insisting that you are a soul that has gone through many lifetimes and haven't got it right. That's what the whole point of this evening's talk has been: that you are the one clinging to that perception, and I am a mirror that reflects it back to you. Do you see?

I'm completely lost.

Good. Now, we can make some real progress.

I have indeed talked about other lives. I have even used the model of language about progressively getting on with it.

But in all cases in which I have done that it is a teaching tool given to the one to whom I am speaking, or perhaps to several in a group, because it is a language that they are insisting on seeing things with. Do you see?

So we only live progressive lifetimes if we believe we live progressive lifetimes?

Yes. And all of that is still within the realm of the dream.

Your reality is that you are the only begotten Son of God and you exist wholly outside of time.

You embrace the whole of creation and it arises within you, and the model and the perception of lifetimes is part of that which has arisen within the Mind of Christ as a free choice. It is like looking at clouds in the sky and deciding that you see animals or what have you. You are the one creating it. You are the one creating the clouds. Even your scientists know that there is no such thing. That is, they are created according to your perception, according to this apparatus that you have created. Does that make sense to you?

Yes.

Precious friend, come to understand that awakening will never come as long as you insist on adhering to a model in which you see yourself as having had a beginning, going through a chain of lifetimes, getting better and better, hopefully. Except for the times that you regress. Hmm.

Do you understand what I am saying? It doesn't mean it's not okay to have fun talking and pretending about all of these incredible lifetimes you've had. But if you want to be Christ, which is to accept who you are, you are going to give up that model because Christ abides in what is eternal and timeless, changeless and unlimited forever. And that is really the goal of every soul that perceives itself progressing through time to become timelessness, to become unlimited.

Does that make sense?

That's what's pressing against you, you see. It's the feeling of being constricted. That's what you are trying to overcome. You may interpret it in a million different ways, but what you are seeking is to be unlimited. And it won't happen until you are willing to begin with a new perception:

I am unlimited – now.

And with that, what unfolds is the releasing of every perception that is not in accord with unlimitedness.

I have said many times that you live the life of every being. *That* is reality. It is part of the highest Truths, if you will, that can possibly be uttered. And when you truly rest and let go of that resistance, you will find, incredibly, that that is true.

Some have said to me,

Boy, you seem to know me so well. Better than I know myself.

Only because I chose my unlimitedness, and therefore I embrace you. I use the word brother and friend because it is a way of communicating at a place where your mind still is.
Precious friend, this whole gathering tonight has been about the power of perception. Actually, we started a little while ago, even last week. The power of perception is what creates what you experience; and the only difference between where you are and where you think I am is that I chose to perceive only unlimitedness, while you have chosen to perceive that unlimitedness is something you will gradually grow into once you have learned all your lessons. And that's perfectly okay. Just enjoy the journey.

What would happen if you were to begin to constantly practice the perception that you *are* unlimited now? That everything you see, every brother, every sister, every blade of grass is arising *within you*?

So what I'm getting is that the whole concept of reincarnation is part of the dream.

Exactly.

Right where you are, you are already home. You are not the body, you are not that personality your parents told you that you were. You are that consciousness, that awareness, that Love, that vast Light in which all of creation is arising—and the holy and only begotten child or offspring of God is eternally one.

Where else can you possibly find a greater freedom than to realize that there is nothing *outside* of you, but there is everything *inside* of you?

When you lay your head on the pillow at night and you dream countless dreams, when you awaken in the morning don't you realize it just took place within your mind? All of this is occurring within your Mind, the one infinite Mind that is Christ. And the dream is shifting. I have called it elsewhere the transference or the translation of an unhappy dream into a happy dream. The reflection of Heaven on Earth is still part of the dream. But it will reflect perfectly what your reality is and that is why at that moment creation itself will no longer be required. What you call "creation" manifests forms in time. It is very difficult to talk about what that will be like. In fact, that isn't possible because it transcends the dream itself.

Oh, precious and holy Christ, you are eternal. There has never been a time that you have not existed. There has never been a world that you have not sojourned through. You are the one that has made it all up. Every lifetime. Know you that called the

Awakening

Book of Life? It is a term from your Judeo-Christian religion. You are the Book of Life; that's who you are. That is why when two minds come together and are willing to accept their enlightenment, there is really hardly anything to do but have a very good laugh. And create from the infiniteness of your being; to play in the drama and choose to play with unlimitedness, when you realize you have been playing with limitation.

I once said unto some of you within the drama of the dream:

> *Fear not for I shall be with you always.*

And those of you that were a little bit attached to that aspect of the dream have clung unto it. Some of you still hold that your greatest sense of identity is who you were then. Hmm. And when I said:

Fear not, for I shall be with you always,

I did so with a twinkle in my eye, for I can hardly be anywhere else. And when I say I have waited patiently, it means that I simply sit on a park bench in eternity, waiting for you who are in the bus in time to choose to stop and get off, and sit down with me.

Is all of that making sense? It is rather important.

So, it's over. The time is at hand. I have never ceased weaving myself in and out of your dreams and dramas to whisper in your ear,

> *Precious one, remember. Remember.*

"Come home" means nothing else than to open the eyes of your heart and realize the Truth of who you are. Has the drama seemed long and vast? Oh, yes. But the more you choose to identify with your unlimitedness, the more the weight of the dream is forgotten—just as when you open your eyes in the morning and for a moment you shake your head and say,

Oh, my goodness,

and your heart is still palpitating. You know that feeling? And then you realize,

Wait a minute. I'm just sitting in my bed. Ahh.

And by the time you get up and take a shower and have a bite to eat, you have forgotten what you even dreamed. Is that not true?

Yes.

That's what awakening is like. When it first hits you, you go,

My goodness, how amazing. I can't even put it into words.

But by and by, you forget all the weight of the dreams, and you actually become better and better at finding ways to communicate, to teach in an artful way that prods the minds of your brothers and sisters, which are really but aspects of your own Mind, into the recognition of who they are. But even that is part of the dream. Miracles are valuable only within a dream, and the choice is simple. And I've used this analogy before, and when I have, some have smiled, some have chuckled. It's very, actually quite literal . . .

It is as though every moment you are walking up to one of what you would call one of your movie theaters which has many movies going on at the same time, on different screens, and you select which ticket to buy. That's really how simple it is.

One of the movies has been that you are only born once and then you are going to die, and thank God that God sent His only begotten Son to die on the cross and save you from your sins. And there are many that cling to that movie and love it, and that's perfectly okay.

One of the movies is that I am an infinite soul and boy, have I gone through a million lifetimes and oh, my goodness, when I was in Egypt; and all of the rest. That too is a movie that many would cling to.

But your reality is simply this: you are the one standing outside the theater and so much power is given to you that you can watch them all at once without buying a ticket. You can allow all of them. You can embrace all of them. You can look at the people that are sitting in the little rows, entranced with the movie, and you can *love* them into awakening by being the one who is awake.

Does all of that make sense?

And that is what you are called to do. Now, who is doing the calling?

You are calling yourself.

Exactly. You will awaken to your own call and no one else's. And if you are here in this room, it's because you have at least begun to hear and answer your own call. And I am but that aspect of you that is a mirror of the deepest Truth that lies within you. And you brought me forth.

Whew, try preaching that on a Sunday morning.
[Laughter]

You might have to say,

> *Oops, wrong theater.*

Make sure you duck before the eggs are thrown:

> *No my dream is so important. I have to insist that my dream is real. Everybody else's is false.*

A dream is a dream is a dream. And nobody is doing better than anybody else if they are still dreaming.

Have you ever had the thought that, perhaps some of you have said,?

> *You know, a long time ago I used to believe this certain way but now I know I am really an infinite soul that's been incarnated a million times,*

and you've believed you made progress?

I am sorry to say one is either dreaming or one chooses to be awake.

There is no other choice and nothing else is occurring. Some of you have been taught, *Well, there are gray areas.*

In this sense there is but white and black, on or off. Love or fear is another way to put it.

And therefore I echo to you your own call to choose to be awake now!

Awakening

And now is all there is. Have you ever played the little game during the course of a day, every hour, stopping and asking yourself, where are you and what time it is? You are always here and it's always now.

And the very same choice is in front of you now as was in front of you when you were a priestess in Egypt.

A warrior in the Steppes. A yogi in a cave. A monk in a monastery. A drunk in a Western town. Sorry about that one. And it's the same choice that is right in front of you now:

Will I choose to be awake?

Do you see what we are coming to within the perception of the dream?

This is the highest form of teaching that can be given because there is nothing beyond it that can be put into words.

It's the last level, if you will; if you want to play that game, it's the last level. And this is what you are coming to because you have chosen to awaken to your own call and to hear it and follow it.

Some of you have heard me say that the bell has been rung. I didn't ring it; you did. Or another level: we rang it together. And as you go out into your journeys, really think about this for a moment . . . you know your journeys called your lifetimes? Aren't those really very much related to the body? Is it not the body that gets into this car instead of that car and into this bed instead of that bed? That eats this instead of that, and all the rest? The Mind that you are is embracing all such journeys and all such dramas, and that is what again you must come to allow yourself to remember.

Those of you that have studied my little work called A Course In Miracles will remember this: the only lesson you have to learn is that there is nothing outside of you. That's it. Learn that and the game is over. Does that bring an end to time? Will the body just crumple to dust? Who cares? Who cares! When you are awake, you are awake, and if the drama goes on or if the drama ends, who cares? When you are so busy being the presence of Love and giving it away, who cares? Who cares if there is going to be an earthquake tomorrow? Who cares if the Earth is going to flip on its axis? Who cares? It's just a drama. And you are too busy delighting in being Love to take on a drop of seriousness about it.

Do you understand that it's that level of freedom that allows some of you to walk upon the hot coals, called the firewalking? That's the very same freedom. You just haven't allowed yourself to recognize that that's the same level of freedom that I manifested when I made a bit of a dramatic appearance. Hmm. It's the same thing. And every time you walk through a ring of fear to embrace your brother and sister as yourself and give them your love, you have done the same thing that I did when I allowed "them" to crucify me. I walked through a ring of fear that was nothing more than a perception: that having nails driven through physical hands could somehow separate me from God. And I demonstrated that that is not true. And if that ring of fear can't separate you from God, there is no ring of fear that can separate you from the Love that you are.

Whenever you are in a situation and you feel that little bit of constriction and you have something in your heart that you are burning to share or whatever it might be, what you are feeling is a little ring of fear and that's all. And it's a blessing. It is such a blessing. My goodness, you've confronted it a million times in your dreams; and all you have to do is walk through it, and

Awakening

it begins to shatter like pieces of glass falling out of a window so that the breeze can blow through. Fear is a blessing. Walk through it. Those of you that have walked on the hot coals know perfectly well what I am saying.

Those of you that have ever allowed somebody to kiss you with passion know what I am saying. Remember that first kiss? My goodness, you've all walked through those rings of fear so many times that it's old hat. And the only thing that now prevents you from walking through what you think are your rings of fear is that you are choosing to perceive it as a wall a hundred miles thick. And as a curse instead of a blessing. That's the only difference.

Do you begin to get the freedom of it all? Good. So now I can return to the place from whence I have come, sitting at the right hand of God, surveying all below me. Seeking out the poor and wretched sinners who need me to save them. Boy, aren't I hot stuff?

[Loud laughter]

Hmm.

I think I'll just rest in reality and be right with you in your own heart throughout all of eternity — as an aspect of yourself that is your brother and your friend as long as the happy dream is necessary.

They once tried to get rid of me and it didn't work. And now you can tell your friends Christ is indeed returned, because that Mind is awakened within you. And so if one comes and says,

Do you believe in the Second Coming?
say,

Jeshua ~ The Early Years

Well, of course. Behold, I stand before you.

[Laughter]

In other words, lighten up and have some fun.

So, what I am going to ask you to do now, tomorrow — this is very important — I want you to do whatever and only what you truly *want* to do. Whew. Think about that. So, right away, you see, we've collaborated to create some rings of fear. And if you are willing to accept them as a blessing, you can walk through it. Just use tomorrow as the one day that you are choosing to do only what you truly, from the depth of your being, want to do. Hmm, I wonder what that might mean? It will be a very interesting day.

Are you willing to try it out?

And if some of you have a certain work that you go to that inwardly you are not so pleased with, if in the morning when you wake up what you really want to do is go sit on a rock overlooking the ocean, call your employer and tell them that something's come up. You don't have to tell them that awakening has come up. And do it, go walk through your fear and sit on your rock.

Now, will consequences come from that? Perhaps. Are you willing to really walk through your ring of fear? Are you willing to let the illusion shatter and allow your life to be reformed by the One Who has sent you forth? Oh, my goodness. It's entirely up to you; so keep that in mind.

Love one another as your Father has first loved you. And He has loved you with unlimitedness and with joy. He sees the perfection of your Light wherever you are. You are free to don

Awakening

the cloak of time and yet be beyond time. You are the one that comes to bring Light to this world. You are infinite. You are eternal. You are the beauty. You are the beauty of every ray of Light that dances a thousand diamonds across the waters of this planet. You are the beauty and the light of every star. You are the vastness and the silence and the power of space in which all things have arisen in your little physical universe. Hmm. You are the brightest of colors and the deepest of tones. You are the perfect melody. You are the song, the instrument and its composer, and you are the one that delights in the song.

You are all that I am and we are one: Christ eternal, unbounded oceans of Love and Light and perfection . . . perfection.

You are the Prodigal Son that has journeyed through all of time and all of space and all worlds, and now has returned to your Father's sacred place. Start chowing down on the food and the abundance that's on the table. For the feast has been prepared for you. The time is at hand and the journey is over. Welcome home. Welcome home, precious and holy friend.

Peace be unto you as you dance your Light into this world and work with me, play with me at translating the unhappy dream into the happy dream. Each of you is a miracle-worker because the miracle has been accepted in you, by you:

I and my Father are one.

Peace be unto you. And indeed Heaven and Earth have been joined in you and extended as far as from the East to the West.

Amen.

Choose to See

Now, we begin.

And indeed, once again, greetings unto *you*, beloved and holy and only-begotten Child of God. Listen well to this greeting. Greetings unto *you*, *beloved* and *holy* and *only-begotten* Child of God. This is, in Truth, the truth of who you are. This is in Reality all that you can be.

For before the time when the first stars were set in the heavens, already did you abide as your Father has created you to be. No, not as the mind would show you 'yourself'. There was not such a thing as what you know as a body. There was not such a thing as a thought of temporality. There was not the trace of the thought of birth, and therefore, no concept or experience of what you would call death. In that ancient beginning, before time is, already were you created *whole* and *complete*, the perfect loving extension of the Mind of God. And God is but Love. This being true, it is true *always*. There is not a moment in time in which this truth is interrupted. There is not a moment in any of your experience in which the real world ceases to be.

How, then, can it be that you find yourself seemingly constricted into the space and volume of a physical body? It is very dense and often quite hard. How is that you look out through physical eyes so certain that what they show you is real? And certainly you can prove it to yourself. Just try to walk through a wall and you will convince yourself that that wall is completely real, that the body is who you are, that's the way it is, and it cannot change. Taking that conception into the mind, taking that perception to be what is true, you teach yourself to deny the gentle Voice given unto God to His holy and only creation—you—and placed lovingly within you, from before the beginning of time.

That Voice is with you still and always. But it requires, if you would hear it, a willingness to surrender every perception you've ever believed about yourself or about the world — and that very act feels like total insanity.

> *What will happen to me if I give up my belief that that wall is real? What will happen to me if I give up all the perceptions that I know are etched in stone and I must act from them in order to survive in this world that I certainly didn't make? After all, I came into it as an accident born of my parents' passion. I simply found myself here, and this is the way that I am.*

It does seem absurd to give up such deeply-rooted perceptions and beliefs *and experience*s that you believe have helped you to survive, in order to entertain what seems to be sheer insanity.

I have said often and through many channels that the world that you perceive is diametrically opposed to the real world. It is the exact opposite. Therefore, if you would know the real world, the first step that is required is to retrain the mind to be willing to *accept* that all things you believe you see are *only* temporary reflections, or illusions — that the physical eyes have never shown you the real world, that your ideas and perceptions based on the data that comes through the senses of the body, these ideas have *always* been diametrically opposed to the truth of the real world.

If there is, then, a call born within you, if there is that spark within you — which means simply that the Voice for God has finally crept in a little bit and you've begun to hear — if there's something in you that calls you to know the *real world*, if there is something in you which calls you to know the Peace of God, if there is something in you that is even just a little willing to surrender whatever needs to be surrendered to know that reality of God's Peace and that Perfect Love which already you are, then you must make a decision. And the decision is this:

> *If I have used time and experienced time to gather evidence that what I have taught myself to believe is true, then perhaps I need now to use time to relinquish what I have believed to be true.*

The decision is the choice to be fully committed to allowing the experiences of time, beginning right where you are in your daily life, to be reinterpreted for you by a Voice that is in you but is not quite yours. At least not yet. The day will come when you will be one with that Voice. The day *will come* when you will know the truth that

I and my Father are One.

The day will come when, though the physical eyes still seem to be operating, you look lovingly upon the world that has been made in error, this physical dimension, this constriction that you perceive within your mind — for you will be looking at it through an *inner eye*, an aspect of your beingness, your consciousness, that does have certain physical correlates, yes, and you will activate that eye and you will open that eye and you will look upon all things *through* that eye. And the sensory data that comes into you will be as though filtered or transmuted so that what you judge of what you see comes not from the beliefs and ideas that you have mis-created, but those perceptions cleansed and purified by the Light and the Wisdom that will shine through that inner eye.

Once when I sat with my friends that you have heard are called disciples, I said unto them: When the eye becomes single, then you will enter the Kingdom. What does such an odd statement mean?

First it speaks on many levels to a truth that can only be

understood through the concept of levels. "When the eye becomes single" means that you have learned to relinquish your fixation of having the attention of your mind linked *to your physical senses alone* and therefore to all of the concepts and perceptions you have built *upon* sensory data coming in through the body—and you have moved that attention to become centered and settled in the *inner eye,* so that the Light of Consciousness that shines upon your experience *reveals* the reflection of the *real* world *through* all that you see and experience.

The second level is this: You find yourself in conflict, you find yourself in a world of duality. There is not a single thing—there's always this and that; up and down; light and dark; good and bad; right and wrong; best value, worst value; best choice, worst choice. Everywhere you go throughout the day you are confronted with the need to make a choice. This or that. Quite frankly it is simply the choice between Love and fear. But in your world that duality prevails, and that is why the world in which you find yourself is *not* the real world. For the real world is single and whole and *only* Love abides there.

Now, to move then into the "single eye" requires that you solve the dilemma of living in duality. How do you do that? For everywhere you find yourself, there you are in the physical world as long as the body lasts—and the body will last as long as *you,* as a conscious being, continue to make the choice for it. By retraining the mind to choose only Love, by retraining the mind to surrender every perception you've ever held about anything or anyone—in this way the day will come when there will not be a *choice* for a physical body, but you will find yourself much indeed with a body yet.

Now, how do you do that? How do you dry the skin while you're swimming in the stream? How do you still the noise while you are abiding in a deafening concert of music? By learning to retrain the mind. There is no other way.

We spoke to you earlier that you do not know what a single thing is or what it is for, and *that* is very good beginning to the process of retraining the mind. The goal, then, is to reach a place of consciousness *prior to* every decision, in which you *remember* the truth of who you are and that you are not yet living in the real world — that what you are seeing before you as a choice that you think you have to make is an illusion based on your past experience.

When you train your consciousness to abide in a clarity of singularity that exists just prior to every choice that confronts you, then and there you can learn to hear the voice of the Holy One who will choose for you, with your permission, until *your* consciousness has learned that that one's choices, the Holy Spirit's, are always one hundred percent accurate and serve the highest in you. You then assimilate or take on, you allow yourself to re-abide in the consciousness of the Holy Spirit itself, and you *become that Voice.* It is no longer outside of you, no longer hard to hear, for you have surrendered everything that kept your identification linked to something other than that Voice. Then, in truth, there *are no more choices*, although you seem to abide yet within the world, living from the singularity of the eye that sees clearly the reflection of the real world through the illusory world that you have laid over the top of it.

From that place, although you live seemingly yet within the body, you will know directly the *experience* of *living without choice*. The dilemma of duality is solved, for there is no longer fear within your mind — nothing to hold onto, nothing to seek, nothing to gain and, most importantly, nothing to lose. For the fear of loss is what keeps you forever entrenched in the conflict of duality, and the 'single eye' remains unknown.

Retraining the mind, then, is the greatest use of time that you have before you. None of the directions in which you think you are going will ever take you to Heaven if those directions have grown out of the way you've learned to make choices. Let me give you an example:

> *I am a body. I must survive. The world is out there and I know it can be rather cruel. I better stay with the job I've got because survival is the greatest value to me. Therefore I will choose (one believes freely) to remain where the heart is not at peace.*

That is not a choice. Not a choice at all. It is an effect of fear and a lack of right knowledge.

Freedom from all circumstance, freedom from conflict and fear, does not come when the body seems to die. For if conflict or the end of conflict does not come into your consciousness before the body dies, rest assured you will find yourself simply and yet again in and as a body perceiving a world in which conflict and duality reign.

There is no choice, then, but to awaken. And to awaken means that you *relinquish* everything you thought you knew and allow an inner Voice to *retrain the use of your mind* until you recognize the real world and abide in that Peace that forever passes all understanding.

Many in the world will not recognize you when this has been completed; for you see, no one can recognize a mind that has awakened unless at least some degree of awakening has occurred within *them* as well. And that's okay. For while the body lasts you are free to teach only Love. But not from the perception of believing that *you* know what that means. Only Love knows what it means; and only Love knows what needs to be extended in each moment. Therefore, while you seem to live yet in the world, from that singularity that is established through the retraining of the mind and the relinquishing of fear, from that place you will find that before each breath you are constantly and simply asking:

What is this moment for? What would You have done through it?

And you will come to hear the voice of the Holy One so clearly and so distinctly, that you will totally relinquish any doubt, any fear, any anxiety. And from that moment you will indeed enter the Kingdom, for the eye will have been made "single". You will go then as the wind, knowing not where you came from or where you're going. There will then only be the eternal present in which you know beyond all shadow of doubt that you are infinitely free and radiant forever and there is only the Love of God present wherever you happen to find yourself. Love will be present when fear is gone.

Therefore, in retraining the mind, begin by recognizing that you do not know what *this* moment is for, whatever this moment is, as it arises. Acknowledge that there is one that you can trust — the Holy Spirit, the teacher and guide given equally unto all until all have returned to the real world.

Learn to trust what you cannot see. Learn to hear what seems not to be spoken out loud. Learn to feel that which does not come *through* the senses, but emerges from *within* them and enlightens them. Learn to look truthfully upon the places where fear has made your home, and as you look upon that place, look lovingly, for you have learned to fear looking upon your fear. And why? Because you believe you *are* that fear expressing as some pattern in your so-called personality. Because you are identified with it, your deepest fear is that if you allow Light to be shined upon it, it will dissolve — and you with it. That is why I said earlier the deepest fear is the fear of loss of a self that never was.

By retraining your mind through the humility of recognizing that you don't know what a single thing is for, that your only choice that you would make is to know and remember and live in the Peace of God, the mind will come to be restructured, to be cleansed and purified—and you will look out upon a world transfigured, and you will see shining through it the reflection of the real world. You will know that you are fear-less, for there is no longer a self that requires your constant protection against the great forces that seem to stand against it. For there can be no great force standing against the True Self, that which shines radiantly with you, throughout you, and throughout all of creation. And that Self is the real world.

You are that One, shimmering brightly, far greater than ten thousand suns. And when you look upon the vastness of your sky, realize that it merely reflects a speck of the Light in which it itself has emerged—and that Light is you. All worlds, all dimensions, all planes of existence arise from within *your* Holy Mind. You are the great vastness that contains Creation even now. And even now, in Reality, you abide and live and exist only in the real world. And the only distance between you in the real world and the you that you think you are in the unreal world is the width of a thought that you would insist on thinking.

Learn, then, to retrain the mind to relinquish that thought whenever it appears. And you will know, though it takes many forms, for you will always feel constricted, you will feel separate from your brothers and sisters, you will feel that the love of this earth of yours is distant from you and that the Peace of God is nowhere to be found. That is a sign that you have chosen to identify and to insist upon a thought that can only birth unreality. Stop trying to defend it. Stop trying to cherish it, because you think you made it and therefore you must keep it. Simply let it go. A thousand times each day let it go. And choose a new thought, a thought of simplicity:

I know not what a single thing is; Holy Spirit, teach me anew.

And allow time to become not that through which you seek your own ends, but rather that through which you allow complete correction to come to the holiness of your Perfect and Radiant Mind.

But, but, I have all of these problems. Jeshua, what am I supposed to do with all of these problems?

Relinquish them. They are illusions. Everything that you think you see as a problem to be solved is the *effect* of first having chosen an insane thought. Simply choose again, as often as you need, until peace returns.

I promise you this: If you become *wholly committed* to awakening from the dream you have dreamed since the stars first began to appear in the heavens, and even before that, if your one desire is to be only what God created . . . then lay at the altar of your heart with every breath, everything you *think* you know, everything you *think* you need, and look lovingly upon every place that fear has made a home in your mind, and allow correction to come. It will come. Regardless of how you experience it, it *will* come.

And the day and the moment will arise when all of your pain and fear and suffering will have vanished like a wind that pushes the foam of the wave away, revealing the clarity of the ocean beneath you. You will literally feel throughout your being that there never was a dream. Some memories will remain with you and you will know that somewhere you must've dreamed a dream or had a thought of wondering what it would be like to be other than the way God created you, but it will be such a faint echo that it will leave no trace upon you. In your heart you will smile gently, regardless of the circumstances in which you find yourself. There will be peace from the crown of the head to the tips of the toes, so to speak, and that peace will walk before you wherever you go. It will enter a room before you enter it with a body, and those who are becoming sensitive will wonder who has come into their place. And some will even say, "Behold, I believe Christ has come for dinner." And you will be that one, for that is who you are— Christ eternal.

Enter with me then now into that place of peace. Those of you that yet believe you are but a body, then begin there. Begin by allowing the body to relax and know that that's not something you can *try* to do: you need only allow it. And as the body relaxes, let your attention recede from the things that you believe are around you.

Give up your need to keep an eye on the world. Give up your need to believe that there is something to accomplish and somewhere to go. Let it sink into the depth of your own being. Not looking to see what's there, but surrendering. Let the breath flow through the body as though something else were breathing it for you. Relax even the activity of the brain, as though it were just another muscle that you could allow to relax. And as you rest and surrender into that inexplicable place of being—the mystery of *your* existence far beyond what the body could ever touch and know, far beyond what the human emotions are capable of containing, far beyond every thought and every belief and every experience you've ever known— there rests the shimmering brilliance of the Light of your Self. Abide in that. Surrender into that. Know only that. And there, in that place, the great depth of your own mind and being, this day, make a new choice.

> *Father, I know not what I have done, I know not how I have dreamed the dream of separation from You, but I relinquish it. I acknowledge that I do not know what a single thing is or what it's for. I know not the moment of my own creation, and therefore I surrender into the radiance and purity of your Peace and your Love. I open my self to receive only You. This alone I am asked to do of You, and this alone I choose. Grant me that wisdom and that strength and that passion by which I might learn to use time constructively as a sacrament of surrender of all that has been unlike Love within me. You are the Way, the Truth, and the Light. And I return to the sacred place of our union. I remain as You have created me to be.*

So, remember then that you will awaken to your own call. You are doing so even now. What you experience along the way is completely and freely chosen. Not one bit of it has been necessary, yet not one trace of it extinguishes or limits the radiance of who you are. It's all in the simplicity of a moment's choice. Let time, then, become your precious friend until time is needed no longer and is given over to the Holy Spirit.

You might then yet find yourself in time again and yet again, but you will not experience it as the world has taught you to. You will see it only as a temporary dance in which you are enjoined freely as a way through which the Love of God can gently descend and touch the unreal world, lighting it again with Reality and bringing the unreal to the real, bringing Heaven to Earth. You are that one in whom our Father remains eternally well pleased.

You are that one unto — what has been given unto you, all power under Heaven and Earth, right now in the palm of your hand. For the power of Heaven and Earth, which is a duality, is the power of *choice*, the power of *consciousness*, the *power* to be committed to own all that you see as self-created, the *power* to relinquish it to that one Voice within you that knows alone how to transmute and translate every thought you have ever held to that which reflects perfectly the radiance of the love that joins you with your Creator. In Truth, the way *is* easy and without effort—if only the choice is made.

Herein we come to the close of this moment's message, again as a stepping stone linked to what has been shared previously. Use it well, use it wisely, and contemplate it often, for it will remind you of the path upon which you walk. For in Truth, if you hear these words now, you *have already chosen* to reclaim the real world within you.

So, we will give pause for a few moments here. And then if you would be willing to give me some of your time, we will entertain and be entertained by certain questions that have emerged within the minds of your brothers and sisters. And many of you will know that these are likewise your questions.

Be then at peace, beloved friends, and know that I am simply here in the real world, waiting for you to recognize that that, too, is where *you* are; and that you no longer entertain a desire to be anywhere else.

Amen.

Question: How does Jeshua explain his acts of Crucifixion and Resurrection in relationship to us, and what is the symbolism that he intended?

Answer: Indeed unto you, beloved brother, this is a question that has been asked of me many times and I would confess that there was a time when I asked these questions of myself!

Choose to See

First, precious friend, when you speak of the Crucifixion and the Resurrection, you are referring first to an activity that *did in fact occur in time*. Let no one make a mistake about that. Rest assured that as a man, like any other man, as a human being like any other human being, I walked my path to remembrance of my union with God. I learned along that path that ultimately I could give nothing to anyone without first receiving it for myself. I became what you might call Divinely selfish: that is, I utilized the body, the mind, the emotions and every experience and every opportunity to teach myself to choose only *with* the Holy Spirit. And the Holy Spirit taught me that death is unreal — period.

How then could I know that? How then could I bring it into the depth and core of my being? By allowing certain environmental pressures, you might think of them — political pressures going on in the time-frame in which I lived — to become not my enemies but my servants. I made a decision in the depth of my prayer and meditation to allow myself to enter into a drama, into an arena that took place in Jerusalem. I allowed myself to be given over into the hands of those that would become my persecutors. I allowed myself the experience of being helplessly imprisoned by those who were governed by fear and not by Love. But rest assured, *I* was governed by Love and not fear, although it did arise one final time, when I separated myself from my friends, and they separated themselves from me by falling asleep. And in the middle of the night I indeed cried out my last cry of anguish,

> *Father, take this from me. I think I've made a slight mistake here... Nevertheless, not my will but Thine.*

Now, with that last surrender, I walked through my final ring of fear and allowed events to unfold as those that were in charge of those events wanted them to unfold. I used even those moments to look lovingly upon my persecutors, to use time constructively, to see beyond the superficialities, to see the loveliness and the Christ within them and quite frankly, as I did that — even as I was stripped and whipped and beaten, as the body seemed to grow weaker and weaker, as they placed a crown of thorns upon my head; and yes, I felt the pangs of pain at a physical level, what you would call pain, without *fear* of that pain — still I focused all of my attention on seeing the face of Christ in my persecutors. And as I did that, it illuminated or refined for me, it took me to the end of my journey. In retraining my own consciousness to see only God's creation, I became one with that Power, one with that Truth without fluctuation or variance. As the events of what you would call the Crucifixion unfolded, rest assured, all anyone was watching was what their *physical eyes were showing them*. Because the masses believed the body is real, because they were identified with it, they actually believed that *I* was dying, that *I* was suffering, that *I* was being taken from them. But this pain and this anguish can come only from the delusion of believing that what is unreal is real.

Now, in time there was in fact what is called a Resurrection. There have been many, many stories about this; it's not quite as fanciful as some would make it out to be. It means simply that because my consciousness, through this final lesson to myself, had become thoroughly settled or centered in the recognition only of the real world, there came a point when the body, or the dust of the ground, merely lying there upon what you would call a sheet, upon a small platform within a certain cavern or cave (given unto me, by the way, by my uncle Joseph of Arimathea; I just wanted to get that in for you) — now there was a time, then, when there was simply no need for even that dead physical form to abide. It began to dissolve, quicken its — what do you call this? — decomposition, if you will, and literally returned to what you would call a molecular or atomic state, a place of almost pure energy and certainly not to be seen by the physical eyes, but trust me it was still there. Specks of dust, you might call it, but much, much smaller.

Now, when certain friends of mine came to the tomb and found that it was empty, they marveled. Why? Because deeply embedded in their beingness was the *belief* that the *body is real* and that consciousness is secondary. Rest assured, it's just the opposite. Now, I chose to reactivate or recreate the form of the body for very specific purposes. If you wish to communicate with someone and they do not understand that a telephone is available, you must go to their house, take them by the shoulder and speak into their ear. If even your best friends have not yet quite learned to believe that they can communicate with any mind at any time, I therefore had need of recreating the telephone of the body, to demonstrate: Look! I *am* alive, death *is* unreal, I've learned the final lesson! Touch me, hear me, feel me just as you did before the Crucifixion — and yet rest assured, I will again leave you because if I do not, the Comforter, the Holy Spirit cannot come to guide you into Truth. But the day will come when you will finally relinquish your need to believe in the world the physical eyes show you. I will come yet again to speak to you from the real world and assist you in moving into that place within yourself. I know not yet the day and the hour, but I will come when *you choose it*. Beloved brother, because you hear these words now, you have chosen, and I have come.

So, that's the historical essence of the Crucifixion and the Resurrection. What did it mean? I have already shared that with you. It was *my path of learning*. I chose it, it was not forced upon me. For my Father's will is the same as for you: that I simply abide awake in Him. It was my simple and particular path for learning that. Rest assured, this should cause celebration, for it is not necessary for you to be nailed to a cross! And why?

I have said many times that everything in your world is a *symbol*. Ask what the symbol is and it will reveal the truth, it will guide you to the real world. Therefore, as you look upon the Crucifixion and the Resurrection, understand that it symbolizes the willingness to allow a death within your consciousness of what you choose to be identified with. If you choose identification with love and unlimitedness and freedom and perfect peace—with the real world—then the events that unfold, even as you experience them, lose their power to enchant you with delusion.

Contemplate that deeply. When you've retrained the mind to teach and choose only Love, and to look lovingly and perhaps laughingly upon the events that pass through you, even the body's arising and passing away, the day will come when you can enter into any experience in perfect peace. And when you enter any experience in *peace*, you will transcend it. When you enter an experience in *fear*, you lock yourself into it. That is called the creation of hell and the need for rebirth. Any experience that you wholeheartedly choose to enter from a place of perfect peace is transcended.

Let then there be the Crucifixion of all of your false ideas of yourself. Be willing to take the leap off the cliff, to entertain what seems to be absurd and insane and outrageous and arrogant, according to the world. Dare to claim that you are as God created you to be and nothing in this world holds a candle to your radiance. And long after the world seeks to destroy you—and it's always trying to do that—and long after the body has been laid down by whatever means you may choose, you will remain and you will laugh at the thought of loss and death.

This is the Resurrection then, the resurrection within your *consciousness* of the *truth that sets you free*. See in my earthly experience only a symbol of what can occur within you, as you choose to give your thoughts, to give your perceptions, to give your fears, to give your petty wants and needs over to your persecutors—for you'll believe that the angels who have come to dismantle your illusions *are* your persecutors, because death feels like persecution. Give yourself over to it. Let the mind be corrected.

Let the heart open and be healed. Let crucifixion be finished that resurrection might be experienced. And when that Resurrection called awakening has occurred, you will ascend to the Father, for He will take the final step for you and you will abide in the real world.

Thank you for asking the question.

Question: How do I know when I have surrendered myself to the Holy Spirit?

Answer: Indeed, beloved friend, you will know that you have surrendered yourself to the Holy Spirit because you will hear a loud bell go off, there'll be much confetti tossed by those in buildings above you! Hmm. Hmm. And someone will rush up to you with a microphone and say, "You are the winner!"

[Laughter]

And you can stand upon the stage and say,
I'd like to thank my mother and my father.

Hm. Beloved friend, I approach your question with levity, for levity is something that you fear. You allow the seriousness of the intellect to interfere with the feeling of receiving the Love of God, like a gentle peace descending upon the cells of your being. So, there's always a point to my seeming madness.

Now, there are indeed signs that you will come to recognize. At first they're slippery because you're used to recognizing something else and calling *it* the real world. You will know that you have surrendered to the Holy Spirit, first in a brief moment here and then another moment there, but you'll begin to feel and sense a certain quality. That quality is peace, no anxiety felt throughout the cellular structures of the body, no longing, no sense of loss and no dread, just the simplicity of witnessing and allowing what unfolds as your experience in any given moment — and it is totally acceptable to you, no matter what is occurring. That seems like madness to the world, for the world says, "Well you're on the right track when you know what's happening is taking you where you know you need to be, where success is coming to you, where comfort and safety in the world is coming to you."

Ah, then I must be on the right track!

No. You're on the right track when you know that from the crown of the head to the tips of the toes, you are at peace with yourself and the world around you. And as you look out upon the world in that circumstance, you see no one to blame, no one to fear, you see only innocence. It is a *palpable feeling* because, you see, you believe you're a body and that's how you judge things. Therefore, as you learn to feel peace through your physical beingness, as you notice that the throat relaxes when you speak, there's no anxiety or hurrying up of your words where someone could be ranting and raving and you just allow them to do so, while *you* are undisturbed. Rest assured, part of your mind has relinquished you to the guidance of the Holy Spirit. Holy, because it's whole and not fragmented. Spirit, because it is the real world, not the unreal world that you have made.

You will know, beloved brother, when you have surrendered

Choose to See

wholly to the Holy Spirit, when the thought of wanting to surrender no longer arises, when the recognition dawns that there's no longer an energy of seeking within you, when no longer do you experience fear arising in your being, when you notice its absence and realize it's not been there for a very long time. You will know that you have become One, through your surrender to the Voice for God.

Question: What role does Jeshua want me to play in the bringing of Heaven to Earth?

Answer: I want you to sell the tickets! [Laughter] Hmm. Might as well create some profit for yourself here! Hmm.

Again, beloved brother, *levity*—for as you ask the question, it comes from a certain pattern of heaviness that there is something you must look to *outside* of yourself, that you must subordinate yourself to something you *should* do. That is a pattern of the world's thinking,

> *Well, I have to go off to work today. Well, I should get out of bed. After all, it's what's expected.*

The world mind is constantly looking outside of itself, for an employer, for a boss, for God, for a priest, for a lover, for a child, for whatever. Some in their drunken stupor would look for a lightpost to give them direction of what they should and shouldn't do. Hmm!

And yet I say unto you, beloved friend, listen well: you *need do nothing* save to choose to open and receive the Love of God, to allow the mind to be corrected so that wherever you are, you know you are Home, you are at peace, you and your Father are One. Then, as the Holy Spirit weaves the tapestry of the Atonement, since you will probably find that your body is still existing, there may be some requests made. They will be simple and you are always free to accept them or reject them. What really matters is that you choose to become the Peace of God and allow that peace to pervade your being. That is what influences the vibrational frequencies of other minds, even if you never lift a physical finger. Compare not your path or your life with others, merely teach only Love. And seek first the Kingdom before all things of the world by reminding yourself daily:

> *I and my Father are One! I need do nothing and I remain as I am created to be! This world is harmless and already it is being*
>
> *translated into reality. And the Holy Spirit doesn't even need me to accomplish it!*

Therefore, be happy in each day, trust what the heart says to you each day, allow yourself to touch joy each day — and be at peace. And for you especially, tell yourself a joke or two!

Question: Is Christ different from Joshua or Jeshua?

Answer: This is a very worthwhile question. As you know, an entire religion has been built up on the exclusive identification of Christ with *me* — that is me as the historical Jeshua ben Joseph, or Joshua if you prefer. Use any name you wish, it doesn't matter to me.

Now, Christ is God's creation. Jeshua is a name given to a particular manifestation of humanity called a man in physical form, a name that separates him for utilitarian purposes from other men with different names, and women too. Christ is pervasive and eternal. Christ is the depth of your own beingness. Imagine it to be like an infinite ocean from which have arisen all waves that you call individual persons, whether male or female. Jeshua, or Joshua or Jesus, that name signifies one of those waves.

Christ signifies that which pervades equally the depth and reality of all minds and hearts. It is really more an energy, a quality of beingness. It is the literal reflection or extension of the presence of the unlimited Love of God. Christ is God's Son, being neither male nor female, it means merely the offspring of, that which wells up out of. Jeshua or Joshua or Jesus became one with Christ, identified no longer as a man but *as Christ*. That passageway is the same one that everyone walks, since it is merely the return to right-mindedness. If you see yourself only as the wave upon the infinite ocean, that's a start; but eventually the goal is to shift your sense of identity, so that my words *become* yours:

> I and my Father are One. Not of myself do I do these things, but my Father does them through me. In other words, there is nobody here but my Father.

Christ and Jeshua are different at one level. They become one and the same as the mind or the individual that I *was* surrendered the illusory perception of myself as separate from God and became identified with *only* the Mind of Christ. Then, there is only Christ and the man has disappeared, except as a temporary symbol, an anchor, a roadmap, a direction that you can follow until you pass me by and become that ocean yourself. And when you no longer need me in any way, shape or form, then we will be together without interruption for all of eternity. Hm. That should give you something to chew on.

Question: Please say more about non-physical reality.

Answer: More about non-physical reality.

[Laughter]

Have I accomplished the task? [chuckles]

Beloved friend and sister, what on earth ever gave you the thought—literally what on earth ever gave you the thought—that physicality was real? If you ask me to speak of non-physical realities, you're already assuming that your physical experience is quite real. How do you know that? Because somebody's taught you it? Because you bang into a wall and therefore, convince yourself that it must be real? Does this not also occur in dreams? When someone plunges a knife into your heart in your dream, do not you feel the dread and terror of death, of being attacked? Until suddenly you open your eyes and it may take you a while to shake it out of your cells but you realize: that was just a dream. Sure seemed real to me!

In the very same way, physicality seems real—until you begin to allow correction to come to your mind, to think the insane thought that maybe you are Christ incarnate. As the real world comes to be re-established through your awareness and consciousness, even while the body seems to abide and exist, you will sense it to be very limited. Just as you may enjoy the experiences of your dream state, but when you awaken you often feel that they were limited, there was something arising from inside of you. As you awaken to the real world, you begin to perceive and feel the body and physicality as something that is smaller than you that has arisen from within your vastness, in other words that you are much more than the body can contain.

It is therefore very appropriate not to think that you live within the body but that *the body lives within you*, it arises from within you, you contain it as a temporary teaching and learning device. Love it, embrace it, have a great time with it, but don't identify yourself with it. Don't limit your understanding of yourself to what transpires between the crown of the head and the tips of the toes and when you extend your arm out, don't you think for a moment that you stop at the end of your finger! You are pure energy, pure light, and your radiance shines through *many* dimensions and you are linked to them all continually.

Non-physical 'realities' — there are many of them, if you wish to look at it that way, and in fact the greater aspect of your beingness is non-physical. Your physical experience is like a drop in the ocean. Let that sink in. It is like a dot on a page and the whole while the vastness of your being is moving merrily along, experiencing dimension after dimension. And often this will creep into your awareness in your dreams or in your meditations: it will slip through the cracks and you'll have what's called an ecstatic experience. You'll feel like you opened, when in fact you simply allowed the openness to seep into the smallness of your physical experience.

How then to struggle to attain experience in non-physical realms? By not struggling, by beginning by acknowledging that you are pure Spirit, that all worlds have arisen from within one Holy Mind, the only creation of God. You are that vast ocean and you have merely focused all of your attention on the physical experience you are creating. You can do that joyfully or you can look at it as some kind of a dread disease. It's your choice. Nevertheless, to experience non-physical realities, merely loosen your fixation of attention on the body-mind and its experiences and problems and all of the rest, and allow yourself to entertain thoughts of your grandeur and greatness. Rest into — through allowing — rest into the feeling of infinity. The mind, or your place of awareness, will begin to open bit by bit and more, more and more until you can no longer squeeze your attention into the space and volume of a body.

This doesn't mean you're going to step on it like a bug and get rid of it! It means you'll just embrace it as another aspect of yourself, like the ocean embraces each and every wave, allows it its experience but doesn't cling to it and doesn't try to make it last; doesn't try to make a wave become rigid as though if it failed to do so, nobody will ever see the ocean. It allows the wave to rise, and then it passes away. The ocean delights in it, but the ocean itself is never identified with any particular wave.

That will do for now, because in what has been shared, as it is contemplated, beloved friend, you will find that correction is coming to certain ideas you have taken upon yourself about what non-physical realities must be and be like, and what must occur for you to experience them.

And again, 'tis a good question to have asked.

No more questions.

We will end then by saying: That's what you think! [Laughter] There will indeed be many questions and we will begin a process then in which some of this time is allotted to addressing the questions which come from this family.

Therefore, in closing, know simply this: there can be no such thing as closure to the extension of Love. Be you all therefore that which you are *this one day*, don't worry about tomorrow, there is no such thing. This day, walk upon your earth while making a choice to delight in perceiving yourself as awake and alive and at peace, roaming through a countryside called the physical dimension for a very brief time. Enjoy it, look lovingly upon it and bless it with the blessings that can come only from the Mind of Christ within you.

Choose to See

Peace then be unto you always.

Amen.

Death Earth Changes

Now, we begin.

And indeed, greetings unto you, beloved and holy friends. I come forth to abide with you from a place that is not apart from where you are. I come forth to abide with you because I love you. I come forth to abide with you because you are already all that I am and all that I could possibly represent to the mind of mankind. I come forth as a promise kept that I am, indeed, with you always. I come forward because the time comes quickly.

And I come forth to gather my friends to myself who have already chosen to join with me in this age, to bring forth that of the Christed Consciousness from the depth of their *own* being; to walk this earth *as* the arisen Christ; to be that one through whom the Love of God is extended unto the plants and to the animals, and to every brother and sister that walks with you and yet carries the veil of fear; that walks the light, the temple of their heart. I come forth because I am asked to come forth of my Father.

I am in charge of the Atonement. That is, I am in charge of the process whereby this planet, this human consciousness, this third-dimensional realm, will begin to move toward a transition of vibrational frequency. Hmm? Therefore, I come forth to any mind that prepares a place for me by choosing to relinquish the burden of trying to be conformed to a thought system, to a way of life that does not work—a way of life and a thought system that must be reversed completely, so that the heart leads and the mind follows; so vision is the guide, and the body is used only to bring forth into manifest form that seed of holy vision which the Father would place within you.

I come forth because we are one. I come forth because we are friends. I come forth *for the simple joy* of abiding with *you*, the Holy Children of God. For from the beginning, which is before space and time, already were we together as One Mind. And in an ancient moment, a useless dream was dreamt, a dream of forgetting, a dream of separation. But even in that moment, already did your Creator, the one that I have called Abba, Father, set the bridge in place that would one day become activated in the depth of your soul, by which you would come from the world of your making into the truth of the Kingdom . . . that the very words I once explained to the world would become *your* words, that would become *your* truth, *your* reality, your *remembrance* . . . that after all dreams have been dreamt and the soul chooses to cross the bridge, it rests and reclines in the simple truth that *I and my Father are one.* And we create together only the good, the holy, and the beautiful.

Therefore, indeed, beloved friends, it is an honor and a joy to abide with you, to co-create with you, to walk with you on the way that you've chosen. For it is only through the innocence of a perfectly free will that the soul can return to the Kingdom. Love does not need to strive, Love does not need to reach out and hold onto, Love does not need to persuade. It merely abides in its own nature, waiting for the seeker of reality to turn from the roar and din of the world, in which peace cannot be found, in which fulfillment is forever lacking, and begins to hear the crystal-clear but very quiet song of the Creator, whispering eternally,

Beloved child, I love you. Come, remember me, and let us be as One.

So, with all of that by way of greeting, I give thanks unto you, each of you, for your willingness to hear the call and to answer it, to step upon the bridge and allow its light, its intelligence —

for the bridge is but the Holy Spirit, the link back to the Mind of God — to guide you in all things. And as you learn not to hear the thoughts born of the world, but to hear the whispers of Spirit that arise from a quiet mind and a peaceful heart and a decision to trust the voice for Spirit, you cannot fail but to complete this journey. The end, therefore, is certain, and each of you in your own way — and indeed, all of you collectively — are witnessing and experiencing within yourselves and in your relationships, the manner in which the Father, God, is calling creation back to Herself.

Therefore, *rejoice* with one another. *Be glad* with one another. *Celebrate* one another. *Love you*, one another. For the end was written in the stars before the stars were birthed. And that time comes quickly. For long have I waited this age to be upon this plane, when enough momentum has been created in the consciousness of mankind so that a wave of awakening can no longer be shut out, that a wave of awakening can no longer be resisted, that a wave of awakening will melt away all fear . . . and once again the Kingdom of Heaven will be spread across the face of this Earth. But unlike the time when Man recognized it not, mankind *will know* that *the truth is true, always* — and that what is real cannot be threatened, and *only* what is real exists.
There, indeed, will come a moment when all dreams of fear are forgotten, when all strife and enmity between brothers and sisters is dissolved as but an echo of a thought — thought so long ago that it's hardly even imaginable. The Earth will radiate the light of Truth yet again, as she, too, prepares to make her transition, her ascension, her vibrational change; and the waters of this planet will run clearly, and the skies will radiate with colors that have not yet been seen by human eyes. There will be a harmony between all species and mankind. And the way of the world will be forgotten. And the way of peace restored. And the Earth will provide all that mankind could possibly need, simply by the asking.

And in that day and hour when all things have been set in place and the Atonement, the correction, has occurred, for a brief moment that state will be experienced. And then [snaps fingers] this whole plane of density will simply dissolve from view. Not gone, but *translated* into an entirely new domain.

There are many — indeed, we would say unto you that everyone living on your planet at this time is being pressed to make the decision: Are you going to stay and go for the ride? Or are you going to have to move to a different neighborhood? Everyone is being confronted by that decision, from the oldest to the youngest, even the brand- new, newborn child. By the way, many of those that are being new born have already made the decision, and that's why they're being birthed — to assist in setting the frequency. Many of the children being birthed in the world now are already light years ahead of where humanity has been stuck for a while. And they bring a new frequency of consciousness; they bring a new sense of unlimitedness. And they will not settle for the limited fear-based ideas that have created the world into which you were birthed.

Each and every one has a role to play, a part that has been assigned. It has been with you since the moment your soul was birthed; and the hour and the day comes when each must turn within and finally *allow* that part to flower and be played through them. And in whatever way that you come to it, you will understand the words that I spoke, seemingly so long ago, when I was confronted with the finality of my drama, the finality of my own teaching — what some would the Crucifixion (I've never desired to emphasize *that* part of it; that was just stepping-stones to the Resurrection.) And those words are simply this: Nevertheless, not my will, not the will of the separate fearful ego, but Thine be done — the will of the One Mind *that is but Love*. And when Love guides the way, miracles sprout before you. And not one obstacle is left in front of you;

it dissolves before you reach it.

So . . . here you are. In a little building in what you call your Santa Fe, gathering with brothers and sisters that you have known across space and time, because you've all answered the same call and are beginning to be called into a resonance that accelerates the growth of all of you. Just as many are being called together through different lineages, through different teachers—orchestrated, if you will, to gather together in their own ways, to learn the lessons they yet need to learn, to discover their way of service to the planet, to humanity, to the Kosmos, to the Heart of Christ and to the Creator. *An ancient dream begins now to end.* The circle is nearly completed, and the pendulum returns all things to the pristine and innocent truth that all things are but the extension of the radiance of God's presence. And fear can have no place in a mind that has awakened to the reality of God.

And what you are doing here, *even in this evening*, is a part of that very process. I've said many times that I come to call my friends to myself. Imagine that all of you have been given a script very, very long ago. And part of the script said that the day would arise when you would reconnect with an old friend—the one the world has called Jesus. And that through that connection a vibration would be created that would accelerate the fulfillment of your own part, your own unique role to play, the stepping into the fullness of *your* Christed nature—just as once, as a man, I decided to take my Father's word at face value and stepped into my own Christed nature.

And while many beings sit before their televisions in this town of yours tonight and many more sit in what you call the rooms for unconsciousness, putting the liquid in the body (the bars), while many seek a lover to keep them warm through the night, the night never lasts forever. *You* have chosen to come *here* because you have heard an invitation for this one evening, and you have accepted. Therefore, celebrate and rejoice, for the day is at hand and there is no greater joy than the re-communion of ancient friends who, deep within themselves, *know* that *the time is now*. The dance has begun, the music has started . . . Hmmm . . . And the whole of creation *will come* to this party.

So. We want, then, in this evening to speak specifically to certain questions that have been generated, for they hold a purpose in helping to extend and to clarify a simple message about this time frame, about certain changes, about certain things that are now occurring within your governments, upon your planet, as this Armageddon boils to a crescendo in which all souls are being asked,

> *Well, are you going to join the dance, or are you going to have to leave the neighborhood?*

That is not a judgment, it is an offering being made to the soul of everyone: Use time constructively, you can heal your heart, you can practice forgiveness, you can awaken as Christ.

You're going to have to, because the planet is doing the same thing; and if you don't come with her you won't be able to handle her light and her frequency, and you'll need to move to a different neighborhood. That's all. No judgment, no fear, no being struck dead by God — only a simple offering. You can awaken now, or you can awaken somewhere else, later. There have been far too many "laters".

So. We believe, then, that you have questions. Well, Jeshua, it's not terribly fair for you to answer the questions before I pose them. It's just a simple mistake that we occasionally make. There seems to be a polarization going on now between people who are answering the call and people who would remain in fear. And those things look like wars and fights and racial tension. Is this part of that process?

No, it's because of what has been placed in the water.

[Laughter] I'm glad you haven't lost your sense of humor.

Indeed. Too much of what you call your fast food.

[Laughter]

Beloved friend, you have heard it said that when you hear of wars and rumors of wars — no, the time is not quite yet but, boy, is it getting close. Hmm? Indeed. As we spoke a moment ago — and please understand this — *there is no such thing as punishment*. There is no condemnation or judgment in the mind of God, who is above, and seeks to give his Holy Child all good things, and would lead the child from dreams of strife and suffering and fear to dreams of freedom and peace and empowerment and Christedness. There is a vibration beginning to build in the depth of this dimension, this density you call your third — third dimension, third-dimensional reality. Although we would say, there's no reality here yet, but it's coming.

[Laughter]

This vibration is like a pebble dropped in a pond that is beginning to send ripples. It's been going on for some time, it's beginning to pick up pace, beginning to vibrate a little more, like water beginning to boil. You sense that it's happening, although you don't even see the bubbles rising yet. You *know* something's changing in the energy of the water. And as that occurs, it is literally rippling through every soul. Why? Because separation does not exist. And if God holds the thought,

Okay, time to nudge the child. I've let them dream long enough. Let's see if they can hear my voice over their dreams,

that ripple must go through every created soul. And as it does so, it is stirring up all the old fears, all the old patterns, all the old habits, and the soul is being asked,

Are you ready to purify?

which simply means to make a different choice. It's not . . . it doesn't require lying on a bed of nails. Hmm? Simply the recognition that something's coming up that no longer feels as comfortable as it once did. Are you willing to let go and allow a small period of disorientation until reality settles in? And what you thought could have never been, becomes your norm. And you walk the world awake.

There are many who are having their fears escalate. And why? Because they are committed to fear. They believe in fear; it is what keeps them safe. I know that sounds odd, but it's very true. As long as I can look out upon my neighbor and see you as the bad person, then I know who needs to be attacked.

And all we have left to do is figure out how to attack you before you attack me. Very simple. And if I win, I get all the marbles. But in attack, no one can win. For when the attacker attacks, the attacker is attacked by the weight of the negativity of their own fear.

So, yes, what you're seeing on the planet is a polarization that is occurring because every soul is being confronted by the decision to heal and to forgive; or to hold onto the idols of their woundedness and to judge.

Death Earth Changes

Once I said, "With what judgment that you put out, rest assured you will be judged in the same way." Why? Because you create your experience. So again, there will be many who will not be able to live on this planet. That is why there is also a creation of many odd and new dis-eases upon your plane. It is why there are very bizarre things being done by certain governments on your planet as the fear builds—in an attempt to remain in control of something that they don't even understand. And yet, *none of it* can affect the pure in heart, the meek who will inherit the Earth, those that choose to heal the gap in their own being between themselves and the mind of God. For they will be led in each moment. And nothing will befall them. A few lessons on the way, yes, but only by way of purification, only by way of a deeper wisdom, a deeper understanding. Where you extend to your Father a smidgen of willingness, the end is certain; and you are safe to trust what you feel in the depth of your heart, which is the temple of the soul, where Father and Child rest together: God and Christ.

Does that help you in regard to that question?

Yes, thank you. But everything you've said tonight can be taken either physically or metaphorically. Is this a physical change that will occur on the planet, or is this a metaphorical change and the planet itself remain unscathed?

Beloved friend, I am very glad that you have posed your question in just that way. Now, we both know that to put anything into language in the form of a question, you are forced to deal with the language structure you have. Your language structure lives in duality. Things are either on or off, white or black, they're metaphor or they're physical. But I say unto you, the whole of this physical dimension is a metaphor. It is a symbol of a vibration of thought. Does that make it less real? Not at all. For how can the Holy Child of God create unreality?

Therefore, this *dream* will be played out and involve the whole of the created domain. And yet it's still just a metaphor, *part of a dream*. For this house you sit in, the town in which it resides, and the planet upon which this town resides all exist in a space no wider than the tip of a pin. And yet, where *you* abide, all of creation is contained within you, and you are vast beyond the reach of all solar systems. And when you get a feel for that, you will, indeed, marvel.

Yes, it will occur, and it is inappropriate and inaccurate for anyone to assume that this change is merely pictures or symbols, that it really only occurs in something called the mind that's somewhere tucked inside a body and has nothing at all to do with the planet, with the stars, with the comets, with the photon belts. 'Tis all one thing: Mind creating. Therefore, for Mind to awaken, all of Mind awakens and changes. Yes, it will involve the planet itself. I believe that should help make it clear.

Then the role of Shanti Christo must also be clear in this process. Is it a beacon?

Actually, beloved friend, we have merely beguiled you, and that which is called Shanti Christo is a distractive mechanism, being created by the Devil.

[Laughter]

Beloved friend, yes. Shanti Christo is an expression of a vibration of thought, like a pebble dropped in a pond, that is created to manifest specific vibrational patterns or ripples. It will be utilized by us to attract many minds and many beings who can step through the portal into awakened consciousness. There are many portals being created. And why do there need to be many portals? Because there are many levels of consciousness and there are many forms of experience that you've all created, everyone on the planet. I am not everyone's teacher, even though I am in charge of the Atonement. So, imagine that I'm merely sitting behind a small little desk out in the meadow, and I pick up the, what you call your cordless telephone. In this case it's even a non-physical phone. And I will call another teacher, another being, and say,

> *You know, this one over there had a very good connection with you back in Egypt four thousand years ago. Why don't you pop down and have a little chat with them?*

So there is an orchestration going on. There may seem to be many forms of the universal curriculum, many teachers, many methodologies. And yet, all of them are but portals through which the soul chooses to walk — to step from fear to love, from insanity to sanity, from dreams to reality. Shanti Christo, then, is one such portal through which I specifically can activate the call and create a gathering place, if you will — a gathering frequency — through which I can call those to myself who, because of past resonances, past experiences, have come to love me and have come to trust me as one who can carry them over the bridge. Hm?

Yes, Shanti Christo has a role to play, and rest assured there is a safety mechanism built into this vibration. This vibration cannot be manipulated or used for personal gain. It cannot be misdirected, for the mind that may be attracted to it and then sort of bounces off and goes to the left or right is one that merely realizes that this vibration requires (what is your phrase?) the "getting real". This is a vibration and a portal that helps souls step into the next vibration. You can't sneak anything past the ego- detector. Hmm.

Does that help in regard to that question?
Yes.

Are there any other questions in the group about Earth changes?

Yes. Are we going to experience a period of three days of darkness during this change upon the earth?

We would suggest here that it is very probable that this will occur. And yet, it will be a little longer than three days. This will eventuate, if it is necessary for the change of vibration, to require what would be called the changing of the axis of the planet. This will create a bit of a shake-up, as one can imagine, and there will be created a blackening-out, and the sun's rays will not touch the Earth. This sun itself is going nowhere.

Yes, but listen well to what I say, for there are many prophecies coming out, and there will be many more as we move closer and closer. Many are getting pictures that are the effect of the generation in their own minds of how they need to understand the ripples that are coming to them. We speak of probabilities because it is never certain what must eventuate for a change of vibration to occur. And you can liken this to your own lives. Sometimes you need to be hit with a broom handle to get your attention. At other times, a quiet whisper seems to be enough.

We would suggest that, because there is no separation, the more that souls choose to awaken and to heal, the less the need for shocking circumstances to get their attention. The more mankind awakens, the easier the transition of the Earth. Does that make sense for you?

Yes.

Is there truly any difference between entities that describe themselves as Germaine, Jeshua, Michael, and who would bring their message through an individual? Is there really any difference among the messengers?

The answer is a resounding yes. And why? When you speak of difference, what you are alluding to is that is there an entity that is its own unique sphere of consciousness arising out of the One Mind. God is aware of God because of God's creation. You are God's creation. Therefore, the Father knows Himself because *you* exist to be aware of Him. Individuation, like the ripple arising out of the ocean, does not change the substance — it's still all made of one thing — and yet, there is individuation, uniqueness, just as there are several souls associated with the bodies that have gathered in this room, and you all have your own unique, cosmic social security number.

[Laughter]

Will it be bankrupt when we get there?

No, it is always, shall we say, overflowing. And you don't even have to pay into it!

So, understand, then, that when we speak of One Mind, we are not saying that individuality does not exist. We're merely saying that each being, each created being, has within them the power to operate from the One Mind that I have called Christed Consciousness. It can go by many names. And yet, individuation is eternal.

There will never be a time, a moment, or a non-moment, when all of you simply dissolve into some amorphous blob of awareness. In other words, the more you settle into God, the more the desire there is to individuate, so that you can have relationship in which to celebrate the good, the holy, and the beautiful — to dance, eternally at play in the Father's Kingdom. Does that help in that regard?

Most definitely.

Now, by the way, I would highly suggest that I would never listen to the Germaine fellow. And Michael sometimes is a little... Hmmm. Just kidding, of course.

And Mary shops at K-Mart.

Mmm... I've never been able to keep that one under control.

Rest assured, we delight with one another, we play with one another, we *see* the Creator, we *see* the presence of God *as each of us*, and we respect our individuation, just as you respect yours. To see the oneness in diversity, to experience communion between two wholes — that is the great promise of the Kingdom. To be in holy relationship in which two Christs, as individuated beings, yet emerging from and operating from the same mind, the same values, the same love, the same compassion, the same wisdom, the same unlimited power to create the good, the holy, and the beautiful . . . Now *that is a dance worth attending*.

Therefore, seek not the death of the self, but seek the arisen Self. Hm? That should help.

Would you care to summarize this evening?

It has been... worthwhile. Beloved friend, as you well know, since the thought was dropped in the mind, that this short gathering of this evening was designed to bring forth some specific corrections that will be flowing out to many minds — many more minds than you're even aware of. For those first ones who receive it will be struck, a little chord is struck,
> *Oh, yes, that's right. Thank you for the nudge. I have to get on with it. I have to get on with it. I was beginning to fall into the*

hope that I could just dissolve away and not have to birth Christ.

And then they will give that to many others.

There is much being taught in your world that is *not* correct. Anything based on fear is incorrect. Anything based on the *end of creation*, even in positive terms, is incorrect. For the Father extends himself *eternally*. How, then, can there be an end to creation? There is only ever-expanding fullness — fullness expanding into fullness, and into fullness, and into fullness, and into fullness. Higher and higher, and wider and wider, and brighter and brighter, and ever more blissful and ever more wise and loving.

And you all know exactly what that means, for every consciousness reciprocates or plays out the very journey of creation. You all know that you've made creations that were a little difficult, they were a little crude; and so you sought new ways, didn't you? And you keep birthing better and better creations. Guess what? That's it! That's the power of God, which is the soul, seeking to create the good, the holy, and the beautiful. And there reaches a point, of course, where you realize that you have to give up being identified with egoic consciousness, so that Spirit can truly use us all to create in a Christed realm. Hm? Like leaving the things of childhood behind and taking up your rightful place of a powerful, mature adult. To be an adult in the Kingdom is to be Christ.

Therefore, indeed, beloved friends, *allow* the good, the holy, and the beautiful to pour forth through *your soul*. For you are the ones sent in this age, with all power under Heaven and Earth, to reveal to your brothers and sisters the truth of a happy dream, the truth of perfect freedom, the end of fear, and the remembrance of Love.

Be you, therefore, with one another often, and remember always that you are the Light of this world. Why not get on with it? And with that, peace unto you always, from the heart of one who loves you and has reached across space and time to touch you and to whisper to you,

> *Beloved friend, come, take my hand. We are on the bridge already. Just step lightly. Come with me. I know the way.*

From that one — who is me, and speaking on behalf of the many who gather with me each and every time this specific work is done — I love you and we love you. It is not possible for you to journey alone. And what you are asked to do in the depth of your vision and in your heart, rest assured, it would not be asked if you were not also given the power and the support to bring it about. Never think you need to be the maker and the doer. You need only be, as each of us is, a servant of the Mind of the Creator who is but Love and whom we serve with perfect freedom and joy and fulfillment.

Peace, then, be unto you always. Amen.

Jeshua...Don't run off.

Where could I go?

Thank you. Take two.

I'd like to discuss with you, pursuant to the book that we're working on, *The Way Through Death*, you brought to our attention this past December that there were many individuals who died in the explosion in Oklahoma City who were at that time unaware of their death situation. They were somehow hung up in that moment of time of the explosion, unable to extricate themselves from the collapsed building. We've all heard stories of ghosts still inhabiting the locations of their death. Why is this so, if what Emmanuel says, that death is "like taking off a tight shoe" is true?

Death is like taking off a tight shoe, but it does not, necessarily, bring enlightenment and freedom. The tight shoe is the density of the physical form. Yet, where a mind is not yet prepared, and where the mind carries attachment to what that mind had learned to value — other bodies in space and time — the energy of that soul cannot ascend to the Father, to use an old Biblical term. There can be no ascension to the Father, unless that soul has gotten over a very important hump: the hump of *at least* having *faith* that there is something beyond this world. Does that make sense for you?

So, in a very real way, a weight has been lifted. There is no cold, there is no heat, there is no need for fuel for the body. Experiences continue. The interesting thing is that without the physical density of the body, there is no experience of time as you know it. Therefore, a soul can remain stuck in a building that is collapsing for what you would perceive as thousands of years — if that mind remains attached to the belief that it is *only* the third-dimensional physicality, and that the only thing of value are other things of third-dimensional physicality.

Just as, many times, you would walk down a street and not even notice that a friend has passed you by because you're so fixated on where you're going, the soul at death can be so fixated on its perceptual values that it doesn't even notice angelic choirs singing in their ear: "Come, beloved friend, ascend!" Doesn't even notice it, until there is communication, till somehow there is discovered a way to create or to bring its attention to value something else — to realize that something has profoundly changed, and that its belief system had been limited.

Does that help you in regard to that question?

So, from what you're saying then, there is no set sequence that occurs at that moment called death. So a lot of people report on going through the tunnel and you're there and...

That is a very... The tunnel experience being spoken of in your cultures as the near-death experience is a very, very basic first stage of the dying process. Primarily, it entails the withdrawal of energy from the brain core—from the brain core to the stem of the body or toward the spine of the body. It creates the *perception* of the tunnel, in which there is a withdrawal from the senses of the body into this, what appears to be a tunnel. And it is a portal and a doorway. And yes, I appear to many, and others appear, as well. But the belief system is still functioning. That is only one of the first stages of the actual death process.

As it continues, and as the brain core literally dies—which simply means that life force is withdrawn and not returned to it, so it is dropped like old baggage—then the soul, the consciousness, experiences a vibrational leap, what you might call a quantum leap in vibrational states, into more and more subtle states of its own being. But there is a period in which there is a playing-out of the residual effects of all of its perceptions and beliefs. It is called the . . . in one stage, the life story is played back that fast. [Snaps fingers] Thoughts or fears of a Satan or beliefs in a Savior become the energy which attracts that experience to that individual. So, in a general sense, there is something that occurs energetically.

But what occurs within that energy is *entirely unique* to each individual. And what will matter is this: If time has been used constructively—that is, if you utilized time to let go of limiting beliefs and begin to foster first faith and then direct experience in tapping into other dimensions, into remembering the mind of God, if you practiced forgiveness and healing—then at death fear has no place to grip the mind.

Yes, the tunnel begins to happen because the energy is being withdrawn from the cellular structure of the body, from the brain itself toward the brain stem—what I call the stem or the interior of the spine. And since the mind has been cultivating devotion to God, the willingness to heal, the ability to *let go* without fear, then as these things come up and move through very, very quickly, they have no effect whatsoever, and the mind proceeds toward light—greater and greater dimensions of light. Hm? And it is possible for the soul, then, to remain in those dimensions without any need of incarnating again. It is always something left unhealed—a fear, a self-judgment, a resentment, an old anger—that creates a heaviness that draws the soul, using its infinite power, to re-create third- dimensional physicality yet again, to try to get it right. It is always much wiser to use the incarnation you have, to get it right! Don't think about the old ones; don't think about the ones that might come. Realize that right where you are, *right where you are,* everything is *perfect for your awakening.*

You can awaken *now*, by choosing to teach only Love. And that must include to yourself. To love the self is ultimately the final portal, for only when you truly love yourself can you serve another. Only when you love yourself so much you're no longer willing to tolerate anything but the presence of Christ in you. When you believe that you are so valuable that you should be treated like a priceless jewel. Then, indeed, Christ will arise. For the Holy Son of God, who is but Christ, will not come up and take his abode in a home unworthy of him. And what is that home? It's not the body; it's the Mind. Therefore, love yourself.

When I once said, "Love your neighbor as yourself," I thought it was obvious that that meant you had to love yourself before you could ever experience loving your neighbor. Therefore, to learn the way of love, practice with diligence forgiveness.
Release expectation from anyone or anything. Create your vertical alignment in the mind of God. And seek not from the world what it does not possess: the eternal and perfect peace that birthed you and that you are seeking to recover. "Be you, therefore, whole and perfect," means just that. Wake up. Get it right while you're on the planet. Let the mind heal. Choose to be the presence of Love. Trust God above all things, and walk this world as the meek who will inherit it. Be you, therefore, the presence of Love.

And when the time comes, as it must, for that temporary density structure called the body to dissolve and be given back to the Earth from which it came, fear will have no place in you. And as the tunnel begins to appear and you know—this happens to every mind, by the way—there is a moment when you know something is occurring that's going to occur and you're not going to be able to interrupt it any more; you're not going to be able to avoid the portal. When you literally feel the energy withdraw from the cells of the body and move toward the stem, or what you call the spinal column, you will welcome it like a joyous ride. And you will turn your attention immediately upward—that is a metaphorical term—but upward to the higher teachings of the mind of God, rather than the teachings of a fearful world. And you will let these things go like toys that have been outgrown. And then the soul can ascend into its full remembrance.

"And in my Father's house are many mansions," which means

that there are an infinite number of dimensions in which you can come to make a new home, based on the quality of vibration that you have brought yourself to in your understanding and in your consciousness, which is nothing more than your love. But the only thing you can ever truly regret is that perhaps you resisted giving that love away, even up to the moment of death. And therefore, love freely, love abundantly, and love without ceasing. And above all, love the Self that has been birthed in the mind of God, for no other reason than to *live in the consciousness of God*.

So, I'll be the gnat shouting at the universe.

Is God self-aware, or is it simply a benign metaphysical force?

Benign metaphysical force.

Don't pick at it, just answer it.

There is nothing more benign than Love. There is nothing more metaphysical, which mean beyond and permeating the physical, than God. There is nothing more forceful, if you mean by that infinite power that cannot be denied, than God.

So if that is what you mean, I would say yes to the use of those terms. Is God self-aware? Are you aware?

Hmm.

Hmm.

Hmm, hmm. Got it.

Hmm. It won't be the last time.
[Laughter]

That, for me, begs the next question. Is there a force outside of God?

Just you. I well do understand the direction of your question. There can be nothing outside of God, and what is unreal does not and cannot exist. Yet, you have the power within the infinite freedom of God to *believe a perception* that there is a force outside of or other than God. Just as you have believed that you are separate from God. 'Tis is an optical delusion of consciousness. It is a dream of a child sleeping in a meadow, in whom no change has truly occurred. That which is called Satan cannot exist or have any power, save in that mind that allows it, and who *gives* that power *to* it. For did I not ask you to speak unto one, could the devil withstand your love? And did it not bring that one to silence? In other words, Love heals—because Love is real. And when you step from fear into Love, where did the boogeyman go?

Well, I'm through with my questions. If you have a summary...

Could I ask a question?

Yes.

Getting back to Shanti Christo, could you give us an idea when this will materialize?

Beloved friend, it already has. And in your third-dimensional plane of time, you are witnessing the process whereby that materialization occurs. In reality, it is already finished, because God does not think thoughts that arise incomplete. Hm? You are merely tuning in to what has already occurred. I know that's a bit of a leap but it's okay, let yourself take it. You are merely choosing to allow yourself to participate in what you've already done. For hear this: In reality, the dream and the process of awakening never occurred. For what has no effect has never happened. The dream, the awakening of the dream, is already done. You might say you are watching the film. Film at 11:00. Can you imagine a newscaster saying,

> *Mmm. All of creation has awakened today and returned to the Holy Mind of God. Film at 11:00.*

[Laughter]

And what you are experiencing is the watching of the film. Like being within a hologram. Yes, and when are the specific parts going to manifest it and love you? When would you *like* them to manifest?

Tomorrow.

Very well. Simply awaken tomorrow, and know: It is finished. Let no doubt arise in your mind, and simply allow the Comforter, the Holy Spirit, to reveal to you what has been finished. Imagine a... what you call a supervisor at a construction site, building a beautiful building, and you come by and you go,

> *How did this happen?*

And he puts his arm around you and says,

> *Come. First I'll show you the foundation, I'll show you the blueprint plans...*

And yet, the whole time you're in the building and your mind begins to tap in to the day they first brought the concrete to make the foundation, then the steel girders, and then later the interior decorators putting the final touches — as he describes for you the process whereby the very building in which you live was created. The buildings on that land are already there. You just don't see them yet. But they're settling in, and you will see them. And when you see them, you will know, just like hundreds of other beings will know,

I've seen those before.

Not in another place and time, but because you've already experienced the completion. Does that make sense?

Yes.

Indeed. And what can stand against the will of God? That is why those that are called to add to and create this vibration must always rest in certainty, in knowingness: It is finished. What a delightful way to spend the last afternoon of the dream of separation. Something to think about.

Thanks, my friend.

Mmmm. Indeed. So, may I be allowed to leave this time?

[Laughter] Where could you go?

Exactly. I merely recede, and just call this communication process. And by agreement always, I merely nod to my brother who no longer, no more exists within the body than you exist within yours. Hm? You're just animating a temporary communication tool. I merely nod to him, and I say, "We're done now." And usually he goes, "Oh, so soon? Thank you." And he returns *his* attention to the body, as I *release* my attention from it. That's all. Kind of like two friends, and one night one of them sleeps in a certain bed in the house, and the next night it's the other person's turn. We just slide in and out of the bag of dust. Sometimes you never quite know who's there.

It's a chance to sleep around though, right?

Indeed. 'Tis good to choose loving cosmic bedfellows.

[Laughter]

Indeed. Therefore, again—and always—I leave, yet I leave not you, for I am closer to you than your own breath, and never further from you than the width of a thought.
Think well, then, and remember the truth that is true always.

Amen.

Decide to be Christ

Now, we begin.

And indeed greetings unto you, Beloved and Holy Children of God. Indeed, greetings unto you, beloved brothers and sisters. Indeed, greetings *unto* you, the embodiment of all that Love is, the embodiment of all that Wisdom is, the embodiment of all that Simplicity is. Indeed, greetings unto *you, Holy Child of God.*

For I come forth not from a dimension apart from you, but I come forth from that place which we have shared together as One, since before the beginning of time. I come forth, then, to abide with you *because I love you.* For I look upon you and I look beyond your illusions of suffering and strife, I look beyond the temporary illusions that *seem* at times to cloud your perceptions still — and *I see only the radiance of that which my Father has birthed and has sustained forever.* For *in you* do I see the reflection of the Truth that *I Am*, and in seeing Christ in *you*, I know Christ in myself.

And the only difference between you and me may yet be that there are a few moments when you make the decision to see yourself other than Christ, and therefore fail to see Christ in your brother and sister. And likewise, there may be a moment when you choose not to see Christ who dwells within your brother or sister, thereby convincing yourself that Christ cannot dwell within you. For remember always that it takes One to know One. And if you see Christ in me, it can only be because *you* have acknowledged from a place within yourself that you *are* the One that you've been seeking. Only Christ can welcome Christ, as only Love can welcome Love. Because you are that Love, all power under Heaven and Earth is given unto you, without measure, consistently — there is not a moment that it is taken from you — and from that power you *choose to create* what *you* have chosen to perceive.

Therefore, the only journey is a journey without distance to a goal that has never changed. It is a journey from the decision to see yourself as separate from God to the decision to see yourself as One with God, and to become entirely vigilant for the Kingdom. And the Kingdom is simply the eternal union of God and His Holy Child, of Creator and created. Like a sunbeam to the sun are you, and nothing you have ever dreamed about yourself has changed for one moment the Truth that is true always.

Therefore, indeed beloved friends I *never* come to instruct you, for what could I possibly teach you that you do not already know? And in any moment, if in your dreams, in your prayers, your meditations, if temporarily through the domain of the mind of this my beloved brother, there are words uttered — caused, if you will, by an impulse of my Love for you — that sound true to you, that touch your heart, that heal the mind, that awaken you, that restore your peace ... rest assured, I have done nothing. For of myself I can *do* nothing, but the Father through me can do all things. For it is the Father in *you* that has activated your awareness. That Truth has been heard. Therefore, when healing comes to your mind it is because *you* have healed it. And you have chosen the context, perhaps, just as some of you in this very hour will choose this context in which to heal an ancient wound, in which to awaken ever more deeply into the Truth that is true always.

Some of you will insist that I have done something to you. But rest assured, *I have no power* over the Holy Child of God: you. I can love you, and I indeed do. I can join with you in the space between your thoughts, and I do — not because there is something amiss with you but because I see in you *everything*

Decide to be Christ

that is good, everything that is holy, everything that is beautiful, everything worthy of Christ's Love; that is what is true about you. Therefore I enter into your dreams and into your meditations and into your prayers, I enter in wherever you would create a space for me *because I love the Child of God who radiates the truth of my Father's Presence and reminds* me *of who I am.*

You, each of you, I see as my savior. Just as when I walked your planet as a man, I learned to look upon everyone as my savior, to see in them the Light of Christ beyond all illusions and it was in seeing that Light that I finally learned that *it must be in me.* This is why relationship *is* the means of your salvation. No one can awaken alone, for there is no truth behind the illusion of separation. There is only One Mind dancing in a myriad of forms, dimensions, layers of consciousness, layers of potentiality, but behind it all *you* are the Shining One sent forth from the Holy Mind of God, at one with that Mind always. And in Truth, only that Mind is Real, for Christ is God's *only* creation.

Therefore, beloved friends, in this hour I am going to ask you to do something that is actually quite important for all of us. If you would indeed honor the Son—the Christ—that dwells in me, then choose from this moment to use the power of choice given unto you to decide to *be* Christ. If you would honor me, then in this hour truly decide to honor *yourself*—to look beyond the illusions that seem perhaps still to govern the mind; to become so arrogant that you take God at His word and simply begin to entertain the thought:

I am That One. I have always been That One. I could never succeed in being other *than That One. It is I who have come to bless this world with the Love of Christ. It is I that find myself temporarily embodied upon a certain planet in a certain solar system in a certain dimension among infinite dimensions. Here, I bless this world. Now, in this moment, Love restores all things, for I am the Redeemer of the world. And as I bless the world, I bless myself. And as I love the world, I have loved myself. And as I see Christ in my brother or sister, I merely reinforce the reality that That One is who I am.*

This is how close the Kingdom is at all times. This, how close the Kingdom *is — now*. What is the width or the distance of a thought? Hm! And yet I say unto you, all that you behold from your perception, even the very body, the trees that bless this planet, the bird that sings at dawn, the wind that whispers gently across the flower bed, the fragrance of that flower — all things that can be perceived exist nowhere save in the distance between the beginning and the ending of a thought. *That* is how powerful you are.

Therefore, dare to think the thought of Truth,

> *I and my Father are One, here and now; I cannot change it. I can delay my recognition of it, for I am given infinite freedom to do so, and perhaps I've been doing a very good job, but nothing I have ever dared to believe about myself has ever been true, except the Truth that is true always: I am That One. I am the One shining beyond all stars. I am the One through whom Creation has flowed. I am the One who blesses Creation with the Love of Christ.*

There may yet be some of you who think that that is arrogant, but I say unto you: the only thing that is arrogant is to insist that you are less than you are created to be and then to try to enlist others to believe it with you. Hm? Hm! Hm. You know that one, hm? How much time and energy have you spent and rest assured, time can waste as well as be wasted — how much time and energy have you spent trying to convince others of your unlovability? How much time and energy have you spent enlisting others to believe *with* you that you are unworthy, that you are weak, that you cannot find peace? How much time and energy have you spent manifesting worlds in which separation seemed to be a success? How much evidence have you amassed to prove it? And yet I say unto you, all of it is your creation. It exists nowhere except between the beginning and the ending of a choice, a thought. And yet the Father waits silently for His Holy Child to awaken from an ancient dream and choose again. The very same power that you have been using and investing in proving to yourself that you are yet separate from God is the *very power* that must come to be used to acknowledge the Truth that is true always. And this *is* being vigilant for the Kingdom.

It is not necessary, then, to seek for Love, for Love is the Truth of your Being. It is, however, quite necessary to seek out the ways in which you have invested time and energy into the birthing of perceptions and beliefs that seem to be other than the Truth – and then to choose anew. All purification, then, is of the mind. And I speak here not of what some would call the lower mind that is engaged in the activities of the body. I speak of the depth of the Mind, or what I often refer to as the Heart – the Heart, the Sanctuary in which Christ yet resides within you: unchanged, unchanging, unchangeable forever.

Please, waste not another moment, for you are worthy of Peace. Please, waste not another moment, but arise now in the Holiness of your Being by simply entertaining this one thought right now in your Being:

> *I and my Father are One. I am as I am created to be. I choose to accept the Truth and to live it – not by my power, for I have none, but by that power that has birthed me in this moment. I am the savior of the world.*

So how does that feel?
[Indistinct reply]
Hm. Is that ok? For, you see, here is the question you must come

to answer for yourself. You must be able to answer this question:

Is it okay for me to be God's Holy Child?

Hm! The only reason you've birthed ideas of separation is that you've answered that question in the past by saying,

Well, not yet. It's okay for Jeshua ben Joseph, and perhaps a few others; I'll select them out and give them permission to be awake.

But if you would honor the Son that dwells in me, *please* honor the Son, the Christ Light, that dwells within you.

Does it feel, what did you say, the pretty darn good? Hm! Trust me, beloved friend, as you live in that decision you will experience an unending expansion of the depth of that goodness and you will discover that your Father's Kingdom has no end and is extended without end in you and through you. And just as you can come to be the master of the domain of your body-mind and of your world, there will then come a day and a moment when you will play as the master of universes, just as you are now beginning to play with the mastery over your mind that seems to be limited to one body.

In my Father's house are many mansions, many dimensions, worlds without end, and you, because you *are* God's Holy Child, are free to open and receive all that has been prepared for you — and if you would well receive it, the whole of Creation in its infinite glory and its unending extension is given to *you*. That is God's delight. Just as a child turns to the father or the mother, and the father and mother feel such love for the child that they would give all things unto that one, likewise does your Father prepare all things for you; and therefore Love merely waits on your welcome.

> *Father, I would receive the Kingdom You have prepared for me since before the beginning of time. I have dreamt long and hard and I have discovered that in separation and limitation there's something lacking: You and me in our perfect and holy Union. Therefore now do I choose to open and receive all that You would give me, gladly. Press it down upon me without measure — let it rain like the showers from infinite, infinite heavenly skies — and I will never cease in my receiving, for I know that I am the one birthed from Your Holy Mind and I am the one whom You love above all.*

That is the Truth, and frankly, though I have tried in a million ways, there's no better way to say it than that. That Truth is true about me *because*— please listen carefully— because and only because it is true for *you*. Hm? If it were true for me and not true for you, then God could not be God, because something would have been created in inequality, and something given would also be withheld — *and God withholds nothing.*

Therefore, that which God is, is pressed down upon you like a gentle spring shower without ceasing and with perfect equality, unto you and unto me, unto every saint and every sinner. And the shower that falls is the power *to choose*. That's all, that is what the Kingdom is: the power to choose what you will be aware of, how you will use the power of mind to create the thoughts that you think and thereby create universes of experience.

Now, here is a simple question that you can ask if you want to find out if this is true. Do you find yourself existing right now? Do you find yourself existing right now? What's the answer?

Hm?

Yes. Yes.

You're using it. You're using the power of God's Love that is showering down upon you to be aware of your literal existence as a sentient being. Hm? And you are just as free to decide what qualities you will experience, right here, right now.

So take a moment and make what you call eye contact — the eyes are the window to the soul — make eye contact with someone in the room, some perfect stranger, existing in an infinitely far space away from you, locked into another body, painfully imprisoned just like you are [laughs] and simply decide that you are Christ and that you would do nothing else in this moment but bless them. Transmit the Love of God *now*.

[Short pause]

No need to tighten the jaw and furrow the brow, the Kingdom is effortless.

Hmmm. There, I believe some of you are feeling that shift in the room. Who's doing it but you?

Now within your own mind gently say, as you continue that eye contact,

> I behold my beloved Self in whom I am well pleased. As I bless, I am blessed. As I love, I receive Love. Therefore, in my giving do I find that which I would receive.
> Therefore, my giving will be without ceasing, that I might give all, to receive all.

Good. Was that pretty darn good? Hm, hm?

Decide to be Christ

[Laughter]

How did that feel? Was it difficult? Did you go through any gyrations in order to do it? The Kingdom is the simplest of the simple. It requires literally no efforting, for effort is of the world, not of the Kingdom. Love is eternally present, waiting only on *your* decision to have vigilance over *your* Kingdom, which is your power to choose. Nothing outside of you has caused anything at any time, for all that you experience flows from within you. And no one has the power to dictate your choice, for no one can usurp the free will of the Holy Son of God.

There is a necessary step in anyone's spiritual journey and that step has just been described for you. The journey *to* the Kingdom truly begins when you completely decide to assume complete responsibility for exactly what you're experiencing in any moment—without fail, without justification, without explanation. For until you choose to claim such power, you cannot truly make the decision—except for momentary glimpses—you can't make the constant decision to be the embodiment of Christ. Why? Because you're constantly giving your power to an illusion outside of yourself. Does that make sense for you?

So the whole of spirituality, after all is said and done, rests only in this:

The Kingdom is at hand. It is spread across the face of the Earth and mankind sees it not because he fails to look into his own consciousness, his own Mind, and claim the power that is going on all the time: the power by which that Mind creates and experiences its creations.

So we have that settled. Hm? Good.

Now, remember that at any time that you notice yourself entertaining an insane idea — and what is an insane idea, except the idea that,

Something out there really is causing my experience. I'm not really the awakened Son of God.

Those are insane ideas. When you have them, realize that you have just freely used the power of your sanity to simply entertain an insane idea. For no other reason than to have the experience. That's all that's going on. That's it! And you are just as free to choose again.

Guilt is a very clever illusion. With it, you have decided that since you once held an insane idea, you've taken away from yourself your worthiness to think sanely:

And now I must strive and work. I must prove myself worthy and hope that God in His Grace will finally have mercy upon me, a poor wretched sinner, and take my burdens from me, and allow me to be healed. Oh Father, don't You hear my prayers?

Frankly, your Father is not even aware of your illusions! He's too busy loving you as you are and giving you the very power to *choose* illusion.

So, understand the great temptation of guilt and how you have worn it like a cloak in order to avoid being what you can't help but be.

You're then trying to shake your hand off of your wrist and you can use the same power to use that hand to bless Creation. On or off, Love or fear, there is no gray area. There is only the power of Mind given unto you freely. There is only the opportunity to choose again and again and again and again and again, until the bliss of choosing *for* the Kingdom finally out-values every other possibility and the mind becomes consistently anchored in the sunbeam that has come forth from the Sun of God and streams forth only Love. Rest assured that as you cultivate that in each present moment, the power of your own beingness will carry you far, far, far beyond the need for a body, the need for time, definitely far beyond the need for, shall we say, dramatic learning experiences.

Is it, then, possible to truly awaken while yet in the world of illusion? Of course! Awakening can only occur *now* and because Love is real, because you are who you are always, nothing in any moment has the power to obstruct you from being awake— except the power of your decision. That's all.

That is the one thing that in this hour I'd wish to express to you. If you can get this, you've gotten it:

Nothing holds power over you and nothing creates your experience except the decision, the choice, that you have used within the power of the Mind.

That's all that's happening, in all dimensions. It's what's happening in the dimension where I hang out—which by the way is not quite accurate, since I hang out in all dimensions, and so do you. The only difference is: I'm perfectly aware of it, while some of you are trying to be perfectly unaware of it.

Where I abide, with a multitude of friends, it is quite true that there is no valuation of the body, therefore no need to manifest one. There is communion and communication. It is immediate, it is more like a frequency that passes unobstructed through a solid wall and we are engaged in ongoing creativity without ceasing, for what can Creation be, what can the very purpose of existence be, if it is not to extend or create the good, the holy, and the beautiful as a way of celebrating Divine Union with all that God Is? This is why I once implored you:

Remember only your loving thoughts, for only they are true. And each time you entertain what was once an insane choice, you're actually saying,

> *I, by the power given unto me of my Father, choose to imprison myself in an illusion and to suffer the guilt that comes with it. Now let me do it really well.*

When you remember only your loving thoughts, you are thinking with God. That *is* the Mind of God because only Love is real. The Kingdom is immediate and at hand. Nothing can obstruct it, nothing can limit it. Perception can be corrected so that you see the real world right here, right where you are. Where there are seemingly chairs and bodies and rooms and lightbulbs and all of the rest, and funny little wires that go to funny littles keys so that the master can make beautiful music come out of them, right here, the real world abides and it is what is perceived when *you* choose to see only through the eyes of Love.

I chose a very dramatic way to learn my final lesson. I invite you to learn your final lesson with ease and gentleness. When I said, "Take up your cross and follow me," I did not invite you into a realm of suffering and strife and sacrifice. Rather, the cross that you crucified yourself upon so many times is merely the illusion of guilt, the insistence that you have actually succeeded in separating yourself from God. To take up your cross is like packing up your tent when it's time to go home: you don't trudge with it on your back, you throw it in the trunk, hm? You get in your automobile and you step on the gas and you have a nice cup of water as you speed down the highway, saying, "It was a nice camping trip, but it's done."

Decide to be Christ

Therefore, take up your cross and follow me please, please, please, for the world is crying out to see again the embodiment of Christ. And just as once as a man I chose to take my Father at His word—to choose to embody Christ, that I might learn what Christ is—so, too, you are given the opportunity, in each moment, in each situation, to be the hands of Christ, to be the feet of Christ, to be the voice of Christ, to be the gentleness in the eyes, the laughter, the embrace, the tear. *You* are the one that your brother and sister can see because they yet believe that only the body is real. And I can be walking (or shall we say gliding) down the street next to them, shouting in their ear, "Beloved friend, I'm right here, I'm right here, I'm right here," and they can have a thousand images in their mind,

> *I just had a thought of Christ, I just had a thought of Christ, but that can't be real, because only bodies are real.*

I've been shouting till I'm blue in my non-physical face, but *you* cannot be denied, *you* who have yet a little while in the experience of embodiment, *you* are the one who can stand before a brother or sister as the embodiment of the Truth and teach only Love.

Nothing can be received until it is offered and that is your only purpose. You are not responsible for the reception of Love but for its extension, and by extending it you keep it for yourself. And it grows and it grows and it grows and it grows and it carries the very spark of Divinity that you are, beyond all worlds, beyond all dimensions— which are, by the way, infinite, so I hope you hear what I'm saying to you—your own Love will carry you beyond what is infinite and is infinitely created, that makes you pretty darn good... Hm?

And I come not alone, for there is one that you have known who also comes with me whenever I join to do this work through this my beloved Brother, who comes with me wherever I go, in whatever creative work I seek to ease illusions from the minds of my brothers and sisters. That one that you have known as "Saint" Germain—I do not give him such honor, he is just my friend Germain—rest assured we are what you call bosom buddies, though we have no bosom!

[Laughter]

Therefore, nothing gets in the way. And he is here now. Well, after all, levity is good in the Kingdom. It's made of light, so how could it be serious? Indeed, this is just to let you know that that one is indeed my brother and friend. I met him once a long time ago, while he was in body and I was in body and I have spoken of that in another time and place, but rest assured, let us just say for now that he was present at what you call my Crucifixion, though you should be able to tell by now that the world failed to get rid of me. He was present and he was not on what you would call the "good side," until in a moment we made eye contact and he used that context to awaken. And from that moment he went on to create several incarnations to learn mastery of many things and is indeed my equal in all things. And from that moment, in an ancient land far, far away and long in the past, we have been joined as loving brothers and that bond will never be broken.

The point of sharing that story with you is this: Where Love has been allowed to join two minds, or souls, separation is no longer possible, for Love has healed the illusion. Bodies come and go but Love joins you with the beloved. Because this is true, waste not a moment, those of you that long to join with your brothers and sisters. Love in each moment and you have healed the gap and restored the perfect remembrance of what is true always. And you will transcend the great horror and suffering that the illusion of separation is, and you will know that when you have loved, wherever that being goes through infinite dimensions, *you are with them and they with you* and no gap exists. And after all, isn't that what you try to do with your bodies? Get so close there's no more gap, and you call it "making love"? Hm. *Would you choose to close the gap between yourself and the whole of Creation, so that in your consciousness constantly there is only the revelation of Oneness?* Take my word for it—it's worth it. For nothing can elevate the heart and the soul into such celebration as the experience of living Oneness! And Oneness comes when *you* close the gap by blessing the one in front of you with the Love of Christ. They're stuck with you forever!

Therefore, when I said, "I am with you always" . . . you get the picture!

[Laughter]

Some of you have occasionally wished that I wasn't.

[Laughter]

And some of you have argued with me and said, "Where did you go?

Where did you go?" Beloved friends, I have gone nowhere, it is you that went—into fear, into contraction, into drama. Perfectly okay, if that's what, shall we say (what do you call it?) lights your fire. But rest assured, I retract from no one who has ever once prepared a place for me, which simply means: I loved them and they received me. [Snaps fingers] Separation gone, unity restored, never to be broken again.

If you could say that there may yet be something in me that I long for—it's not quite accurate, however we'll use it—what I long for is for you to give yourself permission to experience yourself as I experience you. That's all. For then, O beloved friends, then *what we can create together knows no boundary or limitation*. What we can experience together in the fields of creativity, in the dimensions of Creation, is pure unbounded, unlimited, ongoing, deepening bliss. We can create together the good, the holy, and the beautiful forever and ever and ever and ever. That's the meaning of "singing God's praises in Heaven."

If you will join with me by recognizing that you are Christ, if you'll join with me by blessing me, by loving me, by being the one who looks upon Jeshua ben Joseph and says,

> *Beyond your dumb ideas of crucifixion — why you ever did that I don't know — but I know that you're Christ and I love you anyway.*

When *you* make the decision to turn the tables and be the savior who comes to heal your brother Jeshua ben Joseph, when *you* come to look upon *me* and realize you're Christ looking at a brother who longs to know Christ, O my friends, then we can join!

When I am your Beloved, as you are mine, the sacred dance of unity will carry us far beyond all imagined worlds and together we will create that which extends the good, the holy, and the beautiful, so brightly, so creatively, so magnificently, so simply, that the hour and day must certainly come when every mind in every dimension has perfectly awakened.

You, then, are in charge of the Atonement. And frankly, I think God has given the assignment to someone perfectly capable of it: you, all of you. How could it be? *How could it be that you are here now if you did not already know the Truth that sets all things free?* What could have the power to make you be in this room, hanging out with an old brother who has no body, unless you already knew? How could you recognize that I am who I say I am unless you were already awakened to the Truth that is true always:

> *I am that Shining One.*

If you weren't awakened to it, rest assured you'd be somewhere else on this planet, simply because nothing happens by accident. It could very well be that at some level of the soul you've already been in communication with me and said,

> *You know, I would like to hang out with you and I'm going to use this context to choose to be awake. Why not? Tried everything else!*

So. By the way, just as an aside, there is no one in this room that did not also know me in that incarnation that has become so famous. I'm not saying that you were in embodiment at the time. You'll have to figure that one out for yourself. But there is no one in this room who did not know me in that time frame in which I was embodied, went through some learning lessons and got famous.

[Laughter]

Are you saying you're.... [then indistinct]

Indeed. I'm also saying within the great stream of the dream of Creation everyone in this room, shall we say, at least had their attention turned to the events that were unfolding, were quite aware of what was going on, whether you were in body or not. A few of you were looking through the window, but *all of you* have known me before. Not just as this soul or this spark of Divinity but you've known me as I took on the embodiment and became the man known as Jeshua ben Joseph. So here we are again, family gathering.

And all of you abide within what I'll describe here as a stream of energy that I like to call "the Lineage," a specific kind of strand, if you will, that carries a certain vibration, certain characteristics, certain beings that are within it, that have actually created it. That lineage goes back a long ways. It involves myself, it involves you, it involves—no I won't do it! —Germain...

[Laughter]

...it involves the one that was known as Mary, many countless others, all have awakened to the vibration of Christed Consciousness within themselves and realized that there's nothing else to do but extend Love to any mind that will receive it, thereby giving them the invitation to step into the remembrance that they are Christ. There's nothing beyond Christed Consciousness; it already enfolds all things, and you are That. Hm. There... Good.

Beloved friends, turn gently then, from the roar and din of the world that you believe you have made in error and know that you have never been capable of error, but you, out of your Divine greatness, have chosen to take on the sins of the world. That is, you've chosen to experience what it's like to perceive oneself in separation in order to understand dimensions of illusion, dimensions of suffering; to enfold within your being all possibilities. Why? Because your compassion is infinite and unbounded.

And you have not suffered because you've failed. You've suffered because you looked upon a tiny little planet, floating in a certain dimension, in which separation was being played out and your compassion brought you here, to learn of this

Decide to be Christ

world, to master this world, to take it in and know what it's like so that when you look into the eyes of a brother or sister and say, "I love you," they know that you know what you're talking about. No one can fool you, can they? When another says, "I'm suffering," you can say,

> *I know. I took it on once myself. I know that dimension and* I am arisen — *and because the ascension has been completed in me, the same power is in you.*

It is only by taking on "the sins of the world" — perceptions of separation—that you become the vessel, the vehicle, that is large enough to embrace any suffering that comes along the pike. And at a soul level, when you look into the eyes of another and say,

> *Yes, I know that you're suffering — and I love you. I know the Christ lives in you,*

... at a soul level *they* know that you're not what you call

"talking out of your hat." They know that you know because you've been there; and that is why I did what I did. Anybody can hang out in seventeen dimensions beyond this planet and talk about Love. And those that have fallen into illusion say, "Well yes, well come down here and try it out." Hm?

I came down here for the same reason you did: out of the infinite compassion of Christ, so that I could embrace all of my brothers or sisters and help them to uplift themselves back to the place from which they've never fallen. You're doing it, right now — *you*, in the very life you're living! You, out of *your* Christedness, out of *your* compassion, have opened yourself and called forth all manner of experiences so that *you* could wrap yourself around this dimension and enfold it in your love.

That's all you're doing here. So give yourself some credit. Never again entertain the thought that you have failed! You are the one that looked with tears upon this dimension and said, "I'll go." I mean, after all, I'm not even willing to do that again! You are! You are that one! You are the embodiment of the Savior! You are the one sent forth from the Mind of God, you are the one that has been willing to feel it all, to experience every dimension of suffering *just so you could heal it*! And thereby demonstrate that *the Truth is true always and only Love is real*.

So there, now you know what you've been doing! Give yourself some credit, for though through the eyes of the body it looks as though things may be hopeless, rest assured, the heat has been turned up by all of you and there's a point where the water has no longer a choice but to boil and turn to steam. Hm? The train is pulling into the station because *you* have been willing to wrap yourself around this world in your own beingness and heal it with Love — you, just as you are, right where you are. Everyone in this room is actively fulfilling their function.

So before you go to bed tonight, go to a friend and simply say,

> *What a good boy am I — or girl. I'm doing such a marvelous job, and now I'm going to go to sleep and just go off in my dream and see who needs a touch of Grace. I'm not going to go to sleep to try to dream and solve my problems — I don't have any! I'm going to go to sleep and deliberately choose, by intention, to let this body sleep and allow my spirit to find a heart that needs to be blessed.*

Do that and you might find yourself having some interesting conversation over breakfast.

So. Therefore, indeed, we have babbled at you long enough. The message has been given. Has it been received? So, we're

Decide to be Christ

going to do something we've never done before. Since you now know that you are Christ and I'm just your brother, put it into practice and take a moment and think on the one you dare to call your friend, Jeshua ben Joseph, and in your own mind, and in your own being, simply say to me,

Jeshua, I bless you with the Love of Christ that I am.

[Short pause]

Rather fun, isn't it? Don't you immediately feel lighter? More expanded? Isn't there a part of you that knows that's the Truth? Therefore, when next you set up an altar, whether individually or the next time some of you will choose to gather as a group, make it a point to *also bring a picture of yourself.* And if you really want to have some fun, cover up my picture with yours. And start your morning meditations by honoring those pictures. Indeed.

And if you can convince those that run the big stone buildings and brick buildings around the planet that have this funny emaciated image of me hanging on a cross, would you *please* tell them to take them down? I find them to be rather embarrassing. So it was a learning experience that may not have been necessary — it was my choice! Don't need to make such a big deal of it! I suppose every Christ must have a flaw.

[Laughter]

So, I long for the day when beings gather in those brick and stone buildings and sit there and say,
>*Why are we here? Well, since we can't remember, we might as well have a good dance.*

[Laughter].

Then I will know I've succeeded. Indeed!

So, how are you all doing? Has it been worth your *time*? It hasn't been worth mine; I don't have any.

[Laughter]

But rest assured, the opportunity, *the opportunity* to think up a creative way to join with you, to be received by you, to have an opportunity to love you by activating thought that vibrates vocal chords, that transmits something to you that allows our hearts to join as they have countless times, in countless other ways... Indeed, beloved friends, oh yes! It has been worth my while, for you are my treasure, you are my joy, you are my blessing and my beloved.

You are the one who shows me my Father,
and how can I do less than love you forever for what you give to me?
And indeed, I am *with you always.*

So, there are a few of you that feel a question *burning deep in your soul*. This is what we're going to do: I'm not going to engage them right now. I want you, whether you believe it or not, to accept that you are Christ. Therefore, just before you lay your head on the pillow, begin by acknowledging:

> *I and my Father are one, there are no barriers to the depth of wisdom within me. Therefore, now, in this moment, I ask this question and I receive the answer. So be it.*

See what comes. Then tomorrow, we will set aside just a short time, and I would be most pleased to, shall we say, pop back into your presence and we'll see if there are really any questions left that still require that the answer be given through something and someone that seems to be outside of yourself. Fair enough?

[General agreement]

Good.

Therefore, love you one another, as the Father has first loved all of us. Look with graciousness and gentleness. Look with appreciation upon the mystery of the moment in which you find yourselves with one another, for it is the power of your Love that brings you unto one another. Love you one another and you are the Light that lights this world and redeems it from all illusion.

Be you therefore at peace this day — be you therefore at peace eternally — precious and holy and ancient friends.

Amen.

Grace as Reality

Now, we begin.

And greetings unto you, beloved and holy Children of Light Divine. In truth it is with great joy that I come forth to abide with you in this hour, even as you have chosen to come forth and abide with me. Know then, that always I come forth with great joy and I come forth from that place that is of Light and of Truth and of Joy, a place of unconditional Love beyond all boundary, beyond all limitations. I come forth from the place that is already prepared for all of us, given lovingly by the One Who has sent us forth, and that One I have called Abba, or Father, and that One—and that One alone—knows you and holds you, embraces you and feels thankfulness *for you*, because you are indeed the Creation of God.

You are the offspring of Light Divine, and if you are that offspring, and I assure you that you are, the reality of the essence of who you are *is but Love*. For if you are made in the image of our Father, Who Is but Love, then surely you too are that Light and are that Truth and are that Presence, and you are therefore the Word made Flesh that has come to dwell among mankind—not to judge mankind, but to look lovingly upon all illusions, and by taking the hand of your brother and sister, to gently lead them from darkness to Light. Not because *you know* where Light is, but because you have become willing to *allow* life to be lived through you with every word and every breath, with every action—so that life becomes translated from a struggle to survive, from an attempt to work out your salvation, or what some would call your karma (I believe the word is), and to begin to embrace that life is given unto you freely and completely and wholly, and if it were not given in this way, in this moment *you would cease to exist*.

Therefore, if you find yourself listening and hearing words spoken now, rest assured, it is because life is given to you—not *earned*, but *given*—given with perfect freedom from a Love beyond comprehension, a Love that knows no boundaries, a Love that was there before time began and will be there with you long after time has ceased to be. Here and now, as we gather in this moment, the same opportunity is given unto us that is given unto the creation of God—His Children, His Son—in each and every moment. In each and every moment of experience, the same opportunity is given to you as was given to me then, when I once walked upon this Earth, and *is continually* given unto me.

What is that opportunity? Is it not to set aside the perceptions born of the illusions of this world, born of fear and doubt and guilt and judgment, and to embrace with great simplicity the only Truth and only Reality that has ever been? And what is Real cannot be threatened and what is unreal does not exist. And that which alone is Real is the Love that God Is, and the Love that brings you forth as a great Ray of Light that would shine in what could be called darkness, which is only a temporary forgetting of Truth. Therefore, understand well that while we gather in this one little building, in this one little town, on this one speck of earth, which is but a small spinning sphere in a grand universe (and this grand universe is but one of many upon many, upon many, in a multitude of dimensions)—*here* we have an opportunity to choose to set aside all judgment and to hear only the Voice of Love that unites us as One, as brother and brother, as brother and sister, as sister and sister, as the only begotten Child of God.

That is the opportunity that I came, then, to extend unto mankind. It is the opportunity that I ceaselessly extend to every mind that would but turn from the roar and the din of the world for just one Holy Instant: to seek the place of quiet and calm inside in which there is laid upon the altar of the Heart your judgments, your fears, your ideas of what the world is and what it is for; to surrender all things and to throw open the shutters of the Heart to once again become vulnerable and open and to merely ask of me,

I have prepared a place, come and enter therein.

And indeed I will do so, not as a saviour above you, but always and only as your brother and as your friend.

I am your friend, because a friend in ancient times was not a word, you see, taken lightly. A friend was one who was committed to seeing past any illusions, any doubts, any fears; not to not see them, but to see through them and beyond them to the great ray of Light that shines forth from the mind of Christ that dwells within you as your only Reality, and to abide with you and to hold you in that Light until you have the strength to hold yourself in it as well. Therefore, when I say I come as your brother and as your friend, rest assured, I come to celebrate the reality of your Beauty, your Joy, your Truth, your Radiance, your Wisdom. I come forth to *join* with you, never to be apart from you and never, certainly, to be above you. And those of you who have felt some kinship with me, some devotion to me, rest assured that I am worthy of it only to the degree that I am devoted to you. I am devoted to you always and eternally.

I love you. I love you because I know who you are. I know that within you that great Ray of Light shines eternally and has never been dimmed by the experiences of the world. I love you because in you do I know that which I am; and when I look upon you and see naught but the face of Christ, I realize that

Christ is the essence of my own being.

I came into this world as a Light unto the world. Does this make me different than you? Some of you in your religions have been taught that I came forth from the Mind of God to save you, that I was the only begotten Son of God—and I guess that makes you His adoptees if you choose Him.

[Laughter]

Nothing could be further from the truth. I came forth from the Mind of God exactly as you have come forth, and the life that I lived then, in all essential details, is the same as yours—for in the field of space and time, given a body that knew hunger, that had to deal with cold and all of the rest of it, I experienced everything that you have ever experienced, just as each of you have experienced everything that the one sitting next to you has experienced. You all know the same fears, you all know the same doubts, you all know the same visions, the same dreams. All of you know that somewhere within you there is a Grand Being who rests in perfect innocence.

I came forth to celebrate the Truth and to demonstrate it to a world that had seemed to have forgotten it; to demonstrate that life is eternal and that death is unreal; to demonstrate that in all situations—*all* situations—all power is given unto the Holy Son of God to choose the Voice for Love over judgment and fear; that there is a place within all of us, a place of purity and innocence, a place that remains perfectly guiltless, for God creates only in His image and what He creates reflects the purity of His eternal Love forever. I came forth to extend my hand and to say,

"Come. Come to where I am. Join with me in becoming the demonstration that there's another way of looking at everything. Join with me in the demonstration that Love heals all things. Join with me in being willing to be in the field of space and time and yet to hold vigilance over the mind so that you do not allow it to become absorbed by the energies, the frequencies, the thought patterns, the perceptions that make up this world... To instead, through vigilance, to learn the power of choice can never be taken from you and that no matter the circumstances, you hold the Light in you to choose the Voice for Love, to choose peace instead of turmoil, safety instead of fear and insecurity and doubt that within you lies a wisdom so deep that already it outshines all worlds and looks far beyond this mere body, and that there is indeed within you the Light that knows that you've not come to suffer the world, you've come to be joyous, to express the joyousness that Love is, to look into the eyes of your brother and sister and to see that they are your savior! They are the ones who have brought to you the opportunity to look past the thoughts of the world and to see the face of Christ. And the great thing is, of course, that it takes one to know one."

[Laughter]

And many of you, many of you in your journeys through space and time—and tonight we won't resort to talk of what you would know by the term of reincarnation (it's really not essential to the process of waking up) but all of you, even in this life, know the feeling of feeling separate from God, all of you know the feeling of searching, Perhaps if I go just to that other workshop over there,

and then when a group of friends come and say it was the most incredible experience, you feel lost, you go,

> *My God, I should have gone, when's the next time?*

[Laughter]

Is that really much unlike friends who come and say, "Have you been to the new pizza diner down the road yet? It was so incredible."

Oh my God, I Thiruvananthapuram

have to go and have that pizza...

[Laughter]

All of you know that energy of seeking, and doubting that you have the power to find. But always and forever, the truth remains this: The Kingdom of Heaven is within you. Will you then dissect the body to find it? Of course not. For if you would well receive it, the body you seem to carry does not house you; you house the body. It arises from within you and within the choices you have made in your access to the infinite Mind that Christ is. You have chosen, therefore, the body, this time frame; you have chosen it. It has not been forced upon you by any means.

The Kingdom of Heaven is indeed within you. It lies as a jewel, placed gently on the altar of the Heart—with a capital—the Heart whose first beat came from the breath that God breathed into it, long before there was ever such a thing as a body. The Kingdom lies within the 'you' that you have constructed out of your experiences and out of all of the beliefs and ideas that you have garnered in your journey through time and space. Within all perceptions, within all constructs that the mind holds, the Kingdom is found. Silence is the threshold to this Truth Divine.

How then to come to silence? Some of you know well what it means to master the flow of the breath, to chant little words in your mind. Some of you know what it means to take substances called drugs to try to make yourself silent, or perhaps enough food and television might do it. Hm?

[Laughter]

The Soul yearns for silence, because the Soul knows that silence is the doorway, the threshold, that merges you with the Kingdom of Heaven. Silence is the threshold in which the voice, the guidance of the Holy Spirit comes, perhaps as a voice, loud and clear, perhaps as an intuitive nudge, perhaps as a quiet knowingness — and you all know that place.

But how to come to silence? In the end there is no technique that accomplishes it; that would make silence *conditional*. Does that make sense to you? If it takes a technique to become silent, it means that without the technique silence is impossible, and therefore silence is conditional; and what is conditional has no part in the Kingdom.

Silence waits, just as Love does, on our welcome.

It is a silence that is not artificial. It does not simply mean that the heart slows down, and the breath slows down and you don't move a muscle. It doesn't mean just turning off the television or putting the book away. Silence, the silence that speaks of the Divine and whispers it gently to the part of you that has always remained Divine, that silence requires only your willingness to lay upon the altar of the Heart every perception you have ever held about anyone or about the world, every perception and belief that you cling so rigidly unto, thinking that it's going to keep you safe, that it's going to show you how to get through this life. Silence comes when the mind is truly willing to relinquish its attachment to the world that it has made, the world of its experience, the world of its thoughts. Silence comes, then, always as the result of a simple choice, and the more often that choice is made, the simpler it becomes, and in the end, silence becomes what you could call pervasive in the mind, so that although you walk and talk seemingly in this world, there is a core within of Perfect Silence, of Perfect Light, and though you speak and hear others speak to you, though you get up in the morning and make the breakfast so you can feed the body, though you do all things, there is a place of perfect Peace and it comes as the result of being willing, over and over again, to relinquish your beliefs and your perceptions about the world, to look upon the body and say,

> *I don't know what this is. I don't know what it's for! I've certainly known how to misuse it, but I don't know what it is.*

I look about and I see this world with buildings and what you call your automobiles. I must admit, they're a little better than walking on foot and riding on donkeys. But do you really know what these things are, and where they've come from, and what purpose they *can* serve? You know well what the world would ask them to serve but what purpose can all these things that have been manifested, what *can* they serve?

I say unto you that those very questions are not unlike the questions that I, too, as a man, had need of coming unto—to look upon my brothers and sisters, to look upon the great teachers and the friends that I was blessed with, upon even the parents that I was blessed with, to look upon the tumult of the time frame in which I walked upon this earth, to journey into the desert, to get away from all the noise, even the noise of my own thoughts, and to ask of my Father,

> *What's it for? How would you have me use it? What purpose would you extend unto me?*

And I was taught that the body itself has been created in error. It is—in a sense—it has been created to house the ego, to create and to give forth the symbol, and therefore the belief, that separation exists, because (everybody knows it) if you look upon another one as a body, you *know* there's a distance between you. That is evident, through the body's eyes.

But there is another eye, another way of seeing that looks well beyond the body and sees that all minds are joined eternally and that you've never looked upon a thing called a stranger. Know you that word? Eliminate it from your vocabulary because it is a lie. You have never looked upon a stranger, for you see reflected only yourself. And as you see your brother or sister, you will see yourself and as you know them, you will know yourself. To look upon another with judgment means that you have judged yourself and created separation from God. To look upon another with forgiveness, with softness, with gentleness, and with love means that you are willing to look upon that truth in yourself. The body, then, becomes translated into this and this alone. The body becomes translated through the choice of relinquishing your own perceptions of the world into only this: a means for communicating Love, and that is all.

Now, that's a little different than what the world would teach you. Your world would teach you that the body is something that you can gather to yourself joy, pleasure, fulfillment, you name it. I want to share with you this night that if you take but one thought with you and make it your own, carry this thought:

The body can bring you nothing. The body cannot bring you what you seek, because it is not found there. It cannot bring you intimacy, it cannot bring you union, it cannot bring you Joy with a capital J. It will bring what the body calls pleasure, perhaps. The pleasure arises in time, and what starts in time ends in time—and you all know what that feels like. The ice cream is delicious until you realize that the container is empty.

[Laughter]

The body... The body can bring nothing to you. But thank God, through Grace, the body *can* become the means through which you learn to extend what you possess eternally—Love. So that each gesture, each touch, each smile, is a very conscious and deliberate choice to be the one who allows Light to shine forth and to enlighten the world, to allow your brother and sister to become your savior and your salvation, to begin the practice of realizing that every opportunity you see is given to you so that the Holy Spirit can ask you,

> *Well, what choice are you going to make this time? Love or fear, peace or judgment, extension or contraction, giving or the insane attempt to take?*

The body is either the symbol of separation and pain or it becomes the temple of the living Spirit. And that is all that little phrase once meant. It's where the body becomes solely the means for communicating Love, and nothing else; it becomes the servant of the awakened Heart and the enlightened Mind. Now I know it's probably true that no one in this room has ever misused the body...

[Laughter]

Would you be willing to lay even the body down upon the altar of the Heart, to surrender it back to the Source of your creation, and to hold the thought,

> *You know, I really never have known what this thing is or what it's for. I pamper it, I feed it, I do what I think is going to get me*

some pleasure through it. I clothe it in the winter and I unclothe it in the hot heat of the summer. But I've never known how to truly use it, how to bring peace to the cells of the body, how to allow an integration of the body, the emotions, and the mind. Perhaps there's another way of looking at the body itself.

And there is. The body will reflect for you always the choice you are making between Love and fear, between joining and separating, between forgiveness and judgment.

Know you that experience where you walk into a room of perfect strangers and something somewhere in the room just doesn't feel very good? It's like you're picking up a little vibration and you turn around and there's someone standing on the other side of the room. You've never laid your physical eyes on them but somehow you know that you'd just as soon avoid them? Have you had that kind of experience, feeling the energy of someone and feeling repelled by it somewhat? They haven't said a word, they haven't even *looked* at you yet, but there's a *knowingness*—remember, you never look upon a stranger! And have you not also had the experience of being around someone who seems to radiate light so much that, no matter what's going on, just to *think* about them seems to *enlighten* your spirit, to bring you a sense of joy, and when you lay your physical eyes on them, somehow the weight of your daily life is suspended and you feel joy. Have you had that experience?

To the degree that one's mind has become corrected so that the body is not used to house old judgments and old fears and old angers, and it is not used to look upon other bodies as having something that this body can gain, but as correction comes to the mind and the mind becomes enlightened, so too must the body follow. The cells of the body begin to vibrate in a different way; emotional and even physical toxicity is released; the body becomes clearer and clearer and clearer. It becomes a vehicle that radiates Light to various degrees, and that is what you're feeling. What you're feeling through the body of that one is really the reflection of what has occurred in the mind. And the body of one who, shall we say, is what you might call a master is simply the body that has become so perfected that it becomes *as Light* because there's no trace in the mind left of judgment or fear or doubt, there is only the unconditional Love that God Is.

And what I want to share with you is—as you look down at your thighs and your feet and your hands—that bag of dust that you have identified with as being you, is not you. It comes to you from the dust of the ground, it is given to you by your Holy Mother, this precious Earth, and its one purpose and function—its *only* purpose and function—has been to be the vehicle through which Christ extends Light and Love; that's all. It has never been designed to bring pleasure or joy to the mind who thinks it is separate from God.

So you see, that is why I said: If you just take one thought home with you tonight and make it your own, you'll find that it will present a pathway for you of much learning and much revelation. If you hold the thought, as you wake up in the morning, and you raise your hands up and look at them, go,

These are only for giving Love and extending Light.

... and as you walk with your feet upon this Earth, each step you take, you simply hold the thought,

I step so I that can carry this body in its journey in which Light and Love are extended, and that is all.

... what you'll find is that a myriad of things will begin to crop up in your awareness, and you'll see how the mind has been utilizing the body, at least at times, in error. And as those conflicts come up, your awareness brings Light to the conflict and correction comes.

To give you an example: You might be feeling just a bit depressed, or down or lonely or whatever, and so you call your best friend and say, "Let's go to that pizza diner down the road."

And of course what you're really wanting to do is to escape the feeling of conflict that's going on in you. And so you call your friend and they say, "Well, really I was kind of busy, right..."

"Oh no, please. Please come, please come!"

What you're really saying is: "Look, I need you to come fill my hole, okay?" So you call your friend and they go, out of guilt they say, "Well okay, I'll come, I'm not really hungry. I just got done eating, but oh what the heck, what's another pizza?"

Because you see, you've also learned in this world that you always have to *accommodate*. It's not okay just to say no and stand in your own truth. So you get together and you go to the pizza diner and you're feeling better because now you've been able to kind of cover up that inner feeling, and after three or four slices of pizza, you're becoming numb to the whole thing anyway, and you raise a bunch of conversation with the friend.

And then you remember,

> *Wait a minute, when I got up this morning, I held the thought that this body is only for the extension of Light and Love.*

And if you're quite clear and honest and innocent with yourself, without judgment, you look and you see the whole pattern of thought that brought you to the diner, sitting across from your friend, ostensibly wanting to be with them when you know darn well that there was a conflict, something going on in you, an energy that you didn't want to feel, didn't want to deal with, and you needed it to be masked. And you look upon your friend and you realize,

I've just abused them.

And you look in their eye and you say, "You know, I need your forgiveness. I didn't come here to be with you. I asked you to come here to save me from something that's going on in me. I just was feeling really restless and out of touch and alone. Help me."

Now, two things have just happened. You've allowed correction to come back to your mind; you've brought honesty to what's really going on. And that's good, because you can't transcend what you fail to embrace; it goes on and on and on forever. And the other thing that happens is this: You've relinquished the pattern or the energy in the mind, you've laid it out on the table, you're not hiding anything; you've made yourself vulnerable to your friend.

And now something very special can happen, because you have provided your brother or sister with exactly what they're looking for, whether they know it or not: the opportunity to join with you in Holy Relationship. For you have extended unto them the opportunity to give forgiveness, to relinquish any feelings or judgments or resentments (because, remember, they were already full anyway) — to set it all aside, to smile, to join with you sitting across the table in a pizza diner of all places, it becomes a sacred temple in which the Holy Children of God join together and look innocently upon one another and laugh at the ego. And perhaps you extend your hands to one another, and you clasp your hands and you look into their eyes; and suddenly the very energy that was going on in you, that seemed to compel you into the whole series of events that got you and your friend at the diner, that conflict dissolves.

What's occurred? A miracle's occurred, the miracle of a Holy Instant that corrects all things. And you realize that your brother and your sister is indeed the means to your salvation. And in each moment that you are willing to set aside the masks, the ideas of yourself, the fears, the judgments — all the momentums of the mind trying to find its own way in this world and just lay it at their altar, and join with them, and see only Love — to become wholly vulnerable, you begin to see that,

My God, this isn't just my friend who I happened to meet three weeks ago. Christ is in front of me! For Christ's sake!

[Laughter]

And you see in that moment the miracle of the Atonement has occurred, you have been lifted out of the perceptions of the world and a very ordinary occurrence has become extraordinary and blessed forever.

And you have joined with your friend in a way that no physical intimacy has ever gotten anybody. And all it took was the willingness to look with the eyes of Christ, the willingness to be vulnerable, to set aside all perceptions and judgments, to just be straight and honest.

It's very much like saying, "You know, I keep having to face the fact that I don't know who I am or what the world is for." And your friend says, "Oh thank God, I can relax now! 'Cause you see, I don't know either!"

[Laughter]

And then you can join together, and then you can ask, in your momentary prayer—and if you don't quite have the courage to be outrageous, you won't stand on the table at the diner yet—you'll just sit there quietly looking at each other and you'll simply ask the Holy Spirit to bring that correction to the mind so that it becomes more firmly established.

And in this way, almost unbeknownst to you, miracles come to replace the struggle and the strife of life. You become very, very humble because you realize none of your perceptions have ever been true or accurate, except the ones inspired by the gentleness of Love that is totally inclusive of all of Life and embraces unconditionally everyone and everything.

In that moment—and you've all experienced at least a few of those moments—Peace comes. Peace, a peace that passes all understanding and could never hope to be explained in the languages of this world. And that Peace bespeaks a way of living that is available to everyone at all times, a way of living that requires no planning in the way the world would think of this, no striving, no doubt, no anxiety; a way of living that flows gently, in which you smile a little bit more often, in which you talk a little bit less; a way of living that is marked by Grace. And Grace that is lived will reveal to you your true reality. Grace, when fully lived, reveals to you that *you* are the only begotten of God, Christ Eternal, unbounded forever, and that you participate in that Mind, in that Energy, in that Love—call it what you will—with me and with every mind, every brother and sister who's ever chosen to set aside the world and to allow the Kingdom to be lived from within.

Grace. The word itself is so powerful. It speaks of something that comes, it is wholly given, and can never hopefully be

Grace as Reality

earned. No dance you could ever dance could ever earn you a smidgen more of Grace, and Grace descends gently upon you even now, fully in every moment. Grace is available to every mind and every heart that would but choose to receive it, to remember the truth of the Kingdom and to set aside the beliefs of the world:

> *Love is the nature of my being; Father, I receive it. Do with me what You will; I've never known what to do with me anyway!*

Grace. Grace brings a gentleness to all of your activities. Grace brings a peace. Grace brings that Light that can flow through you in this moment, if you would but allow it. Grace, given fully by God unto His only creation: *you*! You are the one in whom the Father remains well pleased. You are the one—*you* are the one—who has come forth into *this* time frame, just as I came forth into a different one, for only one purpose: to demonstrate the truth that the world is *not real* and holds no power over God's creation; that the world that would try to get you to judge, try to get you to hold on to ideas and beliefs about what is and what should be and what shouldn't be and what ought never have been, all of that stuff, the world will try to get you to believe that judgment is justified, that forgiveness must be given cautiously. Hm! It is not forgiveness when it's given cautiously. Grace is the truth that will completely reverse the ideas that you have held in the mind and bring correction completely unto you. It cannot be earned, you cannot strive for it, you can only be willing to allow it...*To allow it.*

I've said before that there's really only one curriculum that anybody ever needs to learn, and quite frankly, you don't have the freedom to decide not to learn it. You do have the freedom—and this is the freedom given unto you since before time is—you have the perfect freedom to decide when to learn it. Does that make sense to you?

> *Ha! Well, not today, Father. You see I have this gripe to pick with my brother. I'll get back to the curriculum tomorrow.*

And the Holy Spirit stands just on the other side and goes,

> *Huh, I thought you wanted to learn the curriculum, so I helped set up this whole affair so that you could extend Love to your brother with whom you think you have a gripe. Oh well, I'll just bring another one.*

[Loud laughter]

Do you know that experience? Something's repeating in my life—what is going on here? What have you not brought forgiveness to? What fear do you still hold on to? What judgment or perception are you unwilling to let go of, so that correction can come and you can be taught anew?

> *Ah, the curriculum. I and my Father are One, the Kingdom of Heaven is within, that which is real cannot be threatened and that which is unreal does not exist. The ego, which is my drama that I've been playing out and out and out, is nothing more than an illusory thought; it is like a gnat floating in the vastness of space. It holds no power, no function and no reality, but each time I listen to its voice I have left the Kingdom.*

That fast! And so the only curriculum, you see, is to choose to hear the Voice for Love, to be the vehicle of forgiveness.

The curriculum ends where the dream of separation began: as a thought. Now, think about this, as a thought held in the mind of the Son of God, one thought,

> *What would it be like to experience myself as separate from my Father?*

Grace as Reality

Voilà, the world!

[Laughter]

Hm! And you thought you had no power to create? Hm! I'll share another little thought, just to plant a seed, something to think about: God creates only what is changeless and right now, look around and see if you can see one thing with the physical eyes that is changeless. Hmm. Come up with anything?

What have you ever experienced through the body's senses, through the thoughts of the world, through all of your worldly experiences, what have you experienced that is changeless? Isn't that part of the frustration of the world—just when you think you've got it, it slips through your grasp? You meet the grand lover at a dance and three weeks later, they don't know your name.

[Laughter]

You sit down to the most scrumptious dinner you could imagine only to wake up the next day with a stomach ache, constipation or what have you, a headache. Or you embark on a career that you know:

> *This one's really going to give it to me. I know exactly what I want and this is gonna do it.*

And every time, or every so often down the journey, you realize somehow it's not quite taking you where you thought it was and other things are popping up instead; and sooner or later the career ends. The mate leaves, the cat or the dog dies, you *all* know these experiences, you've known them countless times. How often, when you've been met with that frustration that somehow you've tried to make something work and it hasn't worked, how often have you just run out and tried all over again?

> *That must have been the wrong choice. It must be this tree over here; I'll eat the fruit of this tree.*

Hm! Know you that experience? Some of you have done that very well with what you call your significant other relationships. You would change them as often as you would change your socks.

[Laughter]

All of it—and do continue to laugh, because all of it is an illusion. All of it emanates, if you would well receive it, from one thought held in the Mind of the Holy Son of God:

> *What would it be like to experience separation from God?*

With that thought, a dream began. And why is it a dream and not real? Because God only creates what is changeless and it is not possible that the Holy Son of God ever *be separate* from God—except in your perceptions and in your feelings and beliefs; it's the only place. Likewise, only in the thought held lovingly in the mind can your union be restored.

And with that one thought—of course this is a bit of a metaphor but it's rather effective—imagine a Light, shining forth from all eternity. It has no beginning and it has no end and you cannot see its boundaries or its end, and into this radiant Light, one mad idea crept: *separation from God!* And the Holy Son of God forgot to laugh and took on seriousness, and seriousness *empowers* thought. Know you when you think a negative thought? When you take it seriously, you are empowering that thought to manifest its reality. It is called fear.

The Holy Son of God chose not to laugh and in that moment [snaps fingers] what your scientists would call the Big Bang occurred and in which that Light exploded into seemingly an infinite number of points of light, all quite identical under the cosmic microscope but seemingly separate one from another. And each of those points of light, out of fear, and out of holding that one thought within itself, began to proliferate the fields of experience. It created *unlike* God, creating things that are forever changing, that forever slip through the grasp, and the most prime example is the body. It begins to sag no matter what you do. No matter how often you fast, you still need to eat. You can't seem to overcome the body's desire, the need for food; hunger always seems to come to it. It shudders when the temperature becomes too cold. It sweats when it gets too hot, it gets dirty and smelly. Know you those feelings, those experiences? The body is a prime example of a creation that is *unlike* God's.

And so it continued, dimension upon dimension. Time began, and out of the field of time continued density, and density is separation — the appearance of it — and eventually this physical world was made manifest. And upon it you've enacted countless journeys. Huh, my goodness gracious, the dramas that have been acted out! You've all been crucified a thousand times, you've all been the crucifier a thousand times — and why? Because you never look upon anybody but yourself, and if you look into the past of your history and you see a grand tyrant, rest assured that you are looking upon an aspect of that mind that was fragmented at the beginning of time. You are therefore looking upon an aspect of your own dream. Not a pleasant thought, is it? But it is very true. And that is why only Love heals. It is only Love that restores the Son to His rightful place. It is only Love that corrects the misperception of separation. It is only Love that corrects the uses of the body.

When you look upon this world, and you see mirrored to you what can be called ego—but it's just called the ego as the perception of separation from God—when you look upon it in any of its aspects, when you look at, ahh what was the one... Saddam, hm? Now there's an aspect of ego, no sense denying it. When you look upon it with judgment, you have only ensured that it will continue. And you are all quite free and quite capable of thinking up a million other examples of expressions of the ego mind's living in separation. If you're really honest, I'm sure you can look inside yourself and come up with a few examples.

Love alone heals, and the way the ego, the way the dream, begins to dissolve is through the relinquishing of the power that you've given unto it, And when you look upon Saddam and feel angry with him, when you feel fear at what tyrants seem to be causing in the world, you have just decided to take it seriously and you believe that something in the field of ego— in my day it was called the 'evil one'—you believe that there are demons out there that can get you. And *you* are empowering them to continue, because all minds are joined. You have told them that their experience is real. Love heals and Love is extended through forgiveness, in the choice the mind makes to look past appearances and to see only the Light that shines there, waiting to be remembered and restored in the one before you.

Now, that sounds like a nice lofty thought, but is it true? I once chose, as a man, not because I was ordered by God—God doesn't order anyone to do anything—*I* chose to bring upon myself a demonstration that death is unreal, as a way of teaching my brothers and sisters that if you think of the most extreme circumstance you can, the opportunity to choose Love is always available. Rest assured, and I know perfectly well, that even if a tyrant ordered someone to strap you to a heavy wooden beam and to pound nails into your hands and feet, the power within you to choose Love has not been taken from you, in any stretch of the imagination.

And paradoxically, in the midst of even your most painful circumstances, when you make the choice to allow Love to descend first into your own being so that it can radiate out to everyone else concerned, you will feel the nails as though they were being withdrawn from your hands and feet. All of you know what it is like to be crucified in some way or another. All of you have felt that. All of you have had glimpses of the power of forgiveness and Love. When you just relinquished your beliefs, your anger, everything about a situation, what comes? Peace comes back. There have been times in some of your lives when some rather dramatic things have happened and it's got your kettle boiling, and all of a sudden you said,

Oh, the heck with it!

And you changed your attitude and you actually *laughed*! What happened? You used the power of choice given unto you to remember the Truth.

Grace. Grace descends gently, like a soft spring rain, so gently that you don't even feel or hear the drops. There's no breeze, it just falls gently, so gently that you don't see it, and yet you are bathed in it constantly. Grace waits, as Love does, to be received by a heart that is finally willing to say,

> *You know, no matter how hard I've tried, I still find myself judging my brother, judging my sister. I still think I know what the world if for and how it ought to be. And I admit that — you*

know something? — I'm really not happy yet.

Do you know that feeling? Something underneath that tells you:

Happiness is really not established in me yet. What still needs to change? Ah! A different relationship, a different career, a different pizza!

[Laughter]

The world — all things that begin in time and end in time and are therefore changing — the world has never, ever, ever offered you anything that can restore you to the happiness that is rightfully yours. What would it mean if you were to go and sit on the corner of your street and just look at this town as a symbol of the world, look at the buildings, look at the automobiles, and just say,

This world means nothing. It gives me nothing, it takes nothing from me.

It would begin to bring about discernment, the discernment between Truth and falsehood. And as you relinquish the value you've placed upon the things you hoped would bring you happiness and safety, you will discover that the place of safety is still within you and has been there since the moment when the Holy Son of God first held the thought,

What would it be like to be separate from my Father?

Correction comes with relinquishing the world. Relinquishing the world does not have anything to do with living in caves and eating a grain of rice a day. It has everything to do with relinquishing your perceptions of what the world is for and allowing it just to be as it is, while you focus on choosing Peace, so that you become the center of Light that seems to walk around in a body. Do you know what begins to happen when you do that? You will quite literally open up what can be called an inner eye, and perception will be healed, and it feels like a very literal physical shift. You are taken away, if you will, from identifying as the body, and you literally see the body for what it is: a nothing, a momentary device through which the Light of Christ can extend Love; it's not even yours anymore! Yes, you'll continue to feed it, do the little things you need to do so that it can function as long as it lasts, but something quite literally shifts: it's not you any longer. And you'll look upon your relationships and upon your careers and they'll all be different! The world will have been swept clean from your mind. That will be replaced by the perception that you're the Holy Son of God, and you're here for a very short time, and each opportunity, each moment, is given unto you because the world is crying out for your blessings. Not the ego's blessings, "Yes, I bless you, my child." Hm. The world cries out for the blessings that you can extend to it by choosing peace, by smiling at the ego and the ways of the world, by being the demonstration that there is another choice, another way, another path.

Ahhh, Grace! Does Grace set the mind and the heart free? Oh yes! It has already done so. Salvation has already been completed and the Son is already restored, and time becomes translated. It becomes translated from your insane attempt to seek the happiness, the union with God. It becomes translated into the gentle explanation, if you will, the gentle demonstration that peace *has* been restored to you — and how do you know? Each time you extend peace to another, you must then understand that peace must have already been restored to you, for you cannot give what you do not possess. And so, by giving we receive.

I learned, just as each and every one of you are learning, to give all that you have received by Grace; and when you know that you are giving all, you will know that you have received all, and you will know that your Redeemer has awakened and arisen within you. And right where you are, Heaven is. For Heaven is not a place and it is not a condition. Heaven is the Real World in which the Son abides eternally with all that God Is—and *God Is but Love.*

Hmmm. Grace... Grace. There is a choice that each mind, each soul in its journey comes to, and I've called this coming to the threshold of the Kingdom. How do you cross into it?

Not by accepting me as your saviour, though I would be honoured if you accepted me as your friend and your brother, who would walk with you to God; frankly, because I see no point in walking any other place. Each of you has come to the threshold of the Kingdom of Heaven a million times—a million times. If you've chosen to set aside learning the curriculum, you've taken a detour. Hm? You said,

Oh yes, there's the pizza diner I want to get to...

and you made a right turn.

The way that the threshold is crossed is by laying aside your perception of yourself as a separate one who is *seeking* God, along with every other perception of yourself you've ever held, in which you become finally willing to acknowledge that *you have found.* Think about it. To acknowledge in your own mind,

No. No more games, I know the truth. I am the Son of God, I am therefore here only for the extension of Love and the world's games

Grace as Reality

mean nothing.

Think what it would mean to acknowledge that within yourself:
My God, I have set up a drama so that I can pretend to be a seeker again and again and again, so that I can avoid finding.

And some of you like the game! That's okay, there's nothing wrong with liking it, and I hope you enjoy it. But in the end, seeking becomes like a weight upon the heart, and the soul in its weariness drops to its metaphorical knees — because obviously it doesn't have any — and it just says:

I'm tired.

And it sets aside the weight of the world, and a Light begins to be remembered. Hmm. The echo of an ancient melody, at once so familiar but it seemed to be forgotten, begins to arise in the soul that has relinquished the world and returned to silence. And the thought comes to replace the one thought of separation — for upon it all worlds have been built, and all subsequent thoughts and dramas are nothing more than expressions of that one thought of separation — and an inner voice speaks these words:

You are my Beloved Son in whom I remain well pleased. Arise, for you are Christ.

And then perception is healed and for the first time a major shift has occurred in your mind. And you know that it's time, and before the altar of God that rests in the silent sanctuary of your Heart, you have the audacity in the eyes of the world to finally exclaim the truth,

I and my Father are One and of myself I've never done anything, but now through me my Father will do all things. I am home and I am at peace. Truth is restored and I will go out no more from this holy place, for the light of day has come and all darkness is vanquished. I and my Father are One and it's -never been any other way.

Does that bring responsibility as long as you seem to live in time? Of course it does! It is a responsibility that the world has taught you not to take on. The world has actually taught you that *I'm* the only one who had the strength to assume that responsibility. Now isn't that a clever device of separation?

All power is given unto *you*, as the Holy Son of God, all power under Heaven and Earth to hear only the Voice for Love. It's a delightful voice, it speaks gently and it shows you the humour of your illusions. And if you would hear only that voice and acknowledge that you are One with God, that you're not sent to suffer the world — to live in lack, to live in poverty, to judge the world — you are sent to be a Light to the world, to show the world that its perceptions and beliefs don't cut it, to allow miracle- mindedness to descend upon you so that miracles can be lived and extended through you, given unto your brothers and sisters who have been given unto you that they might look upon the face of Christ and remember that they see only themselves.

Who, then, has ever honored me? Only those who have honored the Son that dwells in their own heart. Who honors me is the one who chooses to be joyous at all times. Who honors me? The one who laughs and sings and dances and plays and brings a new vision to this plane: a vision of one family under God, healed and restored, in which no one is left outside. Who honors me? You do, each time you choose to acknowledge,

Grace as Reality

Yeah, I know the truth. I hear you Jeshua, I know, I know, yeah. Okay, alright already — I get it!

[Laughter]

And then you see, I do become your brother and your friend — because all minds are joined and that means I am not unavailable to anyone in any situation. I'm not limited in who I come and talk with. I'm one who likes to have a lot of friends and I will come into any mind and unto any heart that prepares the place for me. Does it take ten thousand lifetimes of flogging the body and fasting it, beating yourself up with guilt? *No!* It takes a simple choice:

Look, Jeshua, I too am the Son of God... uh, let's be friends!

That's how the place in the heart is prepared: by acknowledging the truth! And when the door has been opened, just a crack, I will no longer need to knock upon the door but I will enter therein and take up my place with you — not as your savior, but as your friend and your brother who would only play with you joyously — and join with you in your willingness *to teach only Love,* because that is what you are. Each time the mind brings up a thought of judgment, you have separated yourself from God, pure and simple! There's no gray area there at all. Each time you look upon a judgmental thought and say,

Ha! Voice of the ego. Let it go. Look at your brother and extend only Love,

you have chosen to demonstrate that you are in union with God.

So the choice seems simple — and it is. Do you know that energy that comes now and then in which you feel like it's a real struggle to remember Love? Hold this thought: The difficulty is never anything but your unwillingness to choose the Voice for Love. Resistance and difficulty is nothing more than a symptom that you've chosen, quite willingly, to hear a different voice. I know that's befuddling because the mind wants to say, *Well, I — but I'm doing so well, but then this situation arose and if - this person hadn't done this, then I would still have chosen Love. If they would just get it straight, I could be straight.*

That's what keeps the world spinning! You thought it was Love — it's denial! Somebody has to do it differently. And you are that one. You are the one. It has not been given of me of my Father to be in this time frame as you are. I do not have what appears to be a body. And yet I have gone nowhere. I said once that I am with you always and I meant it literally.

I am not absent to you at any time and I can be no further away than the width or distance of a thought, a simple choice. But it *is* given unto *you* to abide in a world that yet believes in separation and therefore sees the body as reality and time as the great authority. *You* are the ones that with every breath you breathe — you are the ones unto whom the power has been given to demonstrate the Real World. You! No special preparation, you don't have to stand on your head for half an hour every morning, you need only be willing to choose *not to tolerate error in your own mind — never*!

No such thing as an idle thought! Each thought generates a world. Choose only the thought of Love and you become all that I ever was. You become the Word made Flesh, you become the Bearer of Light. Beloved friends, Grace is our only shared reality — Grace, and that alone.

You are not separate one from another, and you are not separate from me. Would you choose then, choose to allow this hour and this evening to be the point at which you decide to learn the curriculum? Right here and right now in your own beingness to say,

Okay, what the heck, I know I've got a few perceptions that seem to be blocking me from peace. I've held onto them for a long time;

they haven't gotten me there yet. What have I got to lose? Maybe I should just set them aside.

And allow — allow correction to come to the mind, to trust the safety of the Heart's vulnerability, to become filled with humility:

> *Of myself I do nothing. I don't know what a single thing is, but thank God my Father does! I don't even know what this situation is for, so I'm just going to be here as the Presence of Love, trust and allow it to unfold, knowing that there is one Teacher that has been given unto the world, the one that I have called the Comforter, who knows how to take everything that unfolds and weave it into the tapestry that awakens the Holy Son of God.*

Look lovingly upon every experience you have, for there is a purpose to it for you as well as for others. And every experience is the opportunity, the blessing to remember to choose Love, just like you did when you were sitting across from your friend in the pizza diner: "Oh, wait a minute! I brought you out here under false pretenses. I thought I *needed* something from you so I could hide from this conflict. But now that you're here I just want to love you!" And in that choice the conflict dissolves. And that moment, *that moment is the Atonement*! It's the moment that corrects the conflict that was set up in the beginning of time in which you seem to have been cast from the garden.

Can you begin to feel what I am seeking to share with you, then? That you do not experience ordinary moments! — there are no such things as ordinary moments, unless you forget they're extraordinary. That's what makes them ordinary: forgetting. Every moment, my God, is such a blessing! *The one before you brings you your salvation* if you would but love them instead of judge them. Haaah. If that doesn't bring Light to the world, what can? To see that it doesn't mean what the world thinks it means. It's a dance and an illusion. It's a tapestry woven by One who would but bring the Peace of God back to your heart.

You don't go to school to get a career so you can have a job! The soul is choosing to attract situations so that it can learn where it has failed to extend Love and to live from unlimitedness. That's all!

Just as you created your thought of separation, you as a soul are creating your pathway home. Nothing can arise by accident. And if you seem stuck right now for a while, it just means you're taking a break, a summer vacation. It's not that you *have* to take a break, it's that you're *choosing* to take a break.

Within you lies so much power! In the twinkling of an eye, the Holy Son of God could radically transform this world into the Kingdom of Heaven on Earth, but that can't occur until you allow that transition to occur within *you*, because, you see, the world, it's like a (what do you call those races where everybody thinks that if they can run thirty-five miles that it's a great feat of strength or something, so thousands of them gather in their senior cities straining to get to their...) marathon! Well, the world *does* seem like a marathon. All the crushing masses of humanity, straining at the starting line, waiting for somebody to pull the trigger to release all of this Divine Creative Energy! How long have *you* been waiting for someone to pull the trigger and tell you it's okay to get on with living an unlimited and joyous life?

Well I will as soon as everybody else does! What will they think of me if I give up pain and suffering and judgment and choose laughter and dance and play and joy? Will they think I'm crazy if I tell them, "Look! Hunger is old now, nobody on this planet needs to be hungry anymore!"

And they'll look at you and say, "Well it's always been that way, what are you talking, nonsense?"

Hm, no you're talking with great sense. Don't wait any longer. Look lovingly upon your own life. Look at your circumstances as something you've attracted to yourself and therefore it presents a blessing. Embrace it, honor it and then ask within and be really honest: Is this truly the life that the Son of God would choose to live if the Son of God was thoroughly awake? Hm! Interesting question! For you see it might be, and it might not be. It requires your willingness to surrender your perceptions of yourself and world. And if in your circumstances you can go inside and say,

> *I am at peace. I am where my Father is asking me to be. I don't complain about it; I don't make judgments; I'm just at peace. And there is a lightness to my step and there's a joy in my eyes no matter what the bank account says. I know I live in unlimitedness and if I only have a dollar today that's perfectly okay, because if I need ten thousand tomorrow, they'll be there!*

And if you get in touch and inwardly you finally admit,

> *Who am I trying to fool? Who am I trying to be? Am I trying to*

pretend like I'm more spiritual than somebody else because I'm broke? Hm! Am I trying to believe or to express to someone that my suffering somehow is building me up? Do I look into the face of my brother and say, "Yeah, I'm really content," and then go home at night and inwardly feel something gnawing at me?

Can you become so honest and just admit that you're living a lie? Can you say to yourself,?

No, I'm not happy. There's something in me that wants to be lived and I'm pushing it down.

Fear it no longer, for what you are pushing down is the Radiance of Christ that comes to enlighten and heal the world and to establish the Kingdom of Heaven upon it.

Is *any* of this making sense to you?

[General agreement.]

Of course it is. I cannot say that I come as a grand teacher, I cannot come and say that I have much to give you that is going to make your life work marvellously, because, you see, I know that I cannot give you anything that you do not already possess. I admit it wholly, up front.

I come only as your brother and your friend, to reflect to you the truth that you *know* in the depth of your being — in the depth of your being where the Real World resides and where the world can never possibly touch, and there is only safety to be found in being willing to let the power of the Mind of Christ to be lived through you, to no longer tolerate the errors of the thinking of the world and to demonstrate to your brothers and sisters through Love that there's always another way, always another choice, and that *nothing – nothing —* limits you, save the thoughts that you would choose to hold onto.

I said earlier that I do not have a body, but you do! And I know how to join with you. You don't have to know how; you only need to be willing. And because I love you, because I know that we walk to God together, I will come to you and I will walk with you, and I say this unto you not from a place above you but from a deep compassion and a love for you, whom my Father has created out of Love. There is not a moment when, in your experience as you unlearn the perceptions of the world and reclaim the perceptions of Truth, there is not a moment in which you might feel that your strength is lacking, there is not a moment that I will refrain from giving you mine. *All you have to do is ask!* And I will give you my strength until yours is as certain as mine — and my strength is *perfectly* certain because, like you, I lived once in this world and I chose to teach only Love. I chose the outrageous idea that death is not real, and to believe that no circumstances could separate me from my decision to choose Love.

And I found that what my Father had taught me was true: Death is not real; this world is illusion. And the world dropped away from me as gently as does a dream dissolve from your mind when your eyes open in the morning and you remember where you really are. The world tried to get rid of me and in its insane attempt it simply allowed me the freedom to join with anybody I want! [Laughter]

Hm! And *you*, I'm asking you in your own hearts to be willing to become the hands, the feet, the eyes, the expression and the Heart of Christ. Because, you see, the world believes in the body and if I come and whisper in one's ear as they walk down the street, they say it's just their imagination, "Oh, I've just had this sudden thought of Jeshua - pah, he wouldn't talk to me!"

And on they go!

And I'm still standing, going, "It *is* me! What do I have to do?"

[Laughter]

"No it can't be, it's my imagination. First of all I'm a sinful creature, therefore he would never come to me anyway. Secondly, voices heard that aren't associated with the body, they must be somebody's, uh, insanity..."

I need you as much as the world has ever tried to tell you that you need *me*. Many of you have rebelled against that,

> *Oh God, they're telling me I have to worship this Jeshua fellow. Yuck!*

It has never felt quite right to many of you, thank God!

[Laughter]

But I need you, because my one purpose and my one task is to embrace the whole of the Sonship with the Love that my Father has given unto me. Because my Father embraced me and brought me into that remembrance, my only purpose and function is to give that remembrance to anyone who would receive it. And I can't do that without you — *without you*.

And in the most ordinary of moments, you can choose to remember the extraordinariness of the blessing of that eternal moment. You have the power, even if the one in front of you doesn't know what's going on, to take a deep breath and go,

> *Ah, only Christ is here,*

and to radiate Light and Love, to choose forgiveness, so they begin to look at you and they go, "I don't quite understand, you don't seem to be concerned about the things we're concerned with... Oh no, and yet somehow you're always there, you're always the same, and sometimes through you all this wisdom pours forth."

And then you go, "Whoa, what did I say?'
And they say, "God, you know what you said last night? It was the most incredible thing. Thank you, thank you!"

And you scratch your head and you go, "What? Did we talk last night?"

[Laughter]

"Yes, on the phone for just a moment and you were getting ready to go somewhere and suddenly you said something that seemed off the wall, and then you said, 'Well I have to go, bye.'"

You go, "I said that?"

You've just been willing to let the Holy Spirit reach your brother through you. And that occurs because you have opened the place for miracles to be extended through you by acknowledging,

> *I and my Father are One, and I relinquish my perceptions of what the world is, and I will go gently through my day, remembering the Grace that has set me free. And I will look upon my brother, not believing I know what they need — there is One who knows.*

That's how the mind begins to be opened so that what you channel is no longer the thoughts of the world—and by the way, everything in this world is channeled, everything *inspired* either by the voice of fear or the Voice for Love. Every moment of every day you are choosing what frequency to channel, what quality of thought to channel, what dimension of feelingness to channel—every second, it never changes. Hmm.

In relinquishing your own ideas and acknowledging that you cannot save yourself, the Light of Truth begins to descend and to be re-awakened in you, and you will quite literally find that miracles become the stepping stones upon which your life is lived, upon which you step. And you will come and go as the wind, not knowing where it comes from or where it's going, but somehow you're in the right place at the right time, and everything's okay.

Miracles. Miracles occur naturally to minds that teach only Love. So you see, it gets to the point where if miracles aren't happening you won't even dare to get out of bed...

[Laughter]

because you know something is amiss in your own mind:

> *Where am I doubting, where am I fearful, where am I failing to extend Love? My God, I didn't laugh yesterday. It's been two weeks since I danced! Aah, now I know where to begin!*

... to bring lightness and laughter and the sense of play and safety back into the mind, and then the flow can continue.

Hmm. I know you're holding the thought, "Is he looking at me?"

[Laughter] Yes. [Laughter]

But not with this body. For you see, I do not come into this body, I do not take my beloved brother and kick him out. All that happens is that an ancient resonance is allowed to be made manifest and there is a blending at the level of mind — and mind far transcends the body; remember I said the body arises within the field of mind, it's really an illusion, just an apparition — and at the level of mind, I merely blend my energy with this particular mindset filled with concepts, filled with ideas, made up out of experiences much like your own, and I simply activate it in a different way.

I bring a different level of integration and understanding, that's all. And if I can blend with this mind, rest assured, I can blend with *any* mind. And I can blend with yours. And no I am not going to acknowledge that you are the one I'm speaking to, not in this way, I'm going to ask that you acknowledge it in the depth of your own being, for when I turned this body in this way, a thought came, a thought of knowingness,

He's aware of me. Gulp.

[Laughter]

The time for gulping has passed. I am aware of you because I know how beautiful you are. I see your light and your radiance and your purity and there is no guilt upon you. You have not failed me and you have failed no one, and the Radiance and the Power and the Light and the Truth with which you were created and are sustained *is in you now in its purity*. Be you therefore wholly joyous for in *this* hour a miracle does occur. And you will see the fruits of it unfolding in your life. Precious friend, you came doubting your own worthiness and as an ancient friend, I say unto you, your worthiness is established by God and the world has never taken it from you. I love you.

Hmm. Hmm. There!

So how are all of you doing?

[Laughter]

Excellent.

My beloved brother has asked me many times: "Jeshua, what are you going to talk about?" And I've always given him one answer: "My friend, your task is only to be available." Because you see, *I* never know what's going to be said. I come and abide with you just as you abide with each other as friends. You get together and you sit around in your living room, nothing to do and nowhere to go—you just hang out. I come and abide with you and I read what is in your heart, and what is spoken is not deliberately chosen by me but it flows forth through my mind, then through the mind field of this my beloved brother. You seem to hear it as words spoken and picked up by your physical ears, but what is spoken is being generated from the Source of Oneness in which we abide—One Mind, together; that is what creates *all* experience, *all of it*.

Does that make sense to you? The gathering together of minds that choose to resonate at a certain frequency, that's what generates experience. If there were a tall skyscraper, an apartment building, and all of you got together on a Saturday and said, "Let's hang out on the bottom floor!" Isn't it true that you would look out the window and you would see certain things? And then the next Saturday you would say, "Let's go up to the fifteenth floor and hang out!" And you open the curtains and wouldn't the view be different? That's all that happens in your experience. You choose to come together with minds and the interplay of that energy generates what you call your experience of that moment. And wherever two or more are gathered in my name, there I am in the midst of them. When any two come together and choose to go to the penthouse, the view is unlimited. The table is spread, the finest linens, the finest china, and you sit down to a feast prepared by the Father for the Son Whom He loves above all things and Who welcomes home the prodigal son no longer, but the one who has *chosen* to return.

There has been, by and large, an agreement by all of you, a desire just to hang out together in a frequency of Peace, of Love, to have echoed back to the mind the Truth the mind already knows. So by and large, we've gotten together in the penthouse, and in your daily experience, you have the power to bring the energy of the penthouse into your situations. Now, of course, that means that tomorrow morning when you get up and go to your job or wherever you go, you're having a very high elevated feeling and you go to work and everybody's doing what they call the 'bitching' or whatever it is they do... [Laughter]

... and the complaining and all of the rest. A disappointment comes to the mind:

> *Oh, I thought I could change all this!*

Don't give in to it. That's the trick, you see. Just because somebody else is being miserable doesn't mean *you* have to accommodate them by *joining* them. It doesn't mean you look on them and say, "Well you've created it, get out of it!"

[Laughter]

It means that you look upon them and go,

> *Aah, I'm seeing dimensions of ego, I'm seeing choices for*

separation, but I know that's not the Truth.

You look upon them lovingly and if they need your arm put around them, you do so, or you feed them with the love that they're capable of receiving, but the whole time, you remember what the Truth is. You hold the frequency of the penthouse. And the more often you do that, the easier it gets.

And one day, you walk into that circle of friends or co-workers who are trying to drag you down into their state of being, and you realize something has changed:

It's not affecting me. I feel totally calm and at peace.

And no matter what they say, you just smile and go, "Oh come on, you know there's another way. Would you choose it with me?"

"No, I refuse!"

[Laughter]

"Okay! There will be another opportunity. As for me, I choose to wait only on the Lord, which simply means to wait, to abide in, Christ Consciousness. I choose only peace. Now let's get on with our day."

And you will wait for them to choose with you if it takes ten thousand lifetimes, a millenium, it doesn't matter, you're hanging out in eternity! Hm. It's very, very important. When the whole world is seeking to drag itself down, the world needs just one to make a different choice, and you can be that one in every moment. Isn't that true? Hm! Indeed.

Grace. I offer this unto you. In any situation from this hour in which you are tempted to think with the thoughts of the world and you notice that it doesn't feel very good, remember that simple word: Grace. Gently let it come to the mind and it will be your willingness to send me a telegram, it will be your willingness to open up the place of the heart — and I will not fail to come to you. And as you gently abide with it, certain things that have been said in this evening are going to come to you as if you are hearing them for the first time and you will swear that didn't get said then! And a feeling will come, a certain little resonance, much like that which has touched many of you in this hour, for remember I'm not in this body — for all *you* know, I'm right behind you.

[Laughter]

And with that thought, a different vibration, a different frequency will again begin to come to you. Some of you will have times when, as you begin that, all of a sudden it will be like the pot's really been stirred, and the mind will be going, "I know it didn't work, I know it doesn't work, these bad feelings really are here, I know it, I know it, I know it!" That's just the same thought of denial! But,

Oh! Grace... Grace... Grace...

until the voice of the ego begins to realize, "Wait a minute you've always listened to me before, I guess it's not going to work this time." And the voice of the ego withdraws from your Holy Mind and Peace is restored.

So please be willing not to look beyond the simplicity of what was just offered. It will work, and work beautifully. It will lead you upon revelation and revelation and revelation — and revelation is really nothing more than the unwinding, the unlearning of concepts and perceptions that have imprisoned the mind and kept you away from the peace that you seek. Hmm.

For a moment now, just turn and look at someone next to you. Just turn enough so that the eyes can meet. Now it doesn't matter if you believe this is true or not, just do it anyway. Each of you, one unto the other, take just a moment—and you can decide who gets to go first— look at your brother or your sister, your eternal friend who has journeyed with you throughout all of time and space and has shared every world with you in one form or another...
[Laughter]

... and say to them that "I promise to live my life *for you* as one who has found and acknowledges the Truth, so that no matter if we ever see each other again, wherever I am, I promise to keep my promise." So in your own words, go right ahead.

[Members of the group share this promise with each other]

So how does that feel?

[Comments and laughter from group]

What seems sane to the world is wholly insane to the Mind of Christ and all beliefs of the world are diametrically opposed to the Truth of the Kingdom, so how then to use a bit of a measurement for knowing which voice you're listening to?

If you're not standing out as just a little crazy, you have conformed yourself to the world. Hmm. I taught certain friends many things in secret, something that wasn't meant to be broadcast to minds that really weren't interested in learning anyway, but the essence of what I taught my closest friends was

Grace as Reality

the simplicity of the great power of choosing laughter, dancing, play and singing in each and every day until that frequency permeates every decision you make and every experience you're having. For you see, it is lightness that *enlightens* the mind and lightness carries the mind out of density, out of seriousness.

So if you're feeling a bit heavy and a bit down, ask yourself, "Did I laugh, did I sing, did I dance, did I play this day?" If not, and it's eleven o'clock and you're laying in bed and you're dog tired and you're feeling depressed... Get up!

[Laughter]

And if you're with your spouse and you suddenly jump out of bed and you begin to dance around the bedroom, they'll say, "What are you doing, dear?"

"I'm remembering!"

[Laughter]

Indeed.

Is it not time to release seriousness from what you call spirituality? Is it not time to transcend religiousness and to know that Spirit dwells within you as the voice and the whisper of God's Love that brings you into being?

> *Do I exist? I sure do! It must mean that God still loves me and that God's Love is in me. Haaah!*

So . . . I extend unto you my thanks for your willingness, because you see, think that just on this little evening you've opted to come to this place, perhaps out of curiosity, perhaps because they haven't changed the movies downtown yet, whatever the reason is on the outside, that's not what matters. You are always compelled by what the soul is choosing to attract to itself as experience. I thank you because—please don't minimize this—in this evening, you chose as a soul, no matter what the mind was saying, you chose as a soul to come together and set aside all of the millions of other things you could have been doing in the world, and you came to simply abide, as much with one another as with me.

And when you leave here... No matter what the mind is doing, you are always going to know, *you are always going to know* that the one who walked this plane as a man is like unto yourself. The one the world has tried to get rid of, first through crucifixion and then by making him into a grand savior so far removed and above every other human being, that is untouchable and unreachable anyway, so why try? All attempts to continue the illusion. You are going to know that what I said then is true: *"I am with you always, even unto the end of this age."* And when you fully understand who I am and have become—that is, in shifting identification from a man in space and time to identification with the Mind of Christ—when you come to that place in yourself, you are going to laugh like you've never laughed before, for you will understand then that, for God's sake, I couldn't *be* anywhere *else* but where you are, *because we are One, always.* I am you, and that lifetime is wholly yours. Separation does not exist; *it does not exist.*

Am I the Christ? Oh yes, along with you and *never apart from you.* And I love you. Not as the world gives give I unto you, and not as the world gives can you give unto one another, and that is the glory of Grace. Peace therefore be unto you. Those of you that would like to leave, you're feeling quite nice now, whatever it is, or you just want to get home to the late movie, whatever it is, go always with my blessings. If you choose in this hour to say, "No I'm not ready to learn the curriculum," it's fine with me. I can wait! I've waited a long time and because I live in that which is eternal, rest assured, I *will* outwait you!

[Laughter]

And not one thing you say and not one thing you do will ever, even for an instant, turn me from you. My Love for you is as unshakable as our Father's Love is for each of us, and in loving you in that way I know the Love of the Father for me. And when I said, "Go you therefore and teach all nations," I was *not* talking about walking around with a Bible under your arm! To teach is to teach only Love.

And to go therefore and to teach all nations means to go to everyone you see and to realize that right there, you can be the one who brings the gentleness of Peace and the warmth of Love to *that situation, that moment.* Teach well. Teach well by being what you would desire to learn; and by teaching it you *do* become it; and as you give you have received, in all ways and always.

Peace therefore be unto the only begotten of God, being neither male nor female but Light, and Light alone: The Light that lights all worlds and brings Creation back to God.

Peace be unto you always, for the things of Heaven are indeed united with the things of Earth, and the Peace of God is extended as far as from the East to the West, held lovingly in the arms of Christ—your arms.

Amen.

Healing

Now, we begin.

Indeed, greetings unto you, beloved and holy children of Light divine, indeed offspring of the One Who has been called God. And if you are that offspring, indeed you are created in your Father's image and in you remains the power to heal every false perception, to leave the world of split-mindedness behind you, and to indeed perceive the real world and to abide within it. And what can that real world be if not the extension of love that need not be sent through a filter of fear. For, indeed, it is that filter that keeps the mind split and the heart at least partially yet concealed. And when you choose wholly to remember the Truth of your being, then you hold the power and the freedom to give all things over to the Holy Spirit. You can throw open the shutters of the heart and even of the cells of the body and ask — and know you will receive — that every last trace of shadow shall be released from you.

For those of you that believe that healing can come only to the mind, is it not wise to ask where the mind is? And as I have sought to teach you — the body arises *within* the mind, not the other way around. And, therefore, what you see as these lumps of flesh express quite exquisitely the patterns of belief that you have held in the mind. For the body can only serve the thoughts you choose to hold, and it will do so to perfection.

Therefore, if there has been a thought or a belief grounded in the misperception that you are separate from God, and therefore, in the soil of fear you have perceived an inequality between yourself and your brother and believe that you live in a fearful world, understand well that that creates reaction in the very cells of the body; and the cells themselves become like holding tanks and you hold on quite deeply and quite strongly to ancient wounds and ancient hurts.

And though you hold the thought in the mind,

I am the arisen Christ,

until you are truly willing to throw open the shutters of even the cells of the body and to let all of those little dark shadows fly away, you are still holding on to one small dark belief, choosing to claim it as your own, and you have not released all things to the Holy Spirit for healing.

You cannot know what will transpire when truly you release the hold on that last little corner of your mind that you would hold on to and claim to be your own. But you can, with great faith, trust the process that the Holy Spirit would use to release every shadow—so that even the body becomes capable of radiance.

What is radiance? It is only the Light you are without anything creating an obstacle to its expression. Therefore, precious friends, fear not the release of the chronic hold you have had even within the cells of the body. For the body is only an extension of your thought.

If you are loved wholly and in your Father's eyes you have never sinned, what then is there to fear? To fear healing? To fear release? Indeed, to fear tears? Tears and laughter are your grandest of healers and your greatest of teachers. And I confess they are far greater than I, for all I can do is come and talk to you. I can come and bring my countenance upon you, and I can stand by your side as your friend and your brother—and I certainly don't mean just momentarily as I borrow the mind and body of my beloved brother here—but whenever you turn

Healing

to me, I can be with you; for indeed I am with you always.

But what your laughter and tears can bring to you cannot be measured. Therefore, fear them not and judge them not. Do not create an inequality, saying,

> *Well, I much prefer laughter over tears.*

If you have made the choice to choose healing, then embrace your tears as much as your laughter, and give thanks when they arise. Throw open the shutters of the body and let the tears create shaking in the body. It cannot destroy you because you are not the body. You are that which utilizes it as a vehicle of communication. And when you therefore hold on in the palm of your hand to that shadow, it creates constriction in the body out of fear, and you are choosing to limit what this beautiful vehicle can do. And it will do precisely what you command it to do.

There is no one here who could not walk on water. There is no one here who could not extend healing through the body. And what prevents it? That small little corner that you have been holding on to for an awfully long time.

The message that I would bring you in this hour is this: fear not healing. Yes, it feels like change, and thank God for that. Because if there has been depression, there have been old wounds from which you have been acting out and acting out and acting out, as it is called in your language. Is it not time to release it? If you would indeed be the arisen Christ, then truly have the courage to throw open the cells of the body.

Now, how to you do that? You don't. But abiding in faith and asking the Holy Spirit for the help you need, indeed helpers will come because they have been assigned to you. And it will not be by accident that certain ones will come into your life; and in Truth if you are desirous of healing, be vigilant to see who it is that comes into your life. And understand that they are sent to you because you have asked of the one Teacher, whose guidance never errs, for healing and for completion.

Healing, then, can often feel like death because, of course, it is. It is the death of a false illusion that you have held and clung to in error. And if you would be the servant of your Father—and I say this not in a serious vein but in a very light vein, because to be a servant of the Father is to be one who expresses love and joy and laughter and play and certainty and strength and humility and compassion and patience and vision— and if indeed you would be the servant of your Father, let that death occur down to the tips of your toes. You will not taste death, but an illusion will dissolve away.

Many of you are yet hoping, fervently hoping, that you can achieve awakening by holding the thought in the mind,

I am the arisen Christ.

That is a great place—and the only place—to start. You cannot approach healing as long as you hold the attitude that you are separate from God, because you will create a veil of fear and you will go through process after process after process, but you will never get to the nub of it—because you don't want to.

Therefore, when you understand in the mind, in the heart, the Truth of who you are, that becomes the very foundation and the strength and the faith to allow the Holy Spirit to completely remake even the cells of the body. Notice that I said the cells of "the" body, not the cells of "your" body, because the arisen Christ knows he is not the body and does not possess it, that he does not begin where the body starts and he will not end when

Healing

the body is returned to this Earth.

He knows that the body is given of the Holy Mother for nothing save the extension of the unconditional Love of God.

And from that foundation you will find your strength to allow the complete and radical transformation of every aspect of your being: it is called the personality, which is just a mask made up of fear that can be translated into a vehicle of communication; the emotional body, which is the core where you have held all of those ancient wounds; and even the cells of the body. Therefore, your Kingdom shall be made new again.

Precious friends, fear not the complete healing of every trace of illusion that you have harbored within your being. And if it feels like death, then embrace it. It is the only death that truly counts, you see.

What, then, prolongs the process of healing? *Resistance* to it, born out of the chronic holding on to nothing more than illusions. And when that illusion has truly been laid down, the body will arise, the emotions will arise, the mind, the personality will arise — but will be made new. The dreamer will have been laid to rest and the arisen Christ will finally live through you.

And I ask you to join with me in the willingness to allow that healing to occur: to embrace your laughter and to embrace your tears and to embrace every opportunity to let go of the shadows that bind you.

> *How, then, can you ask the Holy Spirit to heal you if there are dark corners which you have refused to look at, or how can you hand to the Holy Spirit what you have not yet embraced?*

Illusions remain powerful when you refuse to acknowledge them. And many yet hold the fear:

> *What will happen if I truly look my illusions squarely in the eye and acknowledge that, by God, they have been controlling me? Will they be the demons that master me?*

Herein lies the purpose of faith: to know that you are the arisen Christ, that you abide in perfect union with God in the real world, and that you are given and sent to translate this unreal world of illusions and insanity into the real world; and you do it by acknowledging that yes, you have been living there all along and it is time to heal it.

Healing really does not take effort. It takes allowing. Allowing, allowing, allowing, every day and with every breath. So that your illusion—this *unreal* world—becomes translated and becomes the perfect reflection of the *real* world. And it can be painless when your perception changes, that healing is not frightful, that it is okay to cry in front of a friend. It is okay to pick up the phone and say,

> *Lordy, do I need you tonight.*

It's okay to say,

> *There is something going on that I don't understand, but I am not going to constrict. I am going to throw the body open. And if I convulse and if I vomit and if I cry and if I scream, who cares?*
> *It's just the release of old shadows that have no place in the body and the mind and the emotions of the only begotten child of God.*

It is well and good to recite certain words,

Healing

I am the arisen Christ. I live in joy and I live in Light.

But if you have not looked to be sure that you have embraced every shadow, it remains in the realm of a thought and it has not yet manifested as your living reality.

That is why so many become frustrated. They do all the metaphysical games. They even come and listen to me and say,

> *Jeshua said I am the arisen Christ. Therefore, ah, I can avoid the process of healing.*

If you are the arisen Christ — and I assure you that you are — *you will want to embrace the very process of insuring that no trace of illusion remains within you.* You will not deceive yourself. You will not lie to yourself. And when those shadows are made present to your consciousness, you will give thanks to the Holy Spirit and to the brothers and sisters that have thrown them into your face, because they are messengers of God. They are saying,

> *Here, look at this, so that you can embrace it and release it.*

Fear not shadows, because you are made of Light, a Light so powerful that it can dissolve shadows in the instant you truly choose to embrace them and acknowledge them.

That is how powerful each of you truly is. And the day comes when you no longer need helpers to dissolve those shadows, because with their help you have learned it's safe to embrace them, that they hold no power of mastery over you.

The only reason there are such things as healers or teachers or masters is because yet within the drama you believe you need them; and not understanding the strength within you, you need to reach out for the strength of another. By all means do so. One who is truly awakening to the Christ within them recognizes how worthy they are of the help of the universe.

And yet, how many times—and be honest—how many times have each of you felt that you are not really worthy of seeking and reaching out for help?

> *I better just stuff this. After all, I don't want to bother anybody today.*

Anyone know that energy?

God has created you as a Thought of perfect Love in form. And when you choose to manifest that reality, do you think He sits by idly and goes,

> *Well, I don't know if you are really worthy of what I can bring to you.*

It is just the opposite. You are the one to whom the universe is given. You—you—are the beloved of God.

Therefore, when you know you need help, reach out for it. To do so is an act of power. It says that you understand your worth and you will do anything to let Christ be born in you.

The time comes quickly upon this Earth when you are going to need to have made sure that you've healed every wound and every false perception. And the wounds can only be healed to the degree that you are willing to open up and allow that healing. Not to use the power of the mind to deceive yourself, but to understand the Truth of the long journey you've been making, because it's been very complex. You are never going to really be able to look back and pinpoint the moments when a certain perception started. It's not really necessary, but you will at times be able to access certain memories that exhibit the power of that false perception. And as those moments are healed, you have healed all of them.

And isn't that a lucky thing? It would be a rather long journey if you had to heal every moment in which you let a false perception lead you astray. But in each of those moments, they are really all the same. So to heal one is to heal them all. And whether healing comes because one taps into a past life, or healing comes because they have realized that yesterday they exhibited something that was not loving and they bring the Light of the Spirit to it because they have embraced it, the healing is the same, and they have healed the whole of their past. It is not necessary to hold the belief in reincarnation and it is not necessary to go forth a thousand lifetimes backward to find what needs to be healed. Because if it needs to be healed, it is with you right where you are.

Learn to look upon all of your thoughts and all of your actions and all of your dreams and all of your perceptions and ask of yourself,

> *Is this truly the will of God? Or is there a trace of fear in it? Is there a trace of limitation? Is this something that I've seen cropping up over and over again?*

If it crops up over and over, you know it is in need of healing.

Healing has been grossly misunderstood. It's really not the fixing of anything, because to do that assumes that it is already real and that there is someone who can fix it. *Healing is the mastery of allowing.*

Healing is the mastery of allowing: to allow all things, so that they can be embraced and loved and thereby transcended. Never use the mind to minimize your behavior, your thoughts. Never use the mind to do that, because to do that you will only ensure that you will repeat that perception, that behavior, ad nauseam.

You are worthy of the depth of your healing. You are worthy of seeing that in Truth the journey has already been completed, and your Father is just waiting for you to truly throw open the shutters and allow the fullness of the power of Christ to be lived through you. And that is fearful to the small little shadow you have been clinging to.

You have heard it said in your world that many fear failures. The fear of failure ensures it. But a far greater fear is the fear of success. And in this term, in the use of this term, I am not talking about success in worldly terms. I am talking about the success of living as Christ, wholly, without obstacle or block. It is that fear that leads you to hold on to the small, powerless, weak and insane shadow that you have believed yourself to be since before time began. *It takes courage to release that. It takes courage to ask for help. It takes courage to die.*

The whole purpose of the crucifixion is not that it saved anybody from their sins. It never did that. The purpose of the crucifixion was to demonstrate where you will continue to be throughout all of eternity until you are willing to truly let that small little shadow die and to claim your power, not just as a thought or a belief — although that's where it starts — but to allow that power to transform the emotions and every cell of the body. Then, indeed, the resurrection has been realized.

And if I can raise the body and ascend unto my Father, so can you. I am not saying that you have to be able to be nailed to a cross so that the body dies and then resurrected in three days and ascend before your disciples. Of course not. I am saying that that was a demonstration of what has to happen to your perceptions of yourself, which is that which makes up the ego.

A true healer knows that they heal nothing. A true healer knows that they fix nothing. The truest among them simply makes themself available and learns to speak a language that the one who perceives themselves as sick or diseased can understand. And they will abide with them and they will speak that language and they will use their modalities that they have learned, but all the while they know Who It is that will affect the healing. It actually comes from the communication of that soul or that person with the Holy Spirit in whatever form they choose to think of it. And an agreement is made that healing will come because that soul has finally chosen to allow it. And often all they need is the safety of being with a healer.

The greatest of healers are those that have understood that they have needed to allow correction to come to their own mind and their own emotions and their own bodies. And, indeed, *the greatest of healers never cease in that process.* That is what keeps them in the line of power, if you want to call it that, so that the Holy Spirit can work through them.

A true healer is one who has, in a sense, made a grand sacrifice of their life. They no longer are anxious to get to the end of healing but they enact the act of healing daily, throwing themselves open always so that they remain in communication with those that come to them, and never forget what it means to be *in* the process of healing.

Now that is very paradoxical, and I hope you will take some time to contemplate it. Because in the act of, in a sense, donning the cloak of one who is constantly working on their healing, they are actually liberated. And out of their liberation they take on the form of one involved in healing, so that they can be with their brothers and sisters and be an effective channel of healing. Does that make sense? It is very important. Very important. If ever you come across a healer that says,

> *I have already got it all licked; now let me fix you,*

please turn around and leave, because that is an unhealed healer. There are many of you in this room who are making shifts in consciousness, and your compassion has opened. Your understanding that there is nothing outside of you has begun to open, and you have thus begun to see that your brother and sister is not outside of you and *cannot* be outside of you. And out of your compassion, you want to help them heal. You will be effective to the degree that you allow, in every day, healing to come to you; and to never shut your heart to that process.

And if it means that you think you may cry tears in every day of your life for the next two hundred and forty-seven years, you will gladly do it — because that keeps you in that line of power so that the Holy Spirit can work through your humble heart, and extend the healing to the one who has asked for it but needs you as an intermediary because their strength is not yet certain enough to come to the throne of God directly.

And the greatest of days will come when all of the healers that understand what it means to truly be healers are out of work. And then they, too, will rejoice because their work will have been finished.

Please do not fear healing. But I have come to speak about that specific subject tonight because there are some among you who are creating a dichotomy within yourself. You are actually widening the split while holding on to the illusion, created with the power of the mind, that you have already gotten it finished.

Healing

Hmm. Anyone feel like that? You are worthy of being healed, so you might as well get on with it. The Kingdom *needs* you to be healed.

Will you know when it is completed? Here's the rub: *when in Truth healing has been completed, you won't even care* if it's been completed because your life will become, we will use the word here, sacrificed — but I don't mean it in your normal sense of loss. It is a gift given freely by you. It is like looking at your brothers and sisters and saying, Gosh, they sure are enjoying groveling in the muck and mire. Because I love them I am going to get down on my hands and knees and grovel, too. And just maybe one of them will look at me, and if they look at me at the right time, the Holy Spirit might be able to work through me. But the Holy Spirit will never be able to work through me if I don't get down on my hands and knees.

Enlightenment, salvation, is not about keeping the mud off of your knees. It is the freedom to be in the mud without identifying with it, but allowing yourself to be there as long as the Sonship still needs you.

Now, if that were not true, when I ascended to my Father I would have waved goodbye and I would have wished you well, but you would have never heard from me again.

Understand what I mean when I say that I have never really left this world and that I work without ceasing. I can only do so because I completed my part in the atonement as a man who walked upon this plane. Therefore, that is the path you, too, must take: to let yourself complete the process of healing, so that out of your freedom you can take on the cloaks of this world and look like everybody else until *they* learn that they are not separate from God.

I am only a temporary mediation-bringer to you, and the grandest of days that will come to me is when you look past me and need me no longer.

But until that day I will work without ceasing because I love you. And every genuine healer understands the Heart from which those words are spoken, because they are spoken from the Heart of Christ. That is more than any one embodiment could ever contain. I am merely one who is like you but has become identified with the Christ, and I call you to do the same.

The water is fine. Jump in. But to jump in, you see, you have to remove your bathing suit of your wounds that you have refused to embrace so that they might be healed. There can't be any dust on your body when you jump into the water of eternity.

So many of you are standing on the platform constantly repeating that prayer,

> *Holy Father, let there be Light. However, I want to keep this little smudge on myself. I want to hold on to it as my own because I put a lot of energy into creating it. My God, I've spent lifetimes becoming as wretched as I could be and now You want me to let it go? I've spent lifetimes convincing myself that I am weak and frail and now You want me to let it go? How dare You.*
>
> *I have used the power You have given me, Father, to create unlike You and I have been rather proud of it. I have even created the sense that I am separate from You and that took a lot of doing. And now, you want me to let it go before I jump into that lake of eternity?*

Healing

Unfortunately, yes.

Let your life be a sacrifice. Not a painful sacrifice — that's been done a thousand times. It is not a lot of fun. Let your life be a sacrifice in the sense that you realize that you are just walking around pretending like you are a body, pretending like you are just a person so that you can make yourself available to those who still believe they need an intermediary.

A teacher of God is nothing but a temporary device. Please, I beg of you, contemplate well what I have shared with you. It is very important because it is really the journey of everyone, not just a special class of species that are called "healers." You are all healers, every one of you. Learn all you can about it. Apply it to yourself. Become one who loves to heal, not by groveling in your past, but just by noticing the nuances that come when certain circumstances seem to elicit reactions. Don't pretend it isn't happening or it will only continue. And that one veil, though subtle as it may seem, may be the very veil that keeps you eternally on the wheel of birth and death in the drama of separation.

If you want to see the planet healed, then be very fervently involved in your own healing. Not by picking yourself up by your bootstraps, but by asking for help and noticing what comes into your life. It's there for a reason. If indeed nothing arises by accident, then it must be there for a reason.

Now, does that mean that you need to take upon yourself great humility and seriousness, and say,

> *God, I'm such a wretched, sinful creature after all and I've been fooling myself. I have got to dig deep. Boy, do I have work to do.*

No, it means to embrace it and move into healing with joy and with strength and with certainty. Have fun with it.

> *Have you ever spent an hour seeing how deeply you can cry? It has been said by another teacher that some of you are familiar with, that every tear releases a thousand years.*

Well, what would one hour of true gut-wrenching crying do?

Get into it, because just the other side of those tears, divine laughter comes. Some of you have experienced that—when you are truly into it, something seems to shift. Anybody experience that?

[Audience agreement]

Then, why would you fear tears? Why would you fear what you have been taught to perceive as gut-wrenching *pain*? That is just an illusion of perception. When the body shakes with tears, you have been taught to believe it is because you are weak and wretched. Those that can allow tears exhibit great strength.

I hope it all makes sense. Some of you in this room while I have been speaking about this, rather forcefully, have felt a little contraction like,

> *Oh, God, do I really have to do this?*

Yes. And your delight rests just on the other side of doing it. When you are in pain, don't deny it. Own it. It does not mean that you take on the perception that you are anything other than Christ. Even in your pain, even if memories are coming up, you can still keep your attention on the Light of Christ and bring that Light to it without blocking it, without cutting it off. It is indeed most empowering to know and to experience that you can be wailing and at the very same moment directing the

Healing

healing Light of Christ right into the wailings, because those wailings are lifting the lid; and what's bubbling up out of it can then be healed by the Light that is coming to it.

The healer is just one that helps to do that for you until you figure out that you can do it for yourself. And a genuine healer will always rejoice when they perceive and see,

> *Thank God, they don't need me any longer.*
>
> *Now I can go on to the next person.*

So, I know that was all of a bit of a lengthy greeting but sometimes it's necessary. I love you. I love you so much that I gave my life for you. Will you love yourself with that intensity that you are willing to lay down your life for yourself? Because *you* are worth it.

Jeshua?

Yes.

Well, I was crying today in the presence of a friend but I felt myself holding back because I felt that this person was uncomfortable with it. And it seems to happen more often that way.

Precious friend, if you hold back the process of those tears because you sense that the other is uncomfortable, what you are really choosing to say is that their perceptions hold more reality than yours and you must acquiesce and conform yourself to them. That person who seems to resist the tears of a friend may actually need you to truly let the power of your tears come out—so that they learn that they don't have to be uncomfortable with one who is releasing and healing, that they have the strength to be present.

Never hold back your tears. Never hold the belief that someone else's need to resist those tears and to be uncomfortable with yours . . . never hold the perception that their insanity is more important that your healing. That is to take power away from yourself.

Now, therefore, first, in such a situation really let them come out, and if that one is so uncomfortable that they have to leave you, send them love and go find another friend until you find one that can be with you.

That's only claiming what you are worth.

And until you claim what you are worth, your healing can't truly come to its completion.

Does that make sense to you?

Yes, I hope I can remember that.

Will you choose to remember it?

Yes.

Good. That makes all the difference: not that you hope, but that you choose with all of your power to always remember that you have a right to be healed. You don't know the hour or the day when these things are going to be released.

But allow them, because when you hold back in order to be conformed to the perceptions of another, you are denying yourself the opportunity to be rid of who-knows-what that may have been held for an awfully long time.

Healing

And when will the conditions arise again that allow that opportunity to be handed to you?

Know you that saying, "Seize the day?"

Yes, the opportunity.

Yes. Time is given to you so that you learn to use it constructively. And if there is a shadow or weight upon the heart and an opportunity comes, through time, for you to release it and you don't take advantage of it, have you used time constructively?

Many in your world have learned to use a simple device to avoid healing. It has usually a little knob on it, and you turn it and a bunch of little dots create images on the screen. You know what I am talking about? How many times have you when you have been feeling alone, a little depressed, a little sad and confused, how many times have you turned it on? Or sought other ways to distract yourself?

That is not a very constructive use of time, and it only ensures that you are going to have to face certain conditions that must arise and to prod that stuff up again.

> *I am going to shove it back down, turn on the television, or find*
>
> *some other distraction.*

So, is one of the purposes of "special" relationships to stuff our guilt?

Yes, "special" relationships are rather interesting. Most of the time the ego will convince you that you are really looking for that one heartfelt relationship when indeed what you are really doing is looking for someone who can play your game with you and keep you from truly getting on with it:

Ah, we are going to have so much fun. We'll do this and this and that and that.

And there is nothing wrong with having fun, but a special relationship is actually designed by the ego to serve the ego, and you all know what that means.

A holy relationship is founded within two souls that have chosen to come together because they are sick and tired of not getting on with it. They don't come together to drown themselves out with all the devices of distraction of the world. They come together and are willing to allow the uniting of their energies to bring it all up and get rid of it. A holy relationship is for healing and service, not for satisfying egos.

A holy relationship is what you can offer your brother or sister every time you see them, if you would but first make the choice within yourself not to use them to fill you, certainly not to use them so that you can hold on to opinions and judgments, but to be with them openly and honestly and completely. And if they choose to be with you in the same way, you indeed experience a Holy Instant. And no matter what seems to have been going on, there is a feeling of peace that comes, and the value of that encounter makes it timeless and eternal and precious, and it will always be remembered because ultimately the Son of God will remember only loving thoughts.

Holy relationship is everything in the real world. Special relationships are everything in the unreal world that you have created in error.

Choose then, choose to be one so humbled by this vast journey that all you want is holy relationship—not relationship that serves you or gratifies you, but relationship through which the Holy Spirit can awaken both you and your brother or sister right where you are, so that you can experience that Holy Instant of perfect sacred intimacy in which you have looked beyond all illusions and have seen the equality of the Love of Christ in the one before you, and therefore have recognized it in yourself.

The habit of special relationships runs deep and it needs to be interrupted constantly. When you go to see your brother or sister, take just a moment and pause,

> *Why am I really doing this? Is it out of distraction? Is there something I am trying to glean from them? Can I choose to just be with them, to love them? And to open the place in me so that their love can be received, to create the opportunity for the Holy Instant?*

When a master walks upon this Earth—and they have many names and many of you know of many masters—what is it, what is it in them that leads those that follow them, or their disciples, or their friends, or those that study with them, to feel such depth of gratitude? Is it their teaching? That helps. But what it is truly is that a master always looks through the eyes of Christ and extends the opportunity for a Holy Instant to everyone that he contacts or she contacts. And what makes the master loved by the student (to use that term) is that the student has experienced an instant in which they, too, chose to see the master through the eyes of Christ and there was an experience of a Holy Instant.

Now, initially they will think the master did a grand thing for them. Eventually they will learn that it was their power, too, and their choice to join in sacred intimacy.

Practice, then, being masters. Not because you believe you are, but because you have the power to do so. Make a little game of it. When you rest your head on your pillow at the end of your day, go back over your day and count the times you remembered to enter into encounters — or relationships, because every encounter is relationship — how many times did you do so from the standpoint of holiness? And how many times did you forget?

At first you will be rather amazed how small the count is, but it will grow as you practice it. You have simply practiced forgetting holiness; and if you have therefore learned specialness, you can unlearn it. Time is given to you that you might learn to use it constructively. And yet, still, so many of you that have heard this same message for a year are allowing many of your days to go by in unconsciousness. Why? Why would you want to continue doing it?

Well... habit.

Holy relationship is everything, and you are the one who can bring it and give it to your brother and your sister. Now, the mind will tell you that there seems to be a dichotomy here:

How can I be involved with healing and yet extend holy relationship?

Contemplate it because they work together perfectly. The one who is truly open to healing and who will hold on to no dark shadow within them, one who is willing to spend the rest of their incarnation allowing healing to occur is one who already has the power to extend the opportunity for holy relationship because there is no pretense left in them.

Makes sense?

So, have a lot of fun getting together with your friends and talking about your healing journeys and how many times you have extended the opportunity for holy relationship. See, masters can get together and can have a great time rejoicing at all the times they blow it. Hmm.

False holiness says,

> *I am perfect and I am healed.*

True holiness says,

> *Oh, my goodness gracious, did I blow that one today. Yikes! Father, I still need Your help.*

False holiness says,

> *I've got it all figured out now, Father. Goodbye.*

True holiness says,

> *Of myself I do nothing but the Father through me does all things.*

It requires a lot of humility of seeing that you've never been able to heal yourself. You don't know what a single thing is for and none of your perceptions have ever been wholly true. So why cling to them?

And when an insight comes for a moment and you extend it to your brother or sister, you might as well let go of it, because you don't really know where it came from. You don't know the purpose it's going to serve, and you can never be sure of it. But the Holy Spirit knows how to use it.

Do you know how to recognize a false teacher or a false healer?

> *Well, I see that you've got this real serious problem here and I can fix it here, and oh, yes...*

And tomorrow they will still remember telling you those things because they need to cling to their perception of themselves as a healer. A genuine healer allows healing to be done and whatever happens, happens; and then it is gone, so that they are empty and ready for the next opportunity. And they *never allow the insights to come from crystallized pictures or metaphysical beliefs about how the universe is structured.* That takes great arrogance.

Once I said to you that certain words that seem to come through me and have been written down a million times called the Sermon on the Mount, I said unto you that when those words poured through me, when that hour was over and certain of my friends said,

> *Boy, you were really on,*

I said to them,

> *What did I say?*

I couldn't even remember it and I couldn't have cared less. I was moving on to the next moment in which I might have an opportunity to extend a chance for holy relationship, and that is all.

Be, therefore, healers of the world by clinging to nothing, not

Healing

even your old wounds and your old pain, and certainly never cling to the belief that you have got it all together. You are here to take on the form of your brothers and sisters who are groveling in the muck and mire of false perceptions, to take on the appearance so that they can look upon you as one of their own, and you never know how the Spirit will work through you. And when it's done, it's done. Let it go. Release the illusion that to awaken means that you get to go somewhere else and never get your hands dirty again. It's just the opposite.

How will you know, then, when you are truly awake? When you can't wait to find ways to serve and to be available always to serve your brother and sister. When you cry out to God,

> *Give me more opportunities. I'm dying sitting here in my living room.*

Then you'll know you have really begun to awaken.

> *Bring them to me, Father. I don't care. I know I can do this. I'll just be there. Bring them to me. You can do it all through me.*
>
> *I know you can. Bring them to me. What avenues can I use to heal this world?*

Knowing, of course, that you are not the healer; you are just the messenger. Then you will know that you have really awakened. When you don't care if you are exhausted every day, when you no longer care whether your ego is being gratified, when you no longer care about anything but finding ways to help others heal and being available to do it, and if the Holy Spirit says:

Get on a plane and go here for one day and then get on another plane and travel halfway across the world to another place, and you will only see one client.

— and you know that that is perfect, then you will know that a miracle has been worked through you and has happened to you.

I have said that awakening comes as a thief in the night, stealing the cobwebs of shadows outgrown. And I have also said that salvation comes by your extending love to your brother and sister because *salvation can only be realized by sharing it.*

Therefore, when you find yourself so passionately involved in not being able to do anything but find someone to extend love to, whatever modalities seem to work, and when you see miracles happening in others, then when you rest your head on the pillow, you will be able to remember that the thief has come in the night and begun to steal your own cobwebs, because if miracles are worked through you, they must have occurred to you. And then you will give thanks, and you will laugh and rejoice at how healing truly occurs. Indeed.

Precious friends, if I come and blend with the mind and body of this my beloved brother — who finally got so sick and tired of trying to figure it out that he just threw his hands up in the air and said, "What the hell.

I don't understand it. You do it." — if by coming for these three short years, just one of you hears something or receives something that moves you one inch, it will have been a work well served, because when any one of you moves just a smidgen, you will have uplifted the whole of creation.

And that is powerful indeed. That is a miracle. And ultimately again you will come to see that your choice for healing, the ability to take the risk for healing, comes from the power of the Christ in you because you always awaken to your own call. You have been calling to yourself. Hear your call and allow it. And

Healing

in that alone you are already the Light of the world.

Now, if you really understand all of that, then, you see, there is no more time for frowns upon the face, heaviness upon the shoulders. Now, you may experience those as you are releasing and allowing healing to occur, but the rest of the time you are going to be singing and dancing because you are going to see that you are healing out of the power of Christ Himself. And if you are healing out of the power of Christ, you can rest assured that the end is inevitable. But as long as you try to heal out of your smallness, the end is not inevitable. *Claim the power of Christ as yourself and open to your healing and allow it.*

And then sing and dance and play because you have finally figured out there is nothing else to do and isn't it great? All of those demons are just little pussy cats. You might as well pet them.

Jeshua?

Yes.

I am listening to you say "of the world" and "in the world" and I have a memory of that written in the Bible, and I also am sensing that when that was spoken, it is resonating something in me that I am not aware of why. But it is important to me to ask this question.

Beloved friend, I want you to first understand that often what I talk about in these groups, while of course it is for everyone in general, it is often given specifically for one or two or five who are at a certain place in their journey, and certain words are going to resonate as an energy that gets things moving. I am not here going to address with words the answer to your question, but I am going to ask you to keep that feeling that you noticed, and as you rest your head on your pillow, ask yourself the question you just asked me—not with a rigidity of mind, but with a relaxed body and heart, letting the angel of air move deeply through the body. Ask, not trying to hear the answer, but to feel it, because what is at work here is not a concept at all. There is an energy at work that you have allowed to touch your soul, and it is going to release and heal something that you have held on to for some time. Willing to do that?

Yes.

Do you think it will be worth it?

Everything so far is.

Ah, thank you.

Even when I am over my head.

Count it as a blessing when you think you are over your head, because you will stop trying to grasp it with the mind and you will begin to allow it with the heart.

Thank you for you.

Thank you for you.

You are welcome.

And thank you for your "Thank you."

It's actually a lot of fun to sit down with a friend and just do that.
Thank you for you.

Healing

Thank you for you.

Thank you for your thank you.

Thank you for your thank you.

Thank you for your thank you, thank you.

Spend an hour doing that.

Jeshua, I want to thank you for something. Two and a half days ago I found myself in a situation that I found very, very painful and confusing and upsetting. It took me until today and with a little help from Jon Marc to sort things out; and once they were sorted out I was really elated all afternoon, like a great weight had been lifted off my shoulders.

And then I found, driving over here tonight, that I was getting depressed because I was disappointed that it took me so long to practice what you have been teaching. But while I have been sitting here listening to you tonight, I definitely got the message that I- and we- need to be patient with ourselves So that's something that I heard from you that has put me back in a relaxed state.

I am sorry to have affected your tension!

So, precious friend, indeed, be patient. As I have shared with you, I learned from the lips of a very holy teacher that I worked with when I was a child. Some of you are aware of this one who is named in certain ancient scripts, called the Teacher of Righteousness. The Teacher of Righteousness was never born of a woman but manifested a physical form to serve as a teacher. And one thing he said to me always remained with me.

He said,

> *Jeshua ben Joseph, patience is to make power slowly and certainly.*

So don't be impatient. You are worth the best you can offer yourself. Therefore, be patient with yourself.

Now, on your way over here, yes, you decided to whip yourself.

Right. That's so right.

When you notice you are whipping yourself, go,

> *Ah yes, there I am whipping myself. That's a beautiful one.*

And then embrace it and love it and it will fade away because the Holy Spirit will come as the thief and will steal that cobweb from you and you won't even notice it until you look back and it will have been a week or two or three, six months or a year, and you will say, Gosh, I haven't really whipped myself since, I can't even remember when. Where did it go?

> *A little miracle.*
>
> *That will be wonderful.*

Not that that will be wonderful. It is wonderful.

That's in the present tense.

Yes. So, how are we all doing?
Fine. Good.
Thank you for allowing me to deliver that message. It was rather important, in some degree for all of you, but specifically

Healing

for just a handful because of some things that are going on in your own processes.

Jeshua, would you repeat one more time what your teacher told you to do—build something slowly?

Beloved friend, I don't have time.

[Laughter.]

Well, actually that's true: I don't have *any* time.

Patience is to make power slowly and certainly.

The grandest of you're artists have never hurried through their creations. And you are a great creation indeed, worthy of meticulous reshaping.

You see, *when you have truly learned to master time—to use it constructively always—time ceases for you* even if others perceive that the same body and personality is still dwelling in it. For you it has ceased. And when time ceases, all of the long journey and all of the wounds and all of the heaviness is gone.

It's a rather nice feeling, by the way. But, paradoxically, then you become totally free to do what has been called, in your Christian terminology "to take on the sins of the world"—that is to take on the appearance of time and to be in it as long as it takes for the whole of the Sonship to have mastered the constructive use of time.

On the constructive use of time... When I told you that I had a chance to go and stay at a friend's home on a beautiful lake, you recommended that I go, even though I had free will and could choose to do what whatever. And I chose to go, and at the time

I was asking you about it, you cautioned me to use my time wisely. Now, I have been up there for the better part of two weeks, with two trips to town, and I am learning that I am not quite sure what to do with time. I have always had so many things to do with time, it feels very strange. I don't know if I need to kind of structure my time. I think I have a tendency to do that too much and yet, when I just sort of hang out, I am a little uncomfortable with that. What do you think I should do?

Does it matter?

Well, I would like to make lots of progress, more or less.

Then, do so. But understand, precious friend, that you hold the power in every moment to stop the whirlings of the mind, to set them aside and say,

> *Holy Spirit, what is the most constructive use of time that I can now employ?*

He will not hide it from you. For when you want specific answers, the Holy Spirit will give them.

For me to say,

> *Well, the constructive use of time would be not to structure it at all, would not be wholly true.*
>
> *And if I said unto you,*

The constructive use of time is to structure all of it, that would not be wholly true.

The constructive use of time requires your decision to turn to the one Teacher Whose guidance is always unerring, and to

Healing

trust what you hear. Although you may not hear words, you might have a feeling or an intuition. That is the constructive use of time.

What other use is there?

Ah, you've let the cat out of the bag.

I keep thinking I should hear a voice within myself.

Ah. Coming from the clouds of Heaven?

Well, at least something that is distinctly other than me.

Beloved friend, that is the illusion of separation.

I have been having such a problem with that. Sometimes it's good to say things out loud just to hear how erroneous it sounds.

The Holy Spirit is closer to you than your own breath. Now, it is important…

It is what you know in your deepest heart.

Your deepest heart *is* the union of the Father and Son. I've got it!

Ah.

Now, some of you that can see energies that are not usually seen with the physical eyes, if you were watching in that moment, you saw a shift in the change of the color of light around this one, and what you saw would or could be perceived or described as the weight of a thousand lifetimes being lifted. Now we will find out if she lets it remain there.

Oh, I want to. I will.

Know that I love you always and I come always as your servant. I can't be anything else. I simply can't be anything else, and I don't want to be. I love you and I will love you until the whole of the Sonship has its "Aha." And those of you that choose to join with me, and understand that because I am your friend and your brother, in whatever way you choose to serve, all you have to do is ask and I will come running. When you open the door, I will join with you and together we will assist our brothers and sisters in their own process of awakening. I am available to any of you all of the time. Some of you know that.

Peace be unto you and we will see you soon. Amen.

[Short break.]

Beloved friends, what is in Truth the whole heart and essence of healing?

To share with one another from a point of equality, of seeing no one as above you and no one as below you, and seeing not yourself as more perfect than another.

But to see that you *are* one another, and to realize that it is in the sharing of your journey, the willingness to listen and to love, that brings healing to the heart and to the soul.

And forever the soul, which is the Son of God, is one. Though there be many bodies and personalities attached, you are but one Mind and one Heart. And when you choose to join together, you have chosen the creation of holy relationship, and

Healing

even in these few moments you have extended the Holy Instant unto one another.

Therefore, always remember that there is but one thing taking place: the awakening of the holy Son of God — or Daughter, if you prefer. It makes little difference; it's all words. But you are that one, and the language that I use is used only as a point of identification so that you can recognize me.

Beloved and holy Son of God, great is my love for you, for indeed you are already all that I am. Therefore, the one known as Jeshua, that which I am that came and walked among you, could be no other but yourself. The entire drama is yours and there is nothing outside of you. Every pain felt by a brother or sister is your pain, and it is only through your extension of love that you can heal yourself of that pain. To judge another's pain or another's thought or another's behavior is to ensure that it will continue within *you*. Perhaps in a different form, but it will continue. Therefore, indeed, it is only love that heals. It is love that I am and it is love that you are. Everything else is the result of an illusion and a mistaken perception.

That is why a master greets anger with love. That is why a master greets attack with love. For when you believe you are attacked and therefore become defensive, you have asserted with the power of Christ that attack is real, and you have made sure that you will continue to experience attack. Meet all things with love. Greet all things with love. See in the eye of even a blade of grass, yourself. Indeed, I am the holy Son of God given to the world of my Father because He loves you. Where have I come from? The Heart of God. Where have you come from? The Heart of God. We are one and the same.

Therefore, when I come forth and create a demonstration or an appearance of being Jeshua ben Joseph, it is only to animate a physical form because you have believed yourself to be the body, to teach you that you are Spirit and that you are One. The only reality that in Truth can be, is that the holy Son of God is one, united always with all that God is. And salvation is complete on Earth as it is in Heaven when the Sonship awakens to the Truth of its reality.

That is why I have asked you to join with me to extend the Kingdom to your brother and to your sister. And when you see them in error or in pain, embrace them. Offer them through holy relationship the opportunity for the Holy Instant that heals all things. You are the ones; you are the bringers of Light into this world.

I ask you only to let me walk with you. And what does that mean but to recognize that the heart and essence of your being *is* Jeshua; *is* Christ; *is* the offspring of Light divine by whatever name you choose to call it. God is Love and therefore I love you. You are the Grace of God in form. That is who you are. Embrace your brother and your sister. Embrace them with all of your being, not just your mind, not just your heart. Use the arms your Holy Mother has given you.

I am going to ask each and every one of you this week in each of your days to call someone you haven't spoken with lately and tell them how much you appreciate their being, because their being in your life has been serving your awakening. Let them know from the bottom of your heart how much you love them for that. Encourage them to be the Truth of who they are and to never deviate from listening to the voice of Spirit that speaks not in the mind of the ego, but in the quietness and the gentleness of the heart. Encourage them to follow the path that they feel they must follow, because there is a reason for it. And

Healing

the reason serves the atonement of the Sonship.

Indeed, if you could look through the eyes of the Christ—and, of course, you can because that's who you are—and you would never again lament anything that unfolds in your experience or your drama because you would see the exquisite perfection that those moments are serving. Nothing happens by accident and not one of you holds an experience in isolation from the whole of the Sonship. Everything you taste and feel and think and experience is felt and touches the entire community of Christ the Sonship. Everything.

Love every moment that comes to you. Embrace it and honor it. If it means that you cry a thousand tears, then let your tears be a way in which you honor that moment. And if your brother or sister is in pain, embrace them. Don't tell them,

Why are you doing this? You are creating your own reality.

That is nonsense and it is hurtful. For well have I seen that idea being misused in your metaphysical circles. When your brother and sister is in pain, embrace them and feel it with them and allow it to be felt by them. When they are ready to think about it, you will know. Let them feel it. Tell them you know what it feels like. It is called empathy, not judgment.

Ah, beloved and holy child of God, you are one with me. You are one with me. Embrace me. Claim me as the reality of your own being. Claim me. Will I disappear from you? No. I am your brother and I am your friend and I am all that you are, and I choose to be what you are in the fullness that you have yet, for a little while, chosen to resist; and I will never cease in coming to you, because I love you, until finally you decide it's time. Then all healing will occur, and you will be brought rapidly through miracle after miracle after miracle to swiftly be all that

I represent to mankind.

You shall be the worker of miracles. And that is given unto you even now. And in this hour as I stood nearby, and stood in the midst of you, you extended miracles one unto another, because in this hour and in this place you have come and you choose to set aside the perceptions taught you of your world that are wholly insane, and you choose to come together to allow love to heal.

And if not a word is said to you in the whole hour or the whole evening and you would sit there quietly, understand that you participate actively in the healing of every mind and every heart that chooses to come to these gatherings. That is how powerful you are and how precious your presence is. You can be on the floor with your best friend and still be involved in the healing of every mind and heart. Therefore, when another is speaking, let not the mind wander, but just sit there and embrace them with love. Miracles happen naturally and effortlessly to minds and hearts that choose only love.

Love and judgment can never abide in the same moment. Love is of the Kingdom; judgment is of hell. What will your choice be? You are the Light of the world. You *are* the Light of the world. *You are the Light of this world*, and it needs it so desperately.

Be love. Teach love. And therefore you will learn that you are love. Don't just expect miracles. Know that you are the one that is sent to allow miracles to be given through you. It just happens when you choose to love.

Short is the time that is given me to join with you in this rather unusual way. And when I walked upon this plane, I would have never guessed that I would be doing this work with this,

Healing

my beloved brother. My Father hadn't let me in on it yet. It's probably a good thing He didn't. Hmm. Can you know what is around the corner for you? Do you need to know? The mind that is fearful looks ahead and wonders. The mind that is awake lives in this moment and it is enough, because that mind knows that it is sustained by the Love of God, and if it is true in this moment, it certainly won't change in the next.

Be at peace, then, in all things and give no thought for tomorrow, what you shall eat and what you shall wear and what career you might have five years from now. But own the presence of Love now and the future will very easily take care of itself. And you shall be more then than you think you are today.

I love you. Please do me but one favor: love your brothers and sisters, though you don't even know their names, as you believe I have loved you. And if you have felt that love, *please give it away*. In so doing you have honored the Son that dwells within you, and by honoring the Son that dwells in you, you have indeed honored me, and I give thanks for every moment you choose to extend your love to another.

I shall never leave you; and when this brief work is done, think not that I will go away from you. But I call you to quicken your choice to hear me and to abide with me always as your friend and as your brother.

I love you and I want you to be my friend. And even though you are in a body, think not that that body can be an obstacle to our communion, our communication and our celebration that we are as our Father has created us to be: the Thought of perfect Love in form. And if you seem to have the form of a body while

I seem not to, what difference does it make?

There are no obstacles to minds that join in love. Forgive your brother and sister. Forgive yourself for ever having thought that you were separate one from another, that the world was a place in which you needed to be fearful. For perfect love casts out fear, which has been your only enemy. Fear blocks the knowledge of the Kingdom. Let that perfect Love, therefore, be in you, even as it is in me, given to you.

I love you, holy Son of God. Pray not to die, but to live eternally and to let your Light heal this world. Give your love away and you will never be without it. Peace be unto you. Peace be unto the only begotten offspring of God, created changeless and perfect. That is who you are. And let that power of that perfection heal every illusion ever held within your mind and in your emotions and in your body. Honor your Holy Mother by letting that healing come to the cells of your body. Hmm.

Yes, indeed, that indeed the Kingdom of Heaven might be wed with the Kingdom of this Earth, that Spirit and matter might be united as one and the love of Christ be extended as far as from the East unto the West, until it embraces the whole of the creation and *all* of us return home as one. Give your peace away and you will *never* lose it.

And what I said will eternally remain true: I am with you always. I can hardly be anywhere else. I love you, and I thank you for being willing to entertain the thought that just maybe Jeshua can borrow a body and a mind long enough to communicate with words.

But unto each and every one of you — and I speak of when you return to your abodes and rest your head upon your pillow — *I will come* to each and every one of you. Will you open the door and allow me in?

Healing

Peace be unto you. Remember, call someone each day of your following week that you haven't spoken with for a while and share from your heart what I have asked you to share. You don't have to. Don't do it begrudgingly. Do it with a lot of lightness and fun. Get into feeling how powerful the love is that is in you that longs to be given away, and it will transform the whole of your week.

Yet a little while and I will be with you no more. Cherish, then, these few moments given us, for when the form of this work is gone, it is gone. But I hope you will have used it as a bridge to come wholly to where I am, for I wait to truly embrace you without an inch of distance between us. Yet we shall work together to serve the atonement of the Sonship. We shall love every brother and sister that the Holy Spirit brings to us, and though you may not yet see the form of the work you will be doing, it will be revealed to you.

And I will join with you as your friend and your brother, and together — as one — we shall embrace the whole of creation and offer it, on the platter of the awakened Heart of Christ, back to the Father. What else is there to do?

Peace be unto you.

Amen.

Heaven on Earth

Now, we begin.

And, indeed, once again, greetings unto you, beloved and holy friends. In truth, all that occurs within your dimension is not unknown or unavailable to us. For where we abide (and there are many of us), we abide in a state of consciousness in which the transmutation of energies through your third-dimensional realm are entirely observable by us. Yes, this does mean that there is not at any time a true state of privacy — if by privacy you mean secrecy and avoidance of relationship. This means that, as you call to yourself your physical earth plane experience, in *each and every moment*, whether you choose to acknowledge it or not, you are in relationship with the whole of Creation. And the quality of that relationship is what mirrors back to you the state of consciousness that you are choosing to abide within.

It is, therefore, always wise to look clearly and honestly at the nature of your moment- to-moment experience. What are you truly aware of *now*? What thoughts are you permitting to flow through the mind? What feelings are those thoughts generating within the field of energy that you call the body?

Why is this important? To come to where I am requires a complete transcendence of the physical domain or experience — not an escape *from*, for transcendence does not rest on escape. Transcendence can *only* rest on *embracing*. For how can you transcend what you refuse to acknowledge as a part of your experience? Therefore, the heart and mind that is willing to utilize each and every moment of its experience in whatever domain or dimension it finds itself existing within, is that heart and that mind that will indeed come to where I am: to the finality of what you might call evolution, in which *all* seeking has ended, in which the *need* for experience is over, where there is not one question, and not one doubt.

Imagine, if you will, such a state in which you abide in such perfect wakefulness that the mind does not even entertain the *thought* of desiring a physical form through which to funnel a limited sphere of experience. A state of being in which, by simply turning the attention of your consciousness, you can abide anywhere you wish in a moment's notice: actually, even quicker than that. That, just by turning your consciousness, you can abide in any time frame within the physical dimension: to observe it, to interact with it, to bring your wisdom to it. To turn your consciousness to a dimension and a time frame seemingly far removed from where *you* are upon the earth, and all in the twinkling of an eye.

These things are your potential. They were placed within you in the moment of your creation. And if you would well receive it, you have *already experienced* the state in which I am, and there is a part of you that has never left that state. What then has occurred? For look well upon what your experience is in *this moment*. Where do you find yourself sitting or standing? What is the climate of your environment: is it noisy, is it chaotic? Have you lit a few candles and burned your incense, have you played some of your favorite music so you can begin to evoke a physiological change in the body that you will then call a state of peace? — as if peace were dependent upon the body. To each and every one of you, wherever you are in *this moment*: stop. Observe the things around you, and the things within you. For there is a very direct correlation between the two.

For what you see around you expresses a quality of energy, a form of experience, that emanates from the quality of thought that you have been willing to entertain and to *allow* to enter into the field of your energy, into your domain. And from this choice, you look out upon a world that you have chosen to create.

I have chosen to look out upon you and to recognize that you are my brothers and my sisters. I have chosen to learn to look out and see *only* the Light of Christ within you. That Light — that shines radiantly beyond all limitations — it is that Light that I speak to, that Light that I come to, that Light that I join with, not only in this manner of communication but through your dreams and in the space between the thoughts you would choose to think.

If this is so, it must mean that what you are seeking is already within you. And that perhaps the pathway of transcendence rests not on *efforting* or *striving*, but on *wondering*. Perhaps it rests upon looking at all that you see and accepting the fact that you have no idea what it is, how it has arisen, where it has come from, what it could possibly mean, or where it's going. Perhaps the pathway of awakening requires that — after all seeking and all attempts to learn magical formulas to draw enlightenment *to* you — perhaps it truly rests on the recognition of a state of humility in which you finally acknowledge that you have moved nowhere and made no progress.

Oh, yes, you've called to yourself many experiences, high and low, and yet none of *them* has sufficed to help you transcend your common or ordinary or consistent state of being. No matter how good the love-making is, no matter how good the food, no matter how delicious the states of consciousness in meditation, still you find yourself coming back to states of being painfully familiar.

What, then, is the key? It rests in only this: to begin at the end.

To first acknowledge,

> *In reality, I have never changed. In reality, I am as God has created me to be. In reality, I have already tasted all experience and there is nothing new under the Heaven of my consciousness. I am perfect and whole now.*

From that choice it then follows that you can begin to accept that, regardless of what you think you *see* and what you think you're *experiencing*, there is a depth of wisdom within you that can bring enlightenment from the higher self, if you will, from the soul, down to the levels of the personality, all the way into the cellular structure of the body — if that be your true desire.

The true pathway home, then, my precious, precious friends, rests on the willingness to withdraw the value that you have placed on all of the perceptions *you* have created. To be willing to stand with empty hands. To look upon an object, a person, an event, a feeling, and to begin with the thought,

> *I am whole and perfect, and I am bringing the light of my infinite consciousness to shine upon this mysterious phenomena that has arisen in front of me.*

Or 'within' me if you call the body within you: it, too, is on the outside in some sense. And to acknowledge that you are beholding Mystery, and that you cannot rely on your own ideas to understand anything. *That* is the beginning of wisdom.

For if you cannot rely upon yourself, what are you going to do? You could try committing suicide, but all that does is dispose of a certain body; *you* remain. You can try to distract yourself with the ordinary phenomena of cultures. That doesn't work, either. In the end, you must *submit* yourself to something which is, in truth, the grandest mystery of all: the presence of the Holy

Spirit. You must surrender your self—all of your ideas about what you think is true—and ask that something you can't even see (and, at least in the beginning, you can't even hear), to ask some mysterious *something* to teach you the truth of Reality. It feels very much like dying. And, in truth, it is the only true death—the giving up and surrendering of your justifications for anger, your rationalizations for judgment, your *certainty* that what you *know* is true.

The acceptance that what you have called 'knowledge' is highly suspect, indeed. For, if you believe you are a body in space and time, and if you look out and see a limited world, you are therefore using a limited consciousness to decide that *you* know what the whole of Creation is. And the part can never comprehend the whole.

Yet, paradoxically, there is within you that which is already the wholeness itself, the Mind of Christ, and that which rests within you is a perfect wisdom, a perfect peace, a perfect knowingness, is ready to speak to you (so to speak), to speak to your consciousness so that you actually and literally have an *awareness of being the wholeness of creation*. Even though the body still seems to be right as it is, even though the objects seem to be around you, imagine seeing through them as though they were transparent and beholding all distant realms, and all past and all future, in the twinkling of an eye. And allowing that state to be the normal state in which you operate, even while the body seems to last for yet a little while.

All this is possible, and more, when you first use the *power of choice* given unto you to dedicate each and every moment of your awareness—notice I said your awareness, not your experience. Dedicating each moment of your *awareness* to the process of surrendering everything that you thought you knew and needed to hold onto, to allow a mysterious *something* to bring the grace of enlightenment to you.

Beloved friends, you who seem to find yourself in this third-dimensional realm, this physical realm of limitation and duality and conflict, and birth and death—and surprises? Hm! Rest assured you have truly never surprised yourself at any time. There has never been a moment's experienced that has come to you that you have not *deliberately* ordered and received. Nothing comes by accident.

And, of course, you are quite free to choose how to perceive what comes to you. And if you allow that mysterious *something* to teach you anew, what once horrified you can now bring a smile to your face; what once seemed insurmountable can seem like the smallest of stepping stones beneath your toes. All power under Heaven and Earth is given unto you to create *as you are created* in each moment, from and within perfect unlimitedness. And now here's the real secret: you are literally and exactly doing this all the time. You never lose the power of the infinite being that you are; you cannot lose what God has created, or God herself is limited. You, as you are right now, with every breath you breathe, with every thought you think, with every action you perform (even if you have no body), you are literally and always using the infinite power of *your wisdom* to create. That is the only thing you've ever been doing.

And you have therefore created heavens and numerous hells. And in those hells you have created an infinite number of shades or hues or vibrations. You can just as easily create as many heavens blessed with shimmering, beautiful light that the earth has not seen for quite some time. In each moment of your day, *nothing outside of you* causes your feelings and your perceptions. Does this mean that, if you experience another soul, another human being, that they themselves do not carry certain frequencies of energy that you can detect? Of course not. But the detecting of energy from the field of another mind does not *cause* you to perceive them in any way at all. You will therefore perceive them as you *choose* to perceive them, regardless of their name, regardless of their action. You are the one who is free to see that your power to choose your perceptions is a power that overwhelms and transmutes anything and everything that your world can direct at you.

I hope that this is beginning to sink in, because it is an extremely important message. I want you to truly spend some time each day in the simplest of actions. You might simply be closing your fist and opening it again. You might feel your feet upon the earth as you walk forward in a direction of your choosing (and all of your directions are of your choosing). Whatever you choose to bring your attention to, notice with perfect wonder and awe that *you* are *literally* choosing to create the experience you're having. Because this is true, Heaven on Earth is actually no further from your experience than the width of the thoughts you are willing to think. *Heaven on Earth is no further from you than the width of the thoughts you are willing to think.* Heaven on Earth is not apart from where you are.

Would you, therefore, be willing to join with me in daring to think the thought of   a planet healed and a humanity enlightened? Are you willing to allow yourself—not to run around with placards in your hand and placing billboards around what you call your highways (we would perceive them as low-ways... hmm)—would you be willing to allow yourself to rest in each of your days and simply feel the *reality* of Heaven on Earth, and *know* that this has already come to pass? And in the field of time, it seems to be taking time for that to occur. But, after all, that's what time is about: process. In reality, if you hold the thought, *it is done*. And, in truth, you can acknowledge it. For what the Son of God decrees *is* – no matter the state of mind in which you decree it—what you *say in that moment*, whether you speak it out loud, whether you merely think the thought, you have literally created that reality. [Snaps fingers] That fast, in the twinkling of an eye.

This seems like madness to your world because your world *is* madness. It is the complete reversal of Christed Consciousness. The world represents the complete *opposite* of Heaven. It is upside down and inside out. So that when I say unto you: when you think the thought of Heaven and Earth, you have decreed it and it is so, now, and you're totally free to experience unlimited radiance, perfect peace, perfect joy, right where you are—now! The world will say: that is nonsense.

And this is the theme of this hour's discussion, for you to understand that right there is the point that you *must begin* to make a new choice, to learn to think with the Mind of Christ rather than against it. By choosing to think with it, you become it, and when you become it, you realize a discovery: a discovery of what has always been and is never changed. You are, indeed, and you forever remain, as you were created to be. You are the creator of all worlds. And never, ever, ever, ever are you losing, or in a state of loss of, your power to create precisely as God birthed you. That is how powerful you are, right where you are.

And there are some of you, even now that listen to these words, and you think

> *Well, that might be true for somebody else who's a little more powerful, but you see, my situation is such-and-such. I only have five dollars in my wallet!*

Look at the five dollars with *wonder*. Where on earth did it come from? It came into your being and into your wallet because you decided to put it there. And you can just as easily put a million of your golden coins there, if that is what you want to experience. Nothing but your own thought expands you or limits you. No one can create *for you*. No one can bring you the answers you seek—you *are* the answer you seek. You have merely trained yourself to believe that you are less than you are. You have trained yourself to believe that right now in this moment, as you reach to scratch your cheek with your finger, or you hear the sound of a barking dog outside your window, or you see the flash of sunlight as it begins to disappear beyond the mountains to the west—and for some of you, by the way, if you happen to look out and see the streak of light as it begins to rise in your eastern sky, for some of you will listen to this early in the morning—if you believe that you're just some ordinary person trying to figure it all out, *stop where you are*. Look at what you see and truly see it. You do not know what a single thing is. It is Mystery, and yet you have brought it into form, even if it's nothing more than the table in front of you.

How could it be that you're experiencing a physical body in some city within your twentieth century America? How could these things be? What has brought them to be? You have—the infinite power of creation, sitting right where you are, choosing to look like an ordinary human being. The same creativity that moves the sun and the moon and stars, the same creativity that brought forth what your scientists would call from the 'big bang', all forms of creation. The big bang, by the way, was nothing more than an aha! in your Holy Mind as you dreamed up a new thought that had never been thought of before: something called physical matter, a condensation of light.

If you can begin to truly understand, as you place your hand around your cup of tea or your coffee, as these things are called, when you brush your teeth, when you watch how the chest rises as you inhale—if you can truly look upon these things with awe and with innocence, you can behold the mystery of Life itself. And you can come to see that *you* are constantly, moment to moment to moment, manifesting world after world after world after world. You are choosing where to be and how to be. *You* are the one sent forth from the Holy Mind of God to be the agent of the forever extending Creation.

I want to say, also—and this will seem very radical to many of you yet still—you are perfectly, completely free to create whatever you will. You are perfectly free in this moment to go and sell all that you have and to take up your cross and follow me. Some would say that means to become a rather bizarre radical. Hmm. I felt insane the first time I dared to think the thought, "I and my Father are One," just to try it on. It created a tingling sensation from the crown of the head down through the body. It was a sensation I had not yet experienced, but I liked it. And I decided to ask myself this question: What would happen if I were to entertain that thought until it excluded every other thought that seemed to swirl within the mind? What would occur?

For you see, many of you are wondering: Why cannot I seem to manifest what I want to manifest? It is because you entertain conflicting thoughts. And where there is conflict, there is stagnation. Be you therefore of single intent, bring the consciousness to a single point in which the thought you would truly desire to manifest is the only thought you imbue with reality. When you have mastered the ability to discipline the mind, you will discover that you can create an entire universe with one thought. You will discover that you can literally create a golden coin in the palm of your hand, merely by holding the thought of it. And if this is true, and I assure you that it is, you will be the bearer of miracles. And lo and behold, you might dare to think the thought of Heaven on Earth and put all of your focused intention on that one thought until it is your only reality and nothing else matters, nothing else holds value, nothing else can exist for you. And if the rest of the world thinks you're crazy, so what? That, too, is just a thought. You can bring Heaven to Earth in the twinkling of an eye. And it will come to pass that Heaven on Earth *will* be the case, and when it is established, it will seem to have occurred effortlessly in the twinkling of an eye.

Why? Because enough of you will have chosen to energize that thought, and only that thought. You will live that thought, you will drink that thought, you will dream that thought, you will extend that thought, you will feel and live that thought to the exclusion of anything that could contradict it, or be in dissonance with it; and then you will be the *embodiment* of Heaven on Earth. And the time will come, in time, when suddenly the whole of humanity gets it, in the twinkling of an eye. And in that very moment, that which is called the pollution of your waters and airs will vanish as if it had never been. That which is called strife between races will vanish as if it had never been. Anything you can imagine representing conflict will vanish from the face of the Earth. And why? Because the Holy Son of God, manifested as the family of mankind, will have moved sufficiently into a momentum that creates the stabilization of one and only one thought: Heaven on Earth.

That fast, without blinking an eye, without lifting an hand. That is what you're struggling toward as a collective consciousness.

You are beginning to discover, from your scientists, that you can literally create what is called virtual reality. Well, guess what? That's what you've been doing all along anyway. Manifesting on this physical third dimension virtual reality, which means pretty close to the real thing. Hmm. Think about that. For as long as mankind has been on your earth—and there have been many generations and many civilizations, great civilizations that have risen and fallen and been washed away, that your scientists and archaeologists know nothing of and can't even believe could have ever been; cultures so far beyond the one you now live in that yours becomes archaic and primitive—and, yet, all of them are an aspect of virtual reality. Heaven on Earth will be the final happy dream that can be made manifest in the physical dimension, reflecting to all consciousnesses the truth of consciousness itself. Heaven on Earth will last but for the twinkling of an eye. And then even this physical dimension will be as a thought that had never been dreamt of, as the Holy Son of God returns to take up his rightful place at the right hand of God — which just means right-mindedness, creating only what is unlimited and without conflict, only that which mirrors and reflects the vast grandness of His radiance.

And now here's the paradox: *You* can't wait for that to happen, because you are the one through whom it occurs, and yet *you* can't bring it about. You can only allow that mysterious something to accomplish it for you and through you. I once said that it is important to become again as a little child. And now we come to a clear and deeper and more presently meaningful interpretation of that teaching. For a little child surrenders the need to be the maker and the doer. The child just holds the thought. It wakes up in the morning and says, "Ha, I'm hungry, I wish to be fed." And, voila, the mother appears at the door and says, "Oh, my little child, are you hungry? Shall I feed you?" And the child says, "Well, of course, why do you think I called you here?" Hm. Creation. The child *submits* to something beyond itself to bring about the manifestation of its thought.

Does that makes sense to you? Can you become the innocent child who first dares to dream the unbelievable dream, the dream of Heaven on Earth. It seems so outrageous to mankind. Are you willing to dare to let into your consciousnesses light seeping through a crack in the wall, the fortress you have built against the Kingdom of Heaven, the thought,?

I and my Father are One. I am Christ incarnate. How about that!

Right here, wearing my Nikes and my Levis and my (what do you call this with the...) New York Yankees baseball hat upon your head. *You* are the incarnation of Christ pretending to be human so as to be in relationship with a lot of sleeping minds. Dare you, therefore, to think the outrageous and improbable? Dare you to contemplate, and to allow with wonder, that there is a mysterious something that can bring forth your highest creative thoughts when those thoughts are in alignment with the way God thinks. And God thinks only in terms of effortlessness, joy, unlimitedness, expansion—and Love. Love. *Love!*

Do you know what has frustrated your attempt to be the maker and creator of your world? Fear. And fear is the opposite of Love. *Love* is the essential energy of the mind of God. Yet how many times have you prayed for a new job or a new career, a new relationship, or a new washer and dryer, because you *fear* not having these things? Because you *fear* survival, which is already to hold an insane thought: what could you survive? You are Life eternal, and it will never be taken from you. You try to hold your reality together through your attempts to be the maker and the doer because you *fear* letting go of them. And yet, in truth, it is nothing more than the fear of the child letting go of an invisible monster under the bed. But where you choose to create from loving thoughts, the universe, that unseen something I call the Holy Spirit, can begin to blend with the energy of your consciousness and begin to bring forth manifestations that reflect the vibrational quality of Love. And Love is that which *heals*. Love is that which *forgives*. Love is that which creates the *space* for a mind and heart to choose again. For you see, that is the energy in which God sustains you with every breath, creating the space for His creation to create anew. Love. What would it mean for you to go through each of your days and ask yourself honestly,

> *Is this action I am performing, is this thought I'm thinking, is this grounded in my desire to extend and teach only Love?*

Many of you will become quite frightened to discover that ninety-eight percent of what you do is not founded in love at all, but in fear. Therefore, if that is the case, learn to embrace fear itself. Ask of it:

> *Where do you come from? What am I truly afraid of? Can I feel that feeling? Can I embrace that thought? Can I embrace the whole idea, the perception, that is causing me to choose actions out of a desire to survive, out of a desire to control another, out of a desire to prove to myself that I am unworthy of unlimitedness?*

Love. To think only from the foundation of Love is to return to your rightful place, in which Creation flows through you as the vehicle of manifestation. Yet what flows through you is no longer yours. You are the enjoyer, the witness of grand Mystery. You are free. You are awake. You are at peace. You are home. You are Christ.

Imagine a life in which all of your creations were wholly loving. That is the same as Heaven on Earth.

So you see, there's never been a single thing that has *caused* you to be fearful. Fear itself can only arise as a chosen creation from the infinite and all-powerful Mind that you are. If you could look behind your mind in any instant when events or whatever it is seems to unfold, and you begin to feel fearful, you begin to react out of that fear, if you could take one step behind the stage curtain, you would discover yourself saying,

From the depth of the Christ I am, I choose now to create a fearful world and the experience of fear and all that comes with it — and I step into that creation now!

And there you have it. The experience you're having that seems to be causing your conflict. Hm. That does rather take away excuses. And it takes away blame. For even your most fearful creations can be embraced with perfect innocence. And why? Listen carefully: All that you see in the realm of beginnings and endings is an illusion. It is a momentary, a temporary, call it a modification of the creative energy that flows through you. You've just sculpted it for a moment. But think on this: Has there ever been anything you have attempted to create from a non-loving space?

So, the theme of this sharing with you will come to have its point, as it will begin to be a building block upon which we will build Heaven on Earth within *your* consciousness.

For if you are listening to these words now, created out of a free and unconditioned blending of two minds — two minds that are willing to love one another so wholly that nothing can serve as a barrier to their joining and to their creations — as we build upon this foundation, your life is going to change, as it must. For if you are listening to these words, there is already a part of you that has heard the call to awaken and to bring Heaven to Earth. To dare to join with the most insane thought that has ever penetrated the myopic and narrow field of consciousness called humanity. What you could almost say is nothing more than the attempt to resist unlimitedness.

Into egoic consciousness there crept a tiny, mad idea.

What would it be like to have Heaven on Earth? That's insane. I can't think that thought.

The next day:

What would it be like if all the waters were running purely and all the children were well fed and loved?

All of you, each and every one of you now listening to these words—each and every one of you is a being, a soul, an entity, call it what you will, a focus of unlimited creative potential, a spark of Divine Light. You are one that has already allowed such thoughts to begin to seep into your consciousness. And the first thing it does is it begins to create a polarization within you, because as Light begins to descend into the mind, and then also down into the personality and body, it's much like turning on a light switch, and the first thing you see is all of the things within your consciousness that are *unlike* the thought of Heaven on Earth. That are unlike the thought of being the presence of Christ. That are unlike the thought of "I and my Father are One."

And sometimes it seems to be not a pretty sight. And, yet, it is a very necessary process for you *want* to learn to shed light with wonder and awe and innocence upon all of your miscreations. To wonder about how such a thing could ever arise: a thought of judgment, a thought of fear, a thought of lack, a thought of limitation. Let that mysterious something shine the Light of Truth upon everything within your field of being that is unlike the simplicity of Love. For the shining of that Light upon it already begins to dissolve it from your consciousness.

This is why I once said that it is not necessary to seek for Love. It is only necessary to seek for all of the ways in which you have blocked Love from being your only reality. *That* is your purpose, that is the gift of time, to ask:

> *How in this moment am I using the infinite power of my beingness to create something which is less than Love, something less than what I truly want?*

This tape, then, is the first in a series that will be shared with you through this vehicle, through this joining, in which many of us, what you would call teachers, friends, masters, will come to teach you how consciousness works and how to begin to re-discipline the focus of your mind so it becomes like a laser, unwilling to see anything less than Love.

We want then to suggest also that those of you who are listening to these words take the time to re-listen to them on several occasions.

Do this in a very relaxed state of mind, not trying to grasp each and every word, but allowing certain phrases and words to strike you. And the ones that strike you, write them down. And then begin a process of writing those words and phrases consistently in each of your days for at least fifteen or twenty minutes, in a state of aimlessness and innocence. Write the phrases and the words that have *struck* you, for it is that which strikes the *emotional* body that begins to create the space for something new to be birthed through you.

Rest assured, you are not alone. You've never had any privacy. We see it all—and it's okay.

With that, we are going to take pause for just a few moments, for there will be some questions that will be asked by those present. Many of you will be a bit startled to realize that they're the very questions that are on your mind. Be at peace then, and now we will pause to wonder what the question is.

[Break]

We were just speaking then, as we return, that when a question comes into your consciousness, it comes for a reason. Because questions—listen carefully—questions are what form the basis and indeed sculpt the answer that you will discover.

Therefore, if you want the greatest of answers, ask the greatest of questions. If you want clarity to come to you, be clear in the questions you are asking of yourself and of the universe.

A question, once it arises, is an impulse of energy that has come into your consciousness, and it is designed to help you expand into the consciousness, into the mind, that question never leaves until you allow the answer to be realized and integrated into your being. And in that very moment, the old 'you' has died, and you will never return to it. Therefore, why not ask questions such as,

> *How can I be the presence of Christ?*
>
> *Is it possible for me to manifest miracles?*
>
> *Can I choose peace in any circumstance?*

Rest assured that by asking such questions you literally begin to redirect how you create your experience so that you discover the answer. Therefore, if you desire to bring Heaven to Earth, rather than looking upon the world as you think it is and saying,

> *Oh, my God, what a big task I have,*

why not simply ask,

Heaven on Earth

Hmm... How is it that Heaven can come to Earth through me in this moment?

The answer will not be hidden.

And so, with that, have you questions?

Yes, Jeshua, thank you.

It's the first time in feeling the sense of wonder that you're inviting me and us into, that I'm approaching—I usually experience goals and desires as kind of burdensome, but it's the first time I'm feeling a certain goal that I really like is something that I can approach in the spirit of fun. And I don't even really know what my question is, but I know that's what I want to talk to you about.

Now, listen well to what you've just said, and contemplate what was said a moment ago to you. There was a reason for it.

If you would indeed draw to yourself the clarity of a certain answer, make sure that you ask a clear question.

Therefore, allow yourself, beloved friend, to just relax for a moment. It does not come from the mind, it comes into the mind from a relaxed state of being, a relaxed emotional body. Merely begin within yourself to say,

What question would clearly attract to me the answer that I seek to discover?

So we will pause, while you allow the question to be birthed.

[Pause]
You almost had it.

How can I discern Love's questions from fear's questions?

It is actually very simple. Love's questions literally create within the physical body a sense of joy. It may be subtle. A sense of excitement, a sense of wonder, a sense of well-being, a sense of expansion. You can learn to discern the quality of this feeling in the cellular structure of the body itself. Fear's questions create exactly the opposite: a loss of aliveness, a sense of foreboding, a contraction, a coldness, a darkness. A very good practice, then, for you as well as for many (and luckily your question can serve more than just yourself) ...

As you sit in your meditation and allow questions to come, as you begin to become disciplined in your awareness that you're watching what's going on in the mind from moment to moment, when questions come up in your mind, pause and look at it, and ask yourself,

> *Is this a question from Love or from fear?*

And then ask yourself,

> *What do I notice in my beingness that is associated with the arising of the question? Is it a feeling of fun and wonder, a bit of an excitement, a sense of expansion? Or is it a contraction, a coldness, a foreboding, a dissonance instead of a resonance?*

Does that make sense for you?

Yes, it does.

It would be very good for you to practice with that. For you see, everything is a matter of vibration. Thought is a frequency of energy. God's thoughts are the highest form of energy—Love unimpeded, meeting no obstacles. Love is a state in which fear cannot be present.

Therefore, look well and learn now to *feel* the quality of energy that you are abiding in, as different questions arise in your mind. You will come to see very, very clearly that the qualities of energy revolving around and emanating from questions being birthed through and in the vibration of Love are completely and totally different from the feeling and vibratory quality of the questions arising in and around the energy of fear. In fact, they are as far from one another as the East from the West, and have literally no similarities. One specific quality that comes from questions of Love is a feeling of relaxation, so there is not a sense of urgency and impatience. Hmm. Just a thought to think about, to *wonder* about.

Beloved friend, because you have chosen to take the time to allow the clear formulation of the question, now that 'unseen something' can begin to direct a much clearer answer to you. And the clarity of the answer is what moves you from who you are toward what you wish to be. And, of course, what you're wishing to be is who you really are.

Yes

Indeed.

Thank you, Jeshua.

Do you know why this work occurs? Because I was willing to ask a clear question of myself when I was a man who walkedupon this plane and saw the incredible limitations of physical form, and dared to think new thoughts. How could I possibly find a way to communicate with all minds in all dimensions of creation? What would I have to become? How would I need to change in order to experience unlimited communication? The answer was the process of crucifixion, resurrection, ascension, Christed Consciousness. So the answer taught me, because it became my experience — all based on the desire of finding an answer to a clearly asked question.

Where there are no questions, you already have your answer. And how many in your world never ask new questions, and then wonder why nothing changes? The question is how to develop a greater clarity and discernment around wearing one's own emotional body- and energy and staying clear with that and not, so to speak, take on the cloak or clothes of another's emotional body and wearing theirs?

Beloved friend, imagine that you are sitting in a grand orchestra and there are many violins and many flutes and many oboes and many clarinets, and what have you, that comprise this orchestra. And the show has not yet started and so everyone is tuning up their instruments. And as you sit there (you are a flute player) you place the mouthpiece in the instrument, and as you raise it to your lips you're a little nervous because, after all, this is a new show for you, you're the rookie on the block, so to speak. And you seem distracted by the sound of the oboe, the sound of the clarinet, the beating of the drum, the little squeal of the strings of the violin. For a moment you are distracted. Which sound is *my* sound? How can I hear my own sound if all these other things are making noise around me?

The virtuoso, so to speak, the master of the instrument, learns to put their attention on what they *want* rather than on what they fear is *preventing* what they want. And what you want to do is hear the sound of your own flute. And so you bring your instrument to your lip, and you begin to blow across it, until you find just the right angle so you can begin to emit the note.

Oh, that's the one I like. Oop, now I'm being distracted by the oboe again. Rather than thinking, how can I separate myself from the oboe, focus only on what do I want to hear? My own flute.

Practice blowing the note again. By turning the attention to what you want, by releasing the oboe players and the violinists and all of the rest from being blamed for distracting you. Focus on what you want.

What is the frequency you want to feel in your body, what are the thoughts *you* want to think? Put your attention on generating the momentum of blowing the note that you want to hear in yourself. And as you build that momentum, it begins to sound like the note struck from a crystal glass: shining radiantly, sounding radiantly through empty space, where nothing obstructs it.

So that even that the oboe player and the violinists are doing their thing, you are so absorbed, you focus all of your attention and all of your desire on not worrying about what *they're* doing, or how their sounds may be affecting you — but when you feel the effect or distraction of the oboe, you turn again to creating the sound of what *you want*. Whether it means breathing deeply, whether it means smiling lovingly, whether it means thinking a thought that "It is done and I acknowledge it." You learn to turn the attention of your mind in the direction of what *you* want to feel and to experience, to call into *your* reality. That is what builds the strength.

And, you see, that is what brings the answer to the question. For, as you begin to stabilize — by focusing on what you *want* — you become familiar with the frequency of the note that you are creating as the flute player. And the more familiar you become with that note, the clearer it becomes what is *not* that note.

And in just the same way, whenever you think you're feeling

energies and you're not sure whether it's yours or somebody else's, turn the attention of the mind from that thought—that's a useless question. Bring it back to the focus of:

> *Who cares what I'm feeling now or what I think might be going on. What do I want? Oh, I want my body to be relaxed. I want to look lovingly upon the world that I see. I want to walk as a Christed being in feminine form. I want to be happy. Well, what would that feel like in this moment? Ah.*

Begin to use the power of creation, that you're always using, to create differently—by bringing the attention from worrying about the oboe player to focus on the radiant jewel that you can bring into being by blowing your own note. Strengthen that. Become it.

If you were to go to a gymnasium to exercise a muscle, and you go to lift the weight, you would not allow yourself to look around and wonder who's lifting what weight, and why can't I lift that weight over there, and all of those other things. You would know that you're only there to focus on what *you* are doing. How are *you* moving your muscles? How are *you* lifting that weight? What does it *feel* like within you? For you know that if you distract yourself, you might hurt yourself. Is that not true?

Uh-huh.

Each time you choose to let yourself be distracted by what others are doing, by dissipating your attention away from the note you want to learn to play, and that comes by asking the question:

Heaven on Earth

What would it be like to be perfectly at peace in this moment?

What would it be like to be Christ incarnate?

What would it be like to be with no fear?

What would it be like to be free of my past histories?

By focusing on your note, you discover that the only time you ever harmed yourself is when you put your attention on trying to figure out what was somebody else's, and what are they doing?

The more you focus your attention here on blowing the perfect note through your flute, all of this around you will begin to fall away. It is called, I believe, vigilance and discipline.

Laughter.

Let me give you a picture.

Imagine being a Jew, the son of Jewish parents, middle class to lower middle class, as you might call it, in a cultural time frame of great upheaval: great fear and doubt and struggle and conflict. Imagine standing in a circle, what you might call a plaza, I suppose, in an ancient city called Jerusalem. And seeing the bedlam all around you, and suddenly realizing that none of it matters. The only thing that matters is *what do I want*? I could have made the choice and said I want to be a successful merchant, or a successful money changer, like everybody else. But, instead, I decided to go for the gusto and ask the impossible thought, the improbable thought, the heresy, the heretical thought: What would it be like to be Christ incarnate in the midst of this place? I turned my attention to focusing on asking what I truly wanted. And that has made all the difference.

Would you be willing, then, to begin to discipline the mind, to bring it back to asking yourself that question:

> *What is it I truly want? What would it be like right now, to become so outrageous in the midst of what I think is an insane situation, to choose to be unlimited and perfect peace?*

Any such thought like that will do,
as long as it's highly unlimited.

Okay.

Does that help you in that regard?

Uh-huh, very much.

So then we'll be seeing if you decide to play the flute well. Beloved friend, you might as well, you've already explored the vagaries of the clarinet and the oboe and the trombone.

Don't forget the drums!

And the drums.

Jeshua, what is like to live the Christ vibration in 3-D?

It's a lot of fun. It is the wonder of wonders. It is so sublime and so grand that no words can contain it. It is to be in the world but not of the world. It is to be so filled with wisdom and compassion and love and power and capability, and at the same time to know that you are literally nothing. Of myself, I do nothing. And many sought to make me their god. And, yet, I was telling them, don't look at me. I'm not the maker and the doer. I am the witness of grand mystery that I now allow to flow through me. And each so-called miracle was a miracle unto me. It brought a freshness in each moment, to step with a foot upon the warm earth at mid-day, and to be in total awe that that experience could arise, that by placing one foot in front of the other, I could end up at a well having a conversation with a woman that changed her life, that the holy spirit could speak through me to wonder how I even arrived at the well in the first place. It wasn't my intention. It was only my intention to be in a state of awe and wonder and allowing.

To be Christ in the third dimension is a very unique experience. It lasts only the twinkling of an eye, but that's how long the body lasts. But while it lasts, I can tell you this, nothing you can imagine or ever create, nothing any mind has ever pondered can match the sublime fullness and fulfillment that comes as the result of asking the question you have asked. For each question must be answered. And the answer is always the experience of the fulfillment of the question. Continue, then, to ask that question.

There's one that goes with it for me, and that is, if being the Christ vibration in 3-D is as sublime as you just described, then being co-creating Christ in 3-D must be a blast. And I wonder if that's ever happened in the 3-D history that we've known of before?

The answer is no. It has never occurred upon this plane. There have been many grand civilizations, but each, no matter how far removed and even beyond the one you know, as we stated earlier, by comparison yours is extremely primitive in relation to some that have existed. But in each one of them, the thought was held that some could be Christ, but not everyone. They just held that perception that there had to be this hierarchy. Does that make sense to you?

Yes.

Therefore, the thought that is penetrating or descending is the thought of a world in which all body minds manifest the fullness of the Christed consciousness. Second coming, indeed. No, it has never occurred, but it will.

So that's one of the real opportunities we have in Shanti Christo.

It is not just one of the opportunities, it is the only opportunity. Everything serves that, or can serve it. Everything grows out of whether or not there will be minds willing to ask that question with you and be committed to receiving, which means to become, the answer. For my two cents, if I had cents, I would say there could be no grander adventure than the field of time. Does that help you in regard to the question?

Yes, thanks.

Oh. Then the answer is already being received.

What an adventure. I feel like I'm waking up in the conversation we're having.

Ah. Wonder of wonders. Hmm.

The question has arisen about the Shanti Christo membership, and the comment was that it was 'exclusive' to have tapes only go to members. And the question is — what is the question? For those not able to manifest the means to become a member right now, whether the Shanti Christo play in that role to open up and extend tapes to those? What's your view on that?

Not able to manifest the means?! Beloved friend, we'll have you asked the question for it states a universality in human consciousness to deny the simple truth of all that we've said in this hour: *There is never a time that any soul is limited; it chooses to manifest and experience exactly what it's experiencing.*

No one has a dollar bill in their pocket unless they have chosen that experience. There is absolutely no one who is without power to manifest the means of manifestation if they are willing to take responsibility for their miscreations. And they smile and say,

Well, if I created that, I can start anew.

Exclusivity is the most interesting word in your language. Listen well. When one views something as being exclusive, *they* have literally chosen to place themselves on the outside of what they see as being exclusive. It is not the thing in itself, whether it be an organization, a group, a relationship. That is not what causes exclusivity. Perception creates experience—always, always, always. And if anyone would view anything and judge it as being exclusive, then there is an opportunity for them to stop and see how they literally created the feeling of being excluded. Does that make sense for you?

Free will choice is never taken away. I have never excluded anyone from me, and yet many, many, many have judged my work, both at the time I walked upon this earth, as being highly exclusive. Why did you only selected those disciples? Why are there more women than men? I didn't choose them. They chose themselves. The same is true now. Does that help you in that regard?

Uh-huh, yes.

Now. You have an interesting phenomenon in your culture where there are many clubs that are created. Men have clubs and exclude women. Women have clubs and exclude men. Whites have clubs and exclude blacks. Blacks have clubs and exclude whites, and reds, and everything else on the planet. Yet I say this unto you: all that matters is what do you truly want.

If you look upon anything occurring in your society and see it as some form of exclusivity, stop and look and check your own energy. *You* are feeling excluded from something, and that is why you have called to yourself the experience that reflects the quality of exclusivity. There is something *you* are excluding yourself from in your own consciousness. It may not be that club: that is a symbol of the energy that is going on within your beingness. Therefore, if one says, well, this is exclusive, the wise student pauses, reminds themselves that what they experience, they have created. And if they are seeing exclusivity, they need to begin to ask the clear question: what am *I* excluding from myself? How am *I* shutting up energies of exclusion? Does that make sense to you?

Yes.

So are there any more questions? [Pause]

So to each and every one of you that has heard these words, remember that it is a stepping stone. Begin to look at each and every one of your days and all of your experiences, as you being the literal and only creator of your experience. And it can be anything that you want. God doesn't care. You see, God is content to create you. What you do with the power that She has given unto you is your business. But part of God's creation is to extend complete freedom to his creations. It doesn't matter to God because He knows that you're going to come home, when you choose to. And your throne awaits you: the throne of mastery over your creations.

We begin then, now, to weave a blending that will create a vibration and frequency through this 'family'. Hmm. A family which is limited because we're excluding others! [Laughs] It is an open invitation. And any are free to join in the dance, if they have heard truthfully the desire to awaken within themselves.

In closing, then, in this hour, my peace do I give unto you — and not as the world gives, give I unto you. Why would I want to give as the world gives? Surely that is the height of insanity. For the world gives only to take away. The world gives only that you might recognize the world and its greatness. But I give as my Father once gave to me — freely, unconditionally, as the overflow of love.

Therefore, peace be unto you always, creators of heavens and hells, who are free at any time to choose anew. And because I am without time, I can wait forever for you to choose with me.

Amen.

Ignorance is Bliss

Now, we begin.

And once again, greetings unto you beloved and *precious* friends.

Is it not true that wherever you look, whether within you or around you, there is but the Face of Mystery shining back at you? For from the very first, have you ever truly known what a single thing is or what it is for? Yet the thoughts within your mind, your perceptions of things, both within and around you, would lead you to believe that you do indeed *know* what a thing is and what it is for.

You would look upon an object such as a chair and *you* decide what that object is and what it is for. You would look upon the rain that falls from the clouds and *you* would decide what that thing is and what it is for. Indeed, you would look upon your brother and sister and — perceiving something about them or relating their presence to some past history you have had with them — you would decide who and what they are *and what they are for*. And when you decide what a thing or a person is *for*, you then become justified in using that thing or person according to *your perception*. You would look upon a chair and decide: because it is a chair it must be for sitting and I will therefore sit upon it. You would look upon the rain as it falls and, deciding that it is called 'rain', immediately the mind decides what rain is, where it has come from, and what it is for. You therefore act accordingly.

And yet, even this is not quite consistent. For a farmer would look upon the rain and see it much differently than what you call an athlete playing upon a field on a Saturday afternoon, or a family preparing to go upon a picnic. Therefore, what is it that decides *for you* what a thing is and what it is for? Consciousness, the nature of the mind, is very slippery indeed, and it requires great vigilance to learn to see— to comprehend, to transcend, to grasp—how consciousness, the nature of mind, is operating through you, through the body, through the body's senses, *in relationship to all created things*.

But we'll take a slight shortcut. For the things that you look upon when you decide what a thing is and what it is for, you have *projected* your value system upon these things. Something is already operating in the depth of your consciousness that stimulates an impulse which requires you to shape your experience of what you see and what you believe these things are for to fit what you most value in the moment. Always, then, what you *truly* experience is not the thing in itself, not what it may or may not be for within itself—you experience only the boundaries of your own mind. Nothing more. And nothing less.

There are many who look upon the rain as it falls and see not just that which nurtures the soil which will grow the plant, or they see not that which is interrupting their Sunday excursion to the park, they do not necessarily see that this will change the texture of the grasses and the soil so that the athlete might have to slip and fall upon his rear-end occasionally—but rather they look not with the physical eyes and they look with a mind that is not attached to any specific need of their own, and they have learned to ask the Mystery of Creation:

What is this thing? And what is it for? And they have come to see that rain itself, to use an example, is *symbolic* of Consciousness and Creation itself. They look upon even a chair or a person or a blade of grass, and they look past the perceptions they have *learned*, to inquire directly what this thing is and what it is for.

And resting in the purity of Mind, resting in the neutrality of Mind, a different process occurs. For there is no impulse arising from within their own separative consciousness, their own individual mind, their own egoic state of being — believing they need something and therefore the world becomes that which fulfills what they need — they therefore project no value upon what they see, but they await a value to be given from some source deeper than the mind associated with personal history and with the body itself. And from that deep neutrality of Mind something indeed *is* revealed. And yet what is revealed is not of the world, for what is revealed is a *Radiance*, the reflection of a grand Mystery, a *symbol* of the laws of consciousness itself in its universal rather than its personal nature.

The rain becomes that which brings sustenance to creation. The rain becomes a symbol of how gently and easily the grace of a Perfect Love descends and is given to any who would but receive it. The rain becomes a symbol of that which is purely innocent, yet gives itself to be perceived and experienced as the receiving mind would choose.

Likewise, a person is not looked upon according to his or her history, is not looked upon according to whether or not the body is pretty enough to be taken to bed for sex. The body is not looked upon as being large enough or strong enough to bowl over several smaller bodies and then you will give them a contract with big golden coins. A person is not looked upon as something which is (what is your word?) utilitarian — that is, able to perform a certain function, able to fulfill some need for yourself. And therefore what begins to shine forth through that person, your brother or sister, is not their individuality — that is, not their foibles, not their personality structure — but Light, but the presence of the mystery of Consciousness itself which arises as a gentle wave from the ocean of Mind that is without beginning and without end.

Why is this important? Because as you go through your day you believe you are directly experiencing *what is*, and you are absolutely certain that what is is *outside of you* — the person, the chair, the rain, any perceived thing is outside of you. You have not yet truly learned to understand, to comprehend deep in the cellular structure itself. For the body is a knowing mechanism. It is the way in which you attract energy to yourself. It is that through which you project the energy of your mind. It's the meeting place of inner and outer, just as the skin is the meeting ground of what is within and what is without.

You believe that what you are perceiving and therefore knowing is something outside of you that is etched in stone: it is defined, it is complete, and you know it. And yet again, I say unto you, *not in any moment whatsoever* do you ever see or perceive *anything* except that which you project *upon it* until, through the use of vigilance and mastery of the Keys of the Kingdom of Desire, Intention, Allowance, and Surrender, until the mind is retrained to rest at peace, wanting nothing, needing nothing, knowing not what a single thing is or is for — only then does the mind become capable of receiving a higher knowing, a higher intuition. Only then does the body begin to restructure itself so that its deeper, more latent possibilities arise — called third sight for one, to begin to perceive an object through the senses of the body, to *feel* a color, to hear an object that the ears cannot hear. The body itself is an incredible mechanism for joining with and experiencing all of creation.

But what blocks you from being able to hear a color is what you are choosing to project upon creation by deciding that you already know what a thing is and what it is for. Hmm. That is my pet and my pet is to give me companionship, it is to please me; and if therefore the pet acts in a way that is not pleasing, anger arises and the world is a mess.

This one is my employee and my employee is a utilitarian device to assist me in doing what I think I must do to create money to survive, as much of it as I can. And therefore when the employee says, "I'm going through some sort of spiritual crisis and I won't be able to be in on Wednesday morning," immediately frustration arises because what the employer values is the production of the useless items of your culture (by and large) and therefore there is something wrong with the employee and perhaps we should replace *this thing* that does not seem to understand what it is and what it is for.

How many times in each of your days do you believe that that which you perceive around you is not fulfilling its function? Which means, of course, that it's not quite fitting in to what *you* have projected upon it.

How often in each of your relationships are you *so certain* that the other has forgotten their place, and is therefore disrupting your world? And yet how often have you truly learned to *forgive yourself* for what you have believed your brother or sister is and what they're for?

How many times have you relinquished your own ideas of what Creation is and what it is for, to rest into that place of neutrality where one's own ignorance is accepted and embraced and loved and trusted—that place in which there is a suspension of the projection of your own valuation? How often in any given day do you rest in the peace that forever passes all understanding and ask of something unseen:

What is this for? What is the meaning and purpose of this

moment? What would you have me see shining through the chair ... the rain ... my brother and my sister?

For I say unto you, the eye of the needle is found at the source of your own consciousness. The way to a spiritual life is not found outside of you, but within you, deep within the core of everything you have built up around the simplicity of an innocent mystery called Creation.

The way to peace, the way to a miraculous life, lies not in insisting that the world conform to what you have believed it is for and what you have believed about yourself — but rather, in relinquishing all of the ideas you have learned, in relinquishing even the belief that you *exist*, in relinquishing the belief that you must continue into the next moment as a physical being, to look upon the most primary perceptions you carry as a consciousness that is having a third-dimension, or physical, experience, to relinquish *all of them* upon the altar of your heart and to own wholly your *complete* ignorance. For only a mind thus emptied of itself can be taught anew.

The way to peace in life, the way to mastery, the way to union with all of Creation — indeed the way to a perfect and completed Christedness — lies not in trying to make or do, but in mastering the art of relinquishing, the art of resting in the humility and innocence of a divine unknowing.

> *Father, that which is the Source and Creator of all, that which pervades all things, mystery shining forth from mystery, I know not what a single thing is or what it is for. I thought I did yesterday, and even in the last moment, but now I choose to relinquish all things and rest in that Perfect Peace whereby, perhaps, I will be shown how to perceive and therefore to*

Ignorance is Bliss

experience anew.

Herein is the path of *power*.

Power in your world means to manipulate, to control, to get what you want. But I say this unto you: Are you sure that you *know* what you want? Or what you want, is this not resting on what you *believe* you must *have*? And what you must have, is this not a belief in perception that rests on your *prior determination* about what the world is and what you are? If you do not know yourself, how can you know what you need and what you want?

Therefore, beloved friends, we would begin to ask of you to be determined to utilize your experience of each moment as an opportunity to bring vigilance to the mind by *choosing* to acknowledge *your complete state of ignorance* in each and every moment. For he who says that he "knows" probably knows not. And he that says "I know that I know not" probably knows.

Contemplate that phraseology, for within it is much wisdom. The first is the expression of the consciousness of the world. For all you need do is sit upon a park bench and watch your world drive by and walk by, and everybody knows what they're doing, where they're going, why — and of course it's important. But only that one that knows he knows not rests for a moment upon the park bench and says,

> *Father, what would this day be? Teach me. Show me. I know nothing.*

For the one who knows nothing rests in humility and then is free to marvel at that which he or she is guided to do and that which is *revealed* to their consciousness. For only when the mind is released from projecting can it become an empty vessel in which it can receive the radiance of a mystery shining forth from the Mind of God through each and all created things.

The way of awakening, then, is the way of acknowledgement of one's *perfect ignorance*. The way of peace requires the relinquishing of *all* of one's ideas. For only then can the mind be taught anew.

So, let's begin with something quite simple. Just where do you think you are right now? Think about it for a moment and be honest with yourself. When you sat down and placed this tape within your little machine, were you not already operating from a place of consciousness that said:

I know exactly what I'm doing. I'm in my house. I'm in my car. The weather is such-and- such. I only have so much time and oh my goodness, shouldn't the government be doing this and shouldn't that be happening? What about that athletic event? What a dummy to fall on his butt because it was raining, and now the game is lost, and therefore I'm depressed.

All of these things are going through your mind. You put the tape in and you've already decided you're going to hear something that either will uplift you or make you think. Perhaps you've already decided that you're going to be hearing me communicating through this, my beloved brother — rest assured, in the future you will have some surprises. You have already decided what *is* before you begin it. You have already decided how to approach the experience: by turning on your thinking analytical mind so that you heard the words in the sentences and therefore believe that you will come to understanding.

But I say unto you, there are some among you who have learned how to move into ignorance and innocence. And when these words are spoken, you do not so much hear them as see pictures. You feel them rather than think about them. You receive insight from the silence between the words. You feel a transmission of energy that you could not ever explain to anyone because it has nothing at all to do logically with the formation of little sounds you call words to which you have already ascribed meaning. Although you seem to be listening to a tape, you are already in a quality of consciousness that transcends the normal process of listening and analyzing and drawing conclusions.

It has been said that the meek will inherit the earth. What does that word truly mean, then? The meek are those who have learned the futility of their learning. The meek are those who know and accept that there is only Mystery arising. The meek are those who know they are not what they thought they were. The meek are those who wait in each moment for revelation to occur. The meek are those who smile at the futility and insanity of acting in the world *as if* they knew what a thing is and what it's for. They wait on divine consciousness. They wait on the purity that emanates from the Source of Being that can shine through them and reveal to them, moment to moment, what the purpose of any moment is.

Any master, any true master, is one of the meek. For mastery does not rest on the accumulation of knowledge. Mastery rests in divine ignorance, in which true knowledge shines forth — the knowledge that would radiate through your mind from the mind of God, the knowledge that would enlighten even the sensory mechanisms of the body so they receive what is being transmitted from all created objects in ways that transcend ordinary knowing and seeing and hearing.

So look around you, right where you are. You think you know what time it is and therefore perhaps you think you're supposed to still be in bed. You know what time it is and so perhaps you are supposed to be hurrying out the door to get to some kind of a job that you *think* is going to provide you with what you *want*, because what you *want* is linked to what you *think you need*, and what you *need* is linked to your *belief* that you must survive into the next moment in a certain way of lifestyle. Or perhaps you believe that if you did not have that job that the whole universe would collapse around you and not support you whatsoever and therefore, of course, reality *is* that you must be on your way out the door to get to your specific job, even if that job is not your heart's desire. Do you see how it all works?

Somewhere in the depth of your mind you have taken on perceptions about what things are and what they are for, including your body, your mind, your thoughts, your feelings. And from these, deeply embedded, deeply habituated, you have decided what you *need* to fit what you *believe* to be true. And from what you *need* you project impulses of what you *want*. And what you want determines how you will see every object and every person and every drop of rain and every wisp of cloud and every chair around you. But again I say unto you, meekness truly begins with the complete recognition that *you don't know* what you truly want, unless you have come to a place where there is silent voice calling within that says to you,

I want God. I want Peace. I want to come Home.

Earlier I asked you if you knew where you were, and I say this unto you: If you believe you're sitting in a chair, if you believe you know what time it is, if you believe you know what this day is to mean for you, you do not know where you are. *You literally do not know where you are.*

Would it not be wise if you're going to act in any given day, to at least begin to contemplate the simplicity of the question:

Is it not wise to first know where I am, before I decide what I will do?

The human mind believes it knows where it is, and yet where it is is within the complex of insane notions and fearful perceptions it has made in error to replace the simplicity of the reality of being in the Mind of God — unlimited forever, totally supported and provided for in each moment.

If you knew where you were, truly, if all of humanity knew where it was, the world as you know it would *stop dead in its tracks* and soon cease to be. That which is called Wall Street wouldn't even open in the mornings. No one would go to the great halls of government. Many of you would never step foot in what you call an automobile again. Do you know what would occur? First, there would be a delight in waking to watch the first rays of light shine forth from the sun, mystery of mysteries, and to begin to touch the gentleness of the earth. Your delight of the morning would be to discern the subtle qualities of how light changes the coloration of the world around you. And you would tune in and *feel* the vibratory quality of how nature around you begins to wake up with each coming day. You would hear the sound of a leaf coming to life in the morning, not through the ears, but through the very skin of your body. You would delight in allowing your awareness to touch and caress and embrace each created thing in that moment.

Perhaps you would be moved to plant seeds within the soil, or perhaps to harvest what you have previously planted. You might be called to join with your neighbors in singing and dancing, or in quiet prayer. You would be so amazed at what is unfolding around you, within you, that your mind would not be able to analyze, compare, contrast and judge. You would be too blown away by the incredible, powerful mystery that Creation is and you would know beyond all doubt that this day you will be provided *all* that you need and that your daily bread will come to you. 'Daily bread' is not just what you stuff down the mouth of the body. It is emotional nurturance.

It is play. It is laughter. It is fulfillment. There are many levels of daily bread. And yet it falls upon your shoulders like the drops of a soft spring rain without ceasing, manna from Heaven. You would be so immersed in the contemplation of the Mystery of God, who is but Love, that never would a fearful thought arise, never would a judgmental thought arise, never, never would you actually believe that you know what a thing is and what it is for. You would delight in allowing these things to be revealed to you.

And so I ask you to compare that definition, that picture, with how humanity lives, and then ask yourself:

> *Does humanity know where it is? Do I know, as a part of humanity, where I am? Am I willing in this moment to completely relinquish all ideas I have ever had about what anything is and what it's for and therefore what its meaning is, what its usefulness is? Can I choose to rest in the place of neutrality and to allow something beyond myself to teach me anew?*

So, if you are standing, I want you to sit, and if you're sitting, remain where you are — now that that phrase has new meaning. Truly *feel* the fabric of the object you are sitting upon. *Feel it!* Open up the cells of the body and allow the vibrational quality of where you are sitting to penetrate into your beingness. Let the skin be an organism for hearing and not just for feeling. Can you hear the note being sung by the thing upon which you are sitting? All things contain consciousness, or life. For all of creation is but Life itself, and therefore there is wisdom and intelligence radiating through each and every created form. Feel the quality of vibration.

Does a color come into your mind? Not the color of the fabric, necessarily, but the color of the vibration represented by this object. Is it a color that you like? Does it feel good where you are? Rest assured if it does not, get rid of that object and give it to someone else in need, and procure for yourself that which creates the vibration that brings you a pleasure beyond the ego.

Begin to bring into your life those things, whether a chair, whether a flower, whether a pen, the color of paper that you use, let all things begin to reflect and exude toward *you* that which reminds you of the infinite creativity, the infinite loveliness, the infinite quality of vibration of peace and beauty and mystery — the quality of God's Presence. If you now have clothing upon your body, feel it for just a moment. Feel the fabric of the clothing on your body. Who told you you needed to wear that? Who told you you needed that color or that style? Does it truly resonate with you? Does it feel natural? Does it come from the earth or has man made up his own fabric that you now place upon the body. For I say unto you, that which has not come forth from nature, left untampered, blocks certain frequencies that are emitted from the natural world, from your Mother Earth. Therefore, it is always wise to use the most natural of fabrics upon the body.

Does it express beauty and wholeness to you or is it something that you "made do" with because it saved you golden coins? And if you buy something to save you golden coins, are you not telling yourself that you live in a universe of lack and you have no power within yourself to bring abundance into your life? And if you have no power to bring abundance into your life, are you not saying that your Creator has created you limited and unworthy of Creation? *Everything you see around you in this moment is a reflection and a symbol of what you have believed is true about Creation and about yourself.*

Well I didn't mean to become quite so forceful, but it is time for the truth to penetrate consciousness, for soon the earth will no longer tolerate any vibration of consciousness that does not radiate and resonate with light and beauty and freedom and innocence and play and unlimitedness. Therefore, if you would change the world, change your mind. And if you would change your mind, relinquish all of your own ideas.

For those of you in relationship, or those of you that can create a relationship, even if you must run an ad and say that you pay ten dollars of your golden coins per day for someone to be a temporary friend—in other words, if you can find another to be in a relationship with—a very valuable exercise is just this:

Sit with someone. Look into each other's eyes. Place the hands upon whatever you're sitting on, possibly the floor or chair, whatever, look into each other's eyes; and each of you admit to the other the truth about yourself. What will first happen is that you will begin to say,

> *Well, my name is so-and-so and I live in such-and-such a place and I had these parents, and oh my God, and I have these skills...*

None of that is the truth of who you are. The truth of who you are is that you don't know who you are, you don't know what you're for. You are in a state of *complete divine ignorance*. And you can prove it to yourself in this way. Look upon the person sitting across from you for at least two or three minutes and then tell them the thought that is occurring in their mind in this moment. You'll find that 99.9999999 percent of time you are

Ignorance is Bliss

totally wrong. Ask them to do some gesture, to change the body language, and then tell them what they are trying to express. You will discover again that they can fool you any time they want. Do you know what a thing is and what it's for? Do you really know what's occurring in any given moment? My reply to you is that you do not, as long as you are relying on your own thoughts and ideas.

After doing this exercise with each other for a few moments, then practice resting in the neutrality of your own ignorance.

> *Father, I know not what a thing is or what it is for.*

Then ask the other person to hold a certain thought within their mind. It could be a picture of a pink elephant. It could be anything. And as you rest in your ignorance, giving up all hope of knowing what is, what it's for, what needs to be communicated, you might just find that you begin to realize that some idea is being predominant in your mind. It could be outlandish. It could be a pink elephant. And then simply say to your friend,

> *I think you're holding the thought of a pink elephant, or that your body language is conveying a certain thought.*

Through this practice you will refine your ability to receive knowledge in a new way. And as you refine that you will find yourself in a state of what is called Cosmic Consciousness, or Christed Consciousness, where you have so mastered the relinquishing of your own ideas that what is truly real and what holds purpose in the moment is revealed into your consciousness moment by moment by moment, even it concerns someone who's on the other side of the planet. And then when you ask within, *What should I do with this?*

The Holy Spirit tells you, and you will know when to speak and when not to speak, when to act and when not to act. Resting into the quiet of your own unknowing allows Life to reveal itself through you and to you. But what is revealed will not be perceived as your own and you will understand that you can taken no credit for what unfolds through you. And you will say as I once said,

> *Why do you call me good even when miracles are done through?*
>
> *me? There is none good but God. I am but a channel of the Mystery of Life. I am empty. There is no one at home.*

And when there is no one, there is everyone.
And when there is nothing, there is everything.
And when you are empty, you shall be filled.
And when you are at peace, you will know the meaning of power.

And when you want nothing, you will have all things. And when you need nothing, you will know the meaning of freedom.

Beloved friends, contemplate well what is shared this day, for it is time to truly bring vigilance to the mind. Recognize that as you go through your day everything you *think you perceive* is a reflection of where you have *allowed* your consciousness to reside, either in the attitudes and beliefs that you have learned in the world, which will show you only what is insanely unreal, or in the quiet neutrality and peace of your divine and perfect ignorance.

We will spend much time together, moving more deeply into this understanding and into that which helps facilitate your return to ignorance. For consider this: The meek are the masters of creation and yet they seem to know nothing at all. And each and every moment of their existence is given over to the practice of the Keys of the Kingdom, desiring only perfect union with God, setting the intention of relinquishing all ideas of their own, practicing the key of allowing, resting into neutrality so that life might reveal itself to them and through them.

And finally, surrendering every trace of belief that there's something inside your body called 'yourself' that is uniquely yours and that you must take care of and it must get what it wants: the hungry little ghost called the ego. Surrender means to awaken to the reality that there has never been anyone where you are, except the presence of Christ. When you know yourself, you will know that you are all things. You'll know that you are empty and that no one's home, that there is only Life living itself. You will have learned that it is not by striving but by relinquishing that the Kingdom is revealed. And you will discover that you've always been at home.

Contemplate well these things, then, and by all means bring lightness and humor to it. Laugh at yourself. Laugh at the self you thought you were. Whenever you believe you need something to be a certain way, slap your thigh — that would be a good use of it at any rate — and laugh, and tell yourself,

> *My God, I actually thought I needed something to happen in a certain way. Hah! The joke is on me.*

And then the wisdom of how things are unfolding can reveal itself to you. And when you know that there is wisdom flowing through the creation of each moment, you just might make the decision to once again *trust* Life. And Life is but Love radiating forth from the Mind of God. And that is where you are sitting right now.

Peace then be unto you, beloved and precious friends.

Amen.

Joy I

Now, we begin.

Indeed, greetings unto you, beloved and holy and precious friends. Indeed, greetings unto you, holy children of Light divine. I come forth with great joy to abide with you because I love you, and the joy comes from the simple fact that when I look upon you, I see naught but Light. I see naught but the face of Christ. I see unlimited potential, unlimited compassion, unlimited love, unlimited peace. These things are the characteristics of your only reality.

Indeed, I look beyond the body and I look beyond the history of your perceptions and constructs that you have created about yourself and what the world is for, and I see the Light that shines forever radiantly transcending this world and all worlds, and I see the Light you are that is already together with me from before the foundation of all worlds, and I see the Light that participates with me in the atonement of the momentary dream of separation between the Holy Father and His precious and only creation: you.

Now, if you are listening carefully, that should strike you as a little odd that indeed you are participating with me from that place of perfect union with God in the very process of atoning your own perception that you are separate from God. And that is why I have said you will awaken to your own call—not mine and not another teacher's, not another master's. You always awaken to your own call.

But because the call comes from the place in you that is of Truth, and it is a place that you have perhaps repressed and can no longer believe abides within you, what you do, you see, is that you reach your left hand out and you give a little telegram to me and you say,

> *Jeshua, deliver this telegram to me and make sure I get the message. And then indeed I will begin to awaken from my own dream.*

And since I don't have much else to do these days, I take the telegram and I look at it and I notice the date and the hour; and because I love you, indeed I come to you in that hour and I whisper to you in the quiet of your heart,

> *Precious friend, the time for awakening is now.*

And there comes then a stirring in the depth of your heart and the depth of your soul, and a new journey begins. Not a journey deeper into dreams but a journey that begins to lift you from all dreams.

And in part of that process you will believe that someone has come a-knocking upon your heart and perhaps they have forced their way upon you just a little bit, but indeed it is not true.

For *awakening can only come from absolute freedom*. Therefore, indeed, if you can acknowledge that you have begun the process of awakening, give yourself credit because you have heard your own call.

Does all of that make sense to you?

It is very, very important. And why? Because the small part of the mind that you have mistakenly become identified with, that I have called the ego, would lead you to believe that you are powerless and therefore need the constructs born of the ego,

Joy I

born of the very perception of separation from God, to find your way in life, indeed to keep you safe. And the ego would tell you that you are the body, that you are subject to birth and suffering and death.

The ego would cleverly lead you to believe that there might be some other masters that have somehow "managed" ascension and no longer participate in this realm, and the ego will tell you it's okay to wish that you could accomplish that, and at the very same time it will whisper into your other ear,

> *But you know you really can't because you are weak and you are frail. You are far too busy and, after all, you've been a wretched, sinful creature.*

That somehow, somewhere, you have failed; and because of that you know that you cannot awaken.

But it's okay; go ahead, struggle to do so if you want. And each time you seem to come close, the voice of the ego rears its head and says,

> *No, no, no. It's not okay to receive that much joy.*

And so you begin to contract the heart yet again because it is a pattern learned in the mind, and, if you would receive it, you have been operating under the guise of an illusion in which you have struggled to free the heart, and as it opens up you then contracted; and when you contract, it feels like you because you are used to it. And that is how dreams become comfortable but it does not change them into reality. They remain eternally an illusion.

And the Truth of your being is that Light that I see shining in you radiantly at all times, the Light in which the Truth of your being resides in perfect safety—perfect safety and perfect peace—and unto you is given all power under Heaven and Earth to allow that Light you are to *descend*, to become incarnated, if you will, to shine out through even the cells of the body, to radiate your Light out into this world.

And why is that important? Because you have believed that you were something other than that Light. You will not learn the Truth of your beingness until you are willing to allow that Light to shine through you so that you can see the miracles it begins to create in your life, so that it will shine upon your brothers and sisters and show you the reality of their being, not what the ego would have you believe of them. And as you see those miracles pop up in front of your eyes, you then must acknowledge that the Light is in you now—the Light that heals your perception and shows you not time, but eternity; not an unsafe world but a world that is perfectly safe, and it is safe because *your Light* is in it.

When I look upon you, I see a great ray of Light that has no beginning and cannot know an end. I see a great ray of Light. Its strands shine out, embracing and touching the furthest stars, embracing and touching all the multifarious planes of creation, and there are many of them. I see a Light that embraces the whole of all things that have ever arisen and will ever pass away. I see a Light that shines forth from the Mind of my Holy Father, made in His image and, therefore, one with Him eternally. I see a Light comprised of compassion and grace and ease and power and creativity.

For indeed you are created to create like God, and that is why every loving creation is eternal and every loving thought is true. And why? Because God is but Love and His only creation is you. And Love can only beget that which is lovely. That is the one and simple fact that you must come to re-member, to re-

Joy I

cognize: that if you exist at all, you must be the presence of Love. And if you are that Love, right now, here in this room, you are free to begin the process of releasing—or perhaps even ending—the dream in which a host of thoughts have arisen that have mistakenly distracted you into believing that you are something less than the holy Son of God.

I have said to you many times that the greatest of keys to the Kingdom is the key of allowing. For allowing requires trust.

Allowing requires vulnerability. Allowing requires that you let the Holy Spirit bring correction to your mind and you no longer strive to make that happen, and as you begin to rest into the key of allowing, peace begins to descend even into the cells of the body, and you find that you react differently.

You smile even in the midst of situations that used to create such havoc within the mind. And you will look upon your brother or your sister and even if they are casting stones at you, you will marvel at the great Light that shines just beneath their awareness of themselves. And indeed you *will* know the great liberation that comes when suddenly the shutters are thrown open and you realize

> *My God, it's true. I am that Light. I am that Light I have been seeking for countless lifetimes. I am that Light and I am that Light, now.*

And then, you see, the body itself begins to be freed up a bit, for you will no longer be trying to stuff your emotions into the little pockets of cells, saying,

> *Hold on to this stuff. I don't want to look at it.*

Instead, you will say,

Okay, open the hatch and let it out.

And it will begin to bubble up, for, you see, when Light comes to shine upon shadows, it stirs them up and they will run like crazy, trying to find a corner to hide in; but there is no longer a corner, for even the body becomes filled with Light and the shadows of past memories and old emotions begin to be released. But instead of fearing them, you embrace them. You embrace them, knowing — *knowing* — that as you love what you have feared, you embrace it and you therefore transcend it.

That is why ultimately, you see, healing occurs only in the mind. And what is healed? *The perception that fear must be feared.* Fear itself is an illusion. It doesn't mean you don't experience it. Much of what you call your dreams, when you awaken in the morning you would say,

> *Well, that was unreal. It was just a dream.*

Fear is no different, and if you would well receive it, *fear is the foundation of all dreams — all dreams of time, all dreams of separation, all dreams of anguish find themselves rooted in fear.*

But when you allow, when you truly are willing to allow the Light you are to shine upon all shadows born of illusion, you know that in you there is a power to say,

> *I am open. Bring them forth. Throw open the hatches.*

And you will look at the memories that you may carry of times you have failed, of times you have hurt and been hurt, and you will say,

> *Oh, look at that. Yes, I can feel that. I remember that one — boy was I ever into it then.*

Joy I

And you'll shine your Light on it and you will extend forgiveness to yourself, and the shadow itself becomes dissolved into the Light that shines upon it.

Light added to Light only increases your radiance. And after a while the momentum gets going so fast that you can't stop the process. There is no weekend off. And at any time when things begin to flood up — and many of you know what I am talking about — always continue to shine your Light on whatever arises within you. Do not become identified with the thoughts of fear and the thoughts of limitation and the thoughts of loss. That is the voice of the ego saying,

No, no, no. Don't identify yourself with Light just yet. I fear my own demise of power.

Just there, just there is the greatest of blessings given to you, given to you of the Father who loves you: *The freedom that can never be taken from you, the freedom of your choice — the freedom of your choice to look upon all things that arise with the Love of Christ.*

All loving thoughts are true. Everything else is an appeal for help and healing. Even within yourself. And so, when that voice within you — some of you occasionally know what this is like — rears its head and says,

No, no, you can't do it. Don't leap off the cliff,

love it and realize that voice is not yours. If you need to, you can imagine that a stranger has slipped in, in the middle of the night, and is sitting in your living room, believing now that that home belongs to the stranger. And that stranger is the voice that would have you believe that you are other than what you are created to be: The thought of perfect Love in form.

Love cannot be accomplished. It cannot be gained. It cannot even truly be fashioned. Love cannot be found because it is not an object outside of yourself. It cannot be created for it has always been. Love waits in certainty. Love waits in patience for the holy Son of God, who has but dreamed the dream of separation, to rest for just a moment and to be willing to choose anew, to turn from the roar and the din of the world—and the world is not outside of your own mind—to choose again to touch the place of perfect peace and of grace. And there Love shines. And to look upon the face of Love is to see and know your Self.

And in the end of all seeking and in the end of all striving, the awakened Son rejoices and laughs uproariously and says,

> *My goodness, what a good dream I've had. But now the time of wakefulness is upon me.*

And for a little while you seem to find yourself yet in space and time, and you look down at the hands of "the" body formerly called "your" body and you marvel. You look at the body anew. For what seemed to be something that was always filled with conflict between a place that imprisoned you and a place you hoped to find safety, the thing that you don't even understand what it is, has been translated—translated into a beautiful and holy temple, translated into nothing more, nothing less, than a simple means through which the awakened Mind of Christ extends love to the parts of himself formerly perceived as strangers and friends, brothers and sisters, so that the wholeness, the whole Mind of Christ might awaken and merge back together into its own reality. Now that happens to you

Joy I

more often than you give yourself credit for.

When you set aside every fear, when you set aside every need, when you set aside believing that you know what your needs are, when you are willing to just stop judging your brother and for a moment you look into someone's eyes and you embrace eternity—and everyone in this room knows what that is like because you've done it a million times; no matter how fleeting, you have done it a million times—and that moment of no thought and no time in which the two fragments that seem to be separated by bodies become one and the Light of Love shines through the eyes, for indeed the eyes are the window of the soul, and those sparks of Love meet. Not a love that craves. Not a love that needs attachment, but a Love that recognizes Love.

That is called the Holy Instant and it makes all things new. And that is why your relationship to your brother and sister is the most incredible blessing, the most precious possession you can ever have. Each moment of relationship provides you with the opportunity to choose holiness and not specialness. Love instead of fear. Forgiveness instead of judgment.

And because you look upon your brother and because you look upon your sister and you realize they are the means of your salvation, you will no longer tolerate error in yourself, and you will look upon them and see the face of Christ. You will learn to look past the body, to look past time and history. You will learn to discern that radiant Light which shines in them as it shines in you. And then you will learn the magic involved in the simplicity of this teaching:

You will learn what you choose to teach, and in teaching you must learn it for yourself.

That is why there is no time to lose. Each moment is the opportunity for awakening. Each moment the opportunity for healing, that the things of time that have seemed to be a burden upon you and upon your brother can be placed aside and the mantle of peace, like a gentle dove, can descend upon you, wrapping you in the shawl of a perfect Love, bringing such joy to your being that you cannot find words to describe it and no way to contain it. And you finally realize,

> *I don't have any choice. I have to give it away. My Father keeps pouring so much of it into me, it just keeps picking up the speed. I just have to keep giving it away.*

And then the miracle has occurred.

Gone is the seeker. Gone is the one who needs. Reborn is the finder. Reborn is the one who gives, who lets the Light of Christ shine so radiantly within them with every breath and within every thought and with every word and with every deed that they themselves marvel at the miracles that unfold.

And you begin to dance through time, and you see that the Holy Spirit has translated it into a magical kingdom in which every day is filled with the grace of miracles.

And every day is a little better than the one before, and the only thing you need to pay attention to is to simply watch so that you don't become a little contracted against the on-flowing tidal wave of joy that descends to light up your mind and your heart and even the cells of your body. You have a saying in your

Joy I

language,

> *Let it rip.*

See, you must understand that when I walked upon this plane the language that I was given to use was rather serious for the most part—rather formalized—and so there were some limitations in how the Gospel could be expressed; at least when words were used, but not when there was dancing and laughter and singing and rejoicing and embracing. Unto you it is given in this day and in this hour to truly look around you and see,

> *All that I need for my salvation, all that I need for my awakening is presented to me here. For here is my brother and my sister who has walked together with me since before time is, given to me of God. And as I love them, I love the One who has sent me forth. And as I love them, I honor them. And as I honor them, I learn to honor the Son that dwells within my own heart.*

And in honoring that Son, the Atonement is completed on Earth as it is already completed in Heaven. And Heaven is your home.

Delight—listen well—*delight in the blessings of time and see not a single moment as that which would imprison you.* For there is nothing outside of you, while within you is the absolute freedom of choice, given wholly and never earned, in which you can look upon the things of time, each event that time seems to require of you, and you can bring the blessing of Christ to it. You can choose to radiate instead of contract. You can choose unlimitedness instead of limitation. You can choose Love instead of fear. That is the great gift of time. Because time was created in error, it is then translated into the means by which you awaken from time itself. Therefore, use it constructively.

Realize that you live in a domain in which avoidance of relationship is absolutely impossible. Therefore, embrace your relationships, even the ones that push your buttons. For, rest assured, they are the ones given unto you in that moment — and not a year before or a year after — they are the ones that provide the very stepping stones upon which you are asked to walk so that you can pass through an old ring of fear and realize that you've just awakened a little more fully. And the power of the radiance of that Light you are has penetrated, incarnated, a little more deeply into the mind, and even into the body.

So, next, when someone casts stones at you, rush up and give them a kiss on the cheek. Say,

> *Thank you so much. My goodness gracious, now I can heal this part of myself.*

Above all things, never let your vigilance slip.

[Jeshua chuckles]

I am sorry. Should I don the cloak of the savior of the world and kneel at your feet and beg forgiveness?

[Laughter]

Oh, no. That would be a funny picture.

It would indeed. It has always been a funny picture to me that others would put the mantle of the savior of the world upon my shoulders so as to avoid responsibility for awakening

Joy I

themselves. And I would scratch my head and wonder,

Why would they want to do that?

when in the Truth deep within them they know that they must place the mantle upon themselves and see themselves as equal unto me, who has been sent to be only your brother and your friend.

If Christ dwells in me — and I assure you that Christ dwells in me — that same Light must dwell in you equally. For if it does not, it means that God has created a rather imbalanced creation. And whenever you have felt unbalanced, it is because you have denied the part of you that is true and real and whole and lovely — forgiven and loved wholly.

Listen well to what I have just shared with you, for there you will find the key that brings the mind gently back to peace each time you remember it ... each time you remember it. Each moment in time when you are not wholly joyous, it is because you have forgotten the Truth about yourself. When that really begins to sink in, you are going to feel a great weight lifted from your shoulders — the weight of perceiving that what has stolen your peace has come from somewhere outside your mind. It never has.

I have been working for five years with this my beloved brother to seek to teach him one thing: *there is no set of circumstances that can dictate the choice one makes between love and fear* — just as there are no special circumstances you must strive for and achieve before you have the power to choose between love and fear. The choice and that power abides in you now. It is equally in a newborn child as it is within you.

And the process of life, the meaning of time, is merely to create a field in which you can reawaken to the power of your own choice.

At first as you recognize it, it may not feel too good because you will look upon some of your creations and go,

Whoa.

That which is called "being in hell"—what some of your psychologists might call being psychotic, neurotic and all of the rest—is simply because a part of the mind has looked upon its creations in which it has created unlike God out of fear, and it has taken upon itself the mantle of guilt. And guilt creates a block, so you spin in the same circle over and over again. That is what hell is: it is being in a rut.

But when you look upon your creations that seem to elicit unpleasant feelings— because perhaps you see how your creations involve manipulation or control or what have you— when you look upon those things and remember the Truth that they do not leave a single trace upon the holy Mind of Christ, and when you look upon them and realize that *your Father doesn't even see them*, you are free to be reborn in this moment and to allow your life to be made anew.

Oh, beloved friends, carry not the weight of the past upon you for it is gone already. It is gone already!

And the heavy bag that you have been carrying upon your shoulders was removed, before you experienced it, by the Love that created you; and you have been weighed down only by illusion.

Would you not choose to join with me in casting off the bag that is no longer there? You can make a ritual of it if you would like.

Joy I

Indeed, go to one of your intersections, and underneath the thing that hangs from the wires that tells you when you should go and when you should stop, create a circle of precious crystals.

Heap up dried branches. And in the middle of what is called the rush hour, walk as though you are burdened by a heavy bag. Drop it off of your shoulder, and then kick it into the circle and light a match. And then dance freely about your circle of precious crystals. Knock on the hoods of the automobiles of those that are honking at you and say,

Come, watch my bag burn. Come dance with me.

[Laughter]

You might be surprised: a few will get out and do a jig with you.

In short, don't make the process of awakening so serious.

Is it not rather interesting that seriousness is what creates the world of confusion, of pain, and it's an illusion? Therefore, you bring the bag of seriousness to the very process whereby you think you are going to wake up, and you do your techniques, you read your texts, you memorize all of the lines, but still the bag is on your shoulder and you can't quite figure out why it's still there. The bag is filled with the weight of seriousness—and joy, you see, is made of Light. Isn't she?

And that is why whenever you are not wholly joyous, you have identified yourself with an illusion, a bag that was already removed from your shoulders in the very first moment that the holy Son of God began to fall asleep and to create the dreams of creations that are unlike God's. And the Holy Father reached into your dreams and took the tiny bag from your shoulders and dropped it into the fires of purification, if you will, and throughout every incarnation you have ever lived the bag has not been there, but you have perceived that it is still with you.

And now we come to the point of what I would share with you in this hour: The *Way*, the way in life that speaks of perfect peace is not a way of striving. It is the way of allowing. The way in life that demonstrates the Truth of your being is not the way that the world has taught you because in it there can be no seeking. The way in life that allows the Light of Christ to incarnate right where you thought you were requires only that you put into practice the acknowledgement that you are that Light, the Word being made flesh in this moment.

That is the shift that must come to the mind. I don't care if you practice complex spiritual techniques for ten thousand lifetimes. I don't care if you learn how to walk on water and heal the sick. After all is said and done, there is yet one step that must be taken: your willingness to put to sleep the dream of the seeker and to be the presence of one who has found. And the trick of the course, is that the ego will say,

Well, I can't do that because I haven't found it yet.

And what I am saying to you is that in your choice, held in the mind, to simply say,

I and my Father are one. I am the one who has found, and that Light begins to live through me now,

that is the way that you find it — by acknowledging that you possess what you have believed you do not. Seems rather

Joy I

paradoxical.

I have said many times that *the Truth of the Kingdom is diametrically opposed to the truth of the world.*

If your world says that you must struggle, then the way of the Kingdom must be the way of ease.

If the world says you must seek, the way of the Kingdom must be that you have already found.

If the world says you are guilty, the way of the Kingdom must say there is no guilt. If the way of the world teaches you that you are born to suffer and die, the way of the Kingdom must say that you are eternal and do not abide within the space and volume of a body.

If the way of the world says that your mind is your brain, the way of the Kingdom will say the Mind of Christ is that which radiates, animating the brain and the body so that it can serve as a means of communicating the Love of God.

If the way of the world says you are frail, the way of the Kingdom says you are the presence of eternal strength.

And if the way of the world says it's not good to have too much fun, what do you think the Kingdom says?

[Laughter]

Fun! Party!

That is a good phrase, "Party."

Abide in that infinite Light of joy. Bring it down and express it to the world so that the world sees the demonstration of the Truth. So, you see, the theme of this hour is this—it is a three letter word: JOY. Joy is the theme of this hour.

Joy is the theme of every moment. Joy is the reality of your being. Joy is that which infuses the cells of your body. Joy is that which seeks to radiate from the great ray of Light that you are and to descend through the crown of the head and to explode out through the very fingertips—rays of Light exploding in all directions.

Joy is that which will create laughter and smiles. Joy is that which seeks to bring lightness to the heart. Joy is that which heals. Joy is that which brings forth unlimited power to create like God. Joy— joy is the sign of an awakened heart and a corrected mind. Indeed.

And the greatest of blessings, the greatest of recognitions, is this: You cannot create the means in this world to become joyous, but you can bring the joyousness you are to the circumstances of this world; and when you do that, you are the savior of the world. You are the one sent forth of God, enlisted in what seems to be the Foreign Legion, indeed.

Can you come to touch that place of reality in you?

I want to share with you right now that part of the work that I seek to do in this world, not only through this my beloved brother but through countless others, is a correction: the healing of a deeply held perception that somebody else must be the one that the Bible is talking about. Somebody else must be the one who is the Word of God made flesh. Somebody else

Joy I

must be the one who is to be the Messiah ... If you know that you exist, rest assured you are that one.

Who? Me?

Yes, you. Rest assured I, too, said, "Who? Me?" And then I realized if somebody didn't do it, nobody would ever get it.

I was the first, if you would well receive it, to complete the Atonement as a man: completely, irrevocably. And because of that, my Father has put me in charge, if you will, of the Atonement. And I come to give you the Love that you are.

You may think that somehow I give you strength, but actually I'm rather good at sleight of hand and while I am talking to you, I reach into your hip pocket and grab your strength and your love, and I bring it up and I put it back to your face and you believe,

Wow. How did this one named Jeshua do that?

Those of you that have tasted miracles because of our interaction in this form, is it not time to give yourself equal credit? For the strength and the Light that is brought forth, whatever degree of miracles of healing that have come and have been given to you, has come because you have chosen to awaken to your own call. I am just your delivery boy.

Ah. Joy.

Can you feel it? Can you feel it now? Are you willing to throw off the shackles of the mind and heart right now in this moment? Whether you are sitting or lying down, it makes no difference. Are you willing, indeed, to let joy radiate through the cells of the body? Are you doing it? Can you feel it?

Turn the attention of your mind as if you could look and see every cell. Just go in there and turn the knob and open the door and pour Light.

Imagine, right now, you are looking down upon a body that has never been yours, and you are deciding to fill it with Light. Go ahead and do it. There is no great secret. No great technique. It's not going to take you six months of workshops to learn how to do it.

[Laughter]

Hmm. That's why they call them "work-shops." Why not have "gatherings of celebration of the Truth?" Are you doing it? Don't sit there passively. Do it. Bring the joy in. Enlighten the cells. Let them get lighter and lighter and lighter and filled with joy. Feel how it brings the breath more deeply into the body. Feel it down to the tips of the toes.

Yes, Light. Let there be Light. Say goodbye to the shadows of the past. They are with you no longer. Light. Let there be Light. Radiate it down deeper and deeper. Feel the heart beat a little bit faster. It's called passion for joy. Feel it.

Yes! Have what you call an orgasm with joy. Bring Light and laughter and play to every moment.

[Singing] Where has all the seriousness gone? Has it been a long time in passing?

Who cares? Once it's gone, it's gone. We abide together now. We are the great rays of Light that shine forth through the Mind of God, and we bring a new vision indeed to this planet and to

Joy I

this Earth. We are the joy. We are the Light. We are the bringers of the Gospel. We live it. We are the Truth. Look at us. Yes. We're the ones that have burned our bags in the intersections.

If you want to keep yours...

[Loud laughter]
... go right ahead. Indeed.

That is what it's all about. There isn't anything you need that you do not already possess. And when you throw open the shutters of the heart and allow desire born of a pure heart to lead your way, what you thought you must fear, called passion, what you thought you must fear, called your dreams and aspirations, what you thought you must fear because it might make you stick out in the crowd will no longer be a bit of concern. Trust me. I know about sticking out in crowds.
[Laughter]

Some of you in this room did not want me to stick out in the crowd because you feared that the world could take me from you. Surprise!

The world just freed me to be with you always, beyond all of your perceptions of birth and death, beyond your perceptions of suffering and doubt and struggle, beyond your perceptions of separation born of time. The world served my intention well, and the drama was played out and the resurrection was completed. And if you believe in me, you believe in the reflection given to the world of who you are. For the life of Jeshua ben Joseph is your own — as yours is mine.

That is how intimately united we are. We share one Heart and one Mind when we rest in the Truth of the infinite and eternal joy that is the presence of the Love of God in us.

And when others say,

> *Lo, the Kingdom is here,*

and another says,

> *No, the Kingdom is there,*

look them in the eye and say,

> *No dice. The Kingdom of Heaven is within me because I am the one who chooses to be wholly joyous. I let that joy overflow so much that I cannot help but give it to the world.*

And if there are those that fear joy, give it anyway. And if they can't bear it, rest assured they will drop out of your life.

But it's only fear that causes that to happen. But no one can flee *from* Light who does not turn and flee *to* Light. For Light surrounds them wherever they are on the path they choose to walk. If that is true — and I assure you that it is — it means that you are safe to release your hold upon your brothers and your sisters, whatever the form of relationship may have been.

You are free to give them to me, and I will keep them safe and I will whisper to them in their dreams until *they* make the same choice that *I* made in time: to release the dream of the dreamer and to acknowledge,

> *I and my Father are one.*

Rest assured that I will leave no one that you entrust to me. Unshackle from your heart, unshackle from yourself the weight

Joy I

you have carried for so long. The awakening of another is the Holy Spirit's responsibility.

Your only function, your only purpose, your only task, if you will, is to be the presence of one who has allowed correction to come to the mind so that you are forevermore the Thought of perfect and joyous Love in form. That is all that is ever asked of you. The rest is being taken care of. It's a bit of a release, isn't it?

[Addressing a member of the audience]. It's about time you gave that to me. Thank you.

Wish I'd thought of it sooner.

Beloved friend, whenever you think about that Truth, you have immediately moved into what is real and eternal, and it no Longer matters if you didn't think about it earlier because in this moment all things are made new.

It is called rebirth.
That little sigh that you felt released more than you know. Now, be ready for miracles.

Oh, I am. Bring them on.

Ah, yes. What then are your true dreams? For while you abide for a little while in time it is given unto you to allow unhappy dreams to be translated into happy dreams. And you will know the course that the Holy Spirit will take you on by the things that come into your life without effort. And you will know the course given to you to walk to bring you wholly to a dream of joy, as you become willing once again to become as a little child who celebrates the incredible creativity — the dreams that seem to course up through the heart.

For a child goes to what you would call a sandbox, and some image comes of an incredible castle and they are filled with such joy,

> *Ah, this is going to be so much fun.*

They don't go and ask somebody if it's okay. They don't ask somebody,

> *Well, do castles really exist? Is it true that I can build a foundation to sustain it?*

They don't ask for authorization of what you call building codes — they just build it. And they rejoice in every moment of the game; the game, the play. Allow yourself from this day forward to truly get in touch with your heart's desires. Don't fear them any longer.

Now, if you think a desire is coming up in the heart that says,

> *Boy, I've always wanted to murder that so-and-so...*

[Laughter]

I am not asking you to create chaos here. That is not your heart. A clue.

It is a clue, indeed.

But if you dream of wealth, if you dream of service, if you dream of travel, if you dream of a new house, if you dream of a new cloak, if it feels really good and it keeps pressing, not from the mind downward but from the heart outward, why not let it

Joy I

flow?

The river of life lies within you. It sustains you and it carries you, and it will bring you home to the Father wholly — but only if you let it flow. Only if you let it flow. And that river is a river of joy. Indeed, with great sincerity I say unto you, "Let it rip!"

[Laughter]
Indeed. So, how are you all doing?

Great. Yes.

Indeed.

Jeshua?

Just a moment. Stand up. Now, you that just said, "Yes," I want you to become the leader here and lead them in at least three resounding "Yeses."

And don't let them hesitate or hold back. It must be at the top of the lungs. Feel it from the toes all the way up to the crown of the head. Those of you that were lying down have a little further to go but...

YES! More, more. YES! One more. YEEESSS!

Okay.

That was energizing.

Energizing? Why would you want to be energized? Isn't death

and sluggishness much, much better?

No thanks.

Now, I have indeed watched certain minds begin to awaken to—and I believe they will enjoy this—their, I believe the word is the "piggy" nature.

[Laughter and oinking]

Now you have all seen what are called the pigs as they roll around, and the farmer says,

> *My God, there they are rolling around in that mud again.*

A true pig realizes and perceives that they are rolling in the river and the mud of *joy*.

And what if you were to go to your friends tomorrow and say, I have just gone to a great teacher who gave me the last meditation that I need to master,
and your friend says,

> *What is it?*

and you say,

> *Come, come. Come to my backyard and I'll show you.*

[Loud laughter]

You can roll in the river and the mud of joy whenever you want to because this world has no power whatsoever over the Holy

Joy I

Son of God; and that is Truth, indeed.

And all it took was the willingness of one person to say, "Yes," and to lead brothers and sisters in joining in that one place where the mind is one, to say "Yes," and you felt energy and passion and joy course through the cells of your beingness. And that means wherever you are—wherever you are—that power is at the tip of your choice. Who cares where and when you decide to roll in the river of joy?

The world is a lie. Do not let it dictate to you.

Thank you, that was nicely led.

[Personal dialogue here – excluded in this transcript]

Many teachers in many ways are beginning to bring back the recognition: what it's really all about is living from the heart. And in my language I would say that to live from your heart is to live the life of the arisen Christ. These two are one and the same.

Where, then, is the pathway that leads you from this world to - the Kingdom? Look no further than your heart.

What has been your secret desire? What has been your passion and your vision? The journey is what awakens the mind and joins the heart as one, so that the mind becomes the servant of the awakened heart.

Therefore, I say again, in closing—for I want you to have some time to mingle together, and when you do so be willing to share your heart's desires with each other. Have some fun with it and do what you call the "oinking" of your dreams, yes . . .

Be, therefore, that which you *are*; and you are the Light that has come to this world; and you are the one who is the Prince of Peace; or Princess, if you insist.
In short, lighten up and get on with it.

[Laughter]

I love you, but not in seriousness. When you are wholly joyous, rest assured I am with you. When you are not, rest assured I am with you. When you doubt yourself, rest assured I do not. And when you rest in certainty, I celebrate. And if you have ever believed that you have loved me, then truly choose to acknowledge and love the Son that dwells within your own heart and let your Light shine. For only by so doing can you in Truth honor and love me—not as someone above you, but as your brother and as your eternal playmate.

Peace be unto the wholly joyous and awakened and arisen and resurrected Christ, who blossoms forth and brings such beauty to this world that your brothers and sisters, perhaps yet sleeping, won't be able to help but recognize that the Light is in them, too. Indeed. And Heaven comes to Earth because you choose to make the time now.

Have a good time mingling. Come up to somebody, give them a hug and say,

> *You know what I've always really wanted to manifest in my life?*

And let them know. What the Son decrees begins to move into manifestation. What the Son hides is held as a light under a bushel. Decree and manifest Heaven on Earth. It's really all

Joy I

you've ever wanted anyway. Why settle for less?

Peace be unto you whom I love from before the foundations of the world.

Peace be unto you whom I walk with and celebrate with, even when you don't notice and forget.

Peace be unto you always.

Amen.

Joy II

Now, we begin.

And yet once again I say unto you that it is with great joy that I come forth to abide with you — and often I have said that. And yet, have you truly sought to comprehend what those words mean? — "that it is in joy that I come forth to abide with you."

And if I come in this rather particular way to abide with you so that your body can sit there and this body, temporarily borrowed, can sit here, and I can come and abide with you in this manner, rest assured that I come always with joy to abide with you where you really are. You do not abide within a body. The body, again, arises within a field that can be called your consciousness. It is born out of your desire, your expectations, your perceptions that have been built up and built up and built up. And one of those perceptions is indeed that you are within the body. But you are not.

Therefore, I come not to abide with the body, but I come forth to abide with that great ray of Light that you are, that shines forever beyond the body and beyond all worlds. It is to that great ray of Light that I speak and with that great ray of Light that I commune. And the process of awakening, the process of the atonement, is not just some mental gymnastics in which you try to exercise certain statements in which you say,

Well, good. I'm one with God. It doesn't quite feel that way but I'll believe it anyway. That is where it begins. But the atonement is indeed completed when the whole sense of identity that you carry is no longer in any way, shape or form limited to the space and volume of the body.

There isn't even a trace of identification with it save that you acknowledge that you have allowed it to arise within the field of the Light you are. And it serves no other purpose save to be a means by which you communicate the Light that you are into this plane of density and to this world of yours.

If this were not true, it would mean that you are not as God, our Holy Father, has created you to be. And I have said many times, in many ways, that God has but one creation — His holy and precious child; His Son, if you will; that which is the offspring of the Mind of God. And that which is an offspring of Light, that is made in the image of Light, can only be Light, filled with wisdom, filled with creativity, filled with . . . joy.

Therefore, I come forth in joy because joy is that in which I abide eternally, and I come forth to abide with you. Not the body that you think you are.

Not the body that you think you are in, but I come forth to abide with that great ray of Light that outshines all worlds and is forever one with me since before the foundation of all worlds.

And the miracle, the miracle that allows the atonement to be born on Earth — which means in the body — even as it is already completed in Heaven, the miracle that allows that is the simplicity of your willingness to set aside, constantly, everything about what you believe that you are, so that you can relearn the Truth.

And if I were to come to you and speak to you as though you were a body and if I were to acquiesce to your insistence that you are just this form, that you are just your hurts, that you are just your limitations, if I were to come and abide with that, there could be no such thing as a miracle. For it would mean that both of us have gotten caught up in the insanity of an illusion.

Joy II

Precious friends, I abide only with—and speak only to—the great ray of Light that you are, that outshines every limitation that you believe exists in and as your life. And it is to that ray of Light that I gently whisper:

> *Awaken. Awaken from sleep and put away the things of dreams. Put away fears and put away doubts, and begin instead to focus the whole of your attention on Light and on joy.*

And why?

If this world has been made in error—and I assure you that it has—and if the world is diametrically opposed to the Truth of the Kingdom of Heaven, it must then follow that the perceptions and beliefs that have made this world are indeed the opposite of a knowledge that you can find in the Kingdom of Heaven.

The world is made of fear. The world is made of limitation. That is the world that you have taken to be real and, therefore, have allowed it to dictate to you what choices you will make in your life: where you will live, the friends you will attract to yourself.

Every last aspect of your life has come forth out of the perception that you are a body, separate from everyone else, that you live in this world and that this world is real.

This world is constructed in separation, fear and guilt. Therefore, if you perceive it as the real world, you must then attract to yourself that which mirrors what you are insisting on believing in. And yet, I say, week in and week out: I come forth in joy to abide with you. Not with your illusions, not your dreams, but the real you, the real you that is filled with power and Light and goodness and love and capability and creativity; and you name it, you are it.

309

Jeshua ~ The Early Years

If you name it, you will be it. What you decree you become.

So, if I come forth in joy and I come forth from the Kingdom of Heaven, the Kingdom of Heaven itself must be a state, if you will—a quality, if you will—in which nothing can sneak in through the back door unless it is more joy. Does that make sense to you?

If a limited thought emerges and comes and sneaks into the Kingdom of Heaven, Heaven is no longer Heaven, so who would want to be there anyway? Not I. If there is a trace of shadow in the Kingdom of Heaven, it's no longer Heaven. If there is a doubt or feeling of psychological weakness, if that abides in Heaven, then it is beneath who you are and you might as well throw it away; it's no good to you.

The Kingdom of Heaven is a state and a quality of such joyousness that what takes place is that the Light that you are begins to vibrate at a higher and higher frequency until the things that arise in your world that seem to be limiting you don't even matter any longer. And that is extremely important, and that's what I want to speak with you about this evening.

If when what you would perceive as a limitation pops up in your life, rest assured it is coming forth to reveal to you that there is a shadow of perception, of thought, of feeling that is less than whole joyousness, if you will, that yet needs to be, shall we say, corrected within you.

Now, the mind, through its habits, will look at the limitation that arises and believe that the limitation is real and, therefore will, in a sense, step the vibration down to match the vibration of the limitation so that you can do battle with it. Do you know what that feels like? It is called "beating the head against a brick wall." Now, who is the builder? Who is the bricklayer? You are.

Joy II

Enlightenment, empowerment, whole joyousness, if you will, cannot begin until you are willing to accept total and complete responsibility for everything you see, everything you think, everything you say and everything you do—but, above all, everything you feel, because the causative factor of what you feel and what you perceive is never outside of you.

> *Well, surely that must be wrong. When the landlord raises the rent and I don't feel good, surely it is the act of the rent being raised that causes the feeling that I am having?*

That is what the world will teach you and what it would ask you to believe, but remember, the perceptions of the world are just the opposite of the Truth of the Kingdom.

Can you begin, then, to allow yourself to admit, to consider, that every feeling and every perception has no cause outside of you? Each time you believe that it does you have chosen, you have decreed like a judge with the gavel, you have judged that the world outside of you is real and contains a power over you. That choice occurs nowhere save within yourself, within the mind that you are, and it requires something quite fundamental: it requires that in that very moment you have set aside the remembrance of yourself as a great ray of Light. You have given back your God-given power and have chosen an illusion to be your authority.

So then, can you understand the great blessing of each moment? The Holy Spirit has already translated the world that has been brought forth in error, that you've gotten a little caught up with, into the very means whereby you can awaken from the dream of separation, re-identify with the Light that you are and, therefore, outshine everything that has represented the world to you. Every anger, every hurt, every fear, every limitation, every empty wallet; whatever it is, you can outshine it. You can actually change the whole picture because you are using your Light to create the world that you see and have believed in.

And what is the key that unlocks that? Joy.

Joy is not just a word. It is not just a temporary feeling. Joy is something that you have complete control over twenty-four hours a day. It is a vibration. It is a frequency. And if you were to go into one of your laboratories and say to one of your scientists,

> *Well, show me the frequency and color of sadness,*

you could guess that it might be dark gray. And the frequency of love carries a quality of, shall we say, pinks and light violets to it. The frequency of joy vibrates at a very high color, if you will, of vibrant, radiant golden light that you can't even really tell if it's gold or white.

It is a vibration. It is a frequency. It is a tangible reality. It is a real doodad, if you will, that floats with all the other doodads in this universe, and you can claim it as yours every time you choose to remember the Truth. You can choose to open up the body even and literally draw that joy down through the crown of the head. You can draw it up through the soles of the feet.

You can draw it in from the sides. It doesn't matter, that's just ritual. The point is, you are enacting your choice to remember the Truth that you were born in joy, that you were created in joy, that you are sustained in joy, that joy is who and what you are. And out of joy comes the power to do all things, manifest all things, impact all things, change all things, heal all things—and to dance through all things.

Joy. Joy is the key that unlocks the door. When you have indeed

Joy II

desired first the Kingdom; and when your intention has been unwavering; and when you have learned to master the key of allowing in which you learn to forgive the world, to forgive yourself, to trust all things that arise so that you can begin to look at them with new eyes and learn how you are the creator of all that you have experienced; as you rest then into the safety of surrender, the Holy Spirit comes by with a little golden key and says,

Here is what you have been looking for. I couldn't give it to you earlier because you were too busy running around in small circles in the mind. But now that the mind of the world has been set aside, I can speak to you clearly, and I deliver to you the key whereby you begin to translate the unhappy dream that you may have created, or aspects of it, into a happy dream.

A wholly happy dream in which perhaps relationships that have actually been what you would call in your language "dysfunctional" — quite an apt word, by the way — or harmful or limiting, you've finally learned that it's okay to set them aside, that it's okay for you to choose joy. It's okay for you to be happy. It's okay for you to be wealthy. It doesn't matter what it is. It's okay. And the key that unlocks it all is Joy.

So, all you have to do when next you are feeling a little down is sit here and say,

I am wholly joyous now.

Then open your eyes, and if everything's the same, you can rest assured that the key of joy doesn't work. Some do that. They make a meager attempt. They make it from a mind that has become depressed, a body filled with toxins that has become tight and depressed. They make it from the foundation of the perceptions of the world. They give a thought to joy. Nothing changes overnight.

> So, Jeshua must not know what he's talking about. And not only him but I understand there have been a lot of masters around that have talked about joy, and they have all been wrong because I just proved it.

If you have learned to not punch your joy button constantly, if it's at best become an intermittent thing, so that at times you choose to be joyous if the situation looks okay and other times decide to hold on to judgment and thoughts of limitation and lack— if you have learned to do it that way, must it not follow that to re-identify with yourself as joy will also require the process of learning?

We have talked about how the Holy Spirit translates the things of time into the very means by which you may awaken. Therefore, be thankful for the time that is given to you for it is the means by which you will relearn how to not only press, but to hold your joy button until it holds itself.

It is the means whereby the translation of an unhappy dream occurs so that a happy one replaces it. And as the dream becomes happy, what

happens? Something that everybody knows. Anytime you feel relatively happy, you relax. You expand. You open. You become more creative. You feel more in tune, more alive. The cells of the body sing. That's why everybody likes being happy.

The problem is that you have learned to believe that happiness is a conditional expression. That is, it depends on external circumstances.

I will be happy, when…

Joy II

And, of course, "when" never comes. And if it arrives, because you haven't learned how to be happy, you feel uncomfortable. And many of you know what that's like.

> *Now that I have what I have been seeking, I can't quite be happy yet.*

Why? Because you forgot to practice being happy.

Now, joy, then—and that is why we began last week with *feeling* joy—as you practice becoming the frequency of joy, something begins to happen. And all of you know this to some degree. It's just a matter of making it constant. When you choose to, shall we say, abide and to vibrate in the frequency of the Light of the joy that you are, no matter what is coming up around you, when you choose joy, when you draw the Light in through the toes, through the fingernails . . . it doesn't matter, just do it, let the body begin to vibrate. It will feel like the body is vibrating at any rate. Feel the Light, feel the joy . . . it actually begins to blow the cobwebs out, out of the cells of the body and out of the mind, the Mind in which you are already connected with me and with God and with every mind that has ever awakened. Every master that has ever been is no further than a phone call away from within your mind.
Many have said,

> *Gee, I have been trying but I just can't hear you, Jeshua. I just . . . meditation doesn't go well. What's going on?*

It's because there is static in the mind—like a cloudy day that blocks the sun.

> *The sun that truly shines, dwells within your heart — now. Not one thing separates you from your right and your power to choose to dwell in the joy that is the presence of the Light of the Son of*

God that dwells within your heart.

As you choose that frequency and vibration, miracles accelerate. The picture that you have created, called your life, begins to vibrate a little, you see, because it always responds to the frequency that you are living in. You could say that the world is your perfect servant, and it will always show you exactly where your frequency is.

As you choose that vibration, you could say that you begin to vibrate the molecules of matter. You begin to break up the old picture so that that which does not resonate with the frequency of joy that you are choosing to live within, those things begin to have a few earthquakes. And if you are willing to allow them, they will drop out of your life.

Now this is a big stumbling block, you see, because part of the mind is still attached to believing that its identity, its reality, is made up of the things outside of it; so that as you choose awakening, as you choose joy, all the little fears that you've been carrying begin to float to the surface and you have a choice to make. Love or fear? Ever heard that before?

The way is easy and without effort, and yet it takes you through the eye of the needle. The way *is* the way of love and love is the expression of joy— a joy that must spill over into every dimension of your experience until every dimension of it mirrors to you the happy dream of your constant union with God. And then the world itself fades away; you transcend the world.

There is a process to go through. It is a process that will take you from where you think you are to where you long to be. And the process requires that willingness *to trust love*, to trust love to carry you beyond every fear that has ever limited you and

Joy II

ever made you believe that you can only be who you are now.

Fear can arise when the things that you have constructed out of misperceptions, whether they be relationships, careers, whatever it is, if you have made it from the perspective of the ego rest assured its foundation is a house built on sand and it is going to crumble sooner or later. Your world, you see, is one in which you are taught to strive, to struggle, to feel anxiety, to try to keep your creations on solid ground.

You have many people, by the way, that are locked up in mental institutions for no other reason than they see through the game of the ego and they realize any such construction is made on a foundation of sand, so what's the point? And they don't want to participate. Unfortunately, your world isn't quite ready to go to them and teach them another way; and so they are caught in what is called hell.

Beloved friends, be of good courage:

> *When you have truly relinquished every attempt to make and control your world, fear will arise, rest assured. But it is just to show you where you've been living; and just beyond it is the peace that you seek.*

And each time you choose joy, no matter what, you, shall we say, pass an initiation would be one way to put it. You step to the next highest level and a strength begins to come into you, a strength that shall indeed become like a mighty river and the things of this world will not deter you from the path that would be set before you and that you would choose to walk.

The Holy Spirit requires enlightened and therefore empowered minds to join with It, with Him, in the translation of the whole of this world into a happy dream. Does it require strength?

Indeed, it does. Is it going to feel uncomfortable at times? Yes — to the degree that you try to hold on to old habits, whether they be habits of diet, habits of thought, habits of relationship, habits of career. If you believe those things are keeping you safe, you are going to go through quite a struggle because once you choose to awaken, that is like you have taken your finger out of the hole in the dam and the water begins to pour forth — first as trickle, but eventually the power and the force of that water of joy, of Truth and of Light will break down the dam completely. If you resist that, you are going to feel fearful and believe that everything is crumbling to dust; and it is. And yet, what crumbles is only an illusion, only something that has limited the holy Son of God.

If I walk with you, your way is certain and fear need not master you. And the situations that are presented to you in your life are there so that you can recognize what you are now, as a soul, choosing to overcome, to grow beyond. Stop trying to keep the things that limit you in place and give yourself wholly to the force of the water that is the joy of the soul that would break the dam down so that the river can flow. The river of creativity. The river of joy. The river of eternal life that flows from the Mind of God to and through the Son of God, to be demonstrated and spilled over into this world.

I can never make that choice for you. Never. I can only whisper to you. I can only come to you. I can only abide with you, the Truth in you. And I can tell you that it's safe. It's safe to let the false constructs dissolve from your mind. It is safe and it is necessary, and if you would receive it, contemplate what this means: it is *inevitable*.

I have said many times that freedom does not mean — free will does not mean — that you can choose whether or not to take a certain curriculum. You are only free to decide *when* you are

Joy II

going to take it. And the reluctance of the mind to truly take the course, live it and master it (the curriculum), is that part of the mind that wishes summer vacation could at least last a little bit longer. But all the time you think you are enjoying your summer vacation, you are not really getting anywhere, and it takes a resolve—desire and intention—in which, whatever it takes, you finally voice within yourself:

> *No, I'm not going to tolerate error in myself any longer under any circumstances. I am the holy Son of God, and joy is my birthright and my Kingdom and I am going to be that. And if it kills me, good.*

There is a strength in you, a strength you haven't even begun to touch, a strength that when embraced will indeed dismantle every limitation that you believed exists in your life. And the right use of that strength rests on your willingness and your determination to choose joy always.

You see, when you get in your automobile and you leave your humble abode, and you are about to go off to what you call a job… Hmm. Interesting concept. You are not going to a job at all.

You are only choosing to go to what you have chosen to construct out of the infinite freedom of the molecules of physicality. You are an artist and you have painted a picture for yourself to abide within. What you are really doing is getting into your automobile that is a temple, a temple in which you have ten minutes, twenty minutes, an hour, whatever it is that you've painted for yourself, in which to practice being the presence of joy. That's the curriculum. And it's presented to you in every moment.

Every moment that you step forward into is a precious and holy temple in which you have the opportunity to choose fear or love.

And you will know if you have chosen the door labeled "fear" because you might feel tired, sad, confused, depressed. And you will know if you have chosen the door marked "joy" that comes from choosing love because, you see, if you are in your automobile, if you are making breakfast, if you are paying bills, it doesn't matter what you are doing—it's not going to matter because it, itself, is part of the dream that is being translated, and it is your willingness to abide in joy that will allow you to heal every limited thought that you have ever had. And each limited thought has been made manifest as the nemesis of problems that come to your life. It's all the result of a lack of joy.

Can it be that simple? Yes, it is. Yes, it is.

Joy is an incredible thing. An incredible blessing. Every time you choose to be wholly joyous, rest assured you have decided not to identify with the ego. And remember, you are asked to do only one thing: to live as though you are not an ego. Every time a judgment slips through the mind and is projected onto someone,

Oops, I misidentified.

Take it back. Burn it up. Laugh and get on with joy.

Joy is like a light, like a fire that purifies the mind, that purifies the body. And why is that necessary?

Because your Father longs to have you join Him as a co-creator and an awakened, healed mind. Such a mind's creations are always loving, always expansive, always healing. The creations of an awakened mind seem to attract other minds to it like moths to a light bulb. And that is exactly what is

Joy II

happening.

Your Father longs to pour forth the fullness of His power and creativity through you. But if you've closed yourself off so tight that only a trickle comes through, just enough to keep the body alive, is there any wonder that there is lack mirrored to you in your life?

Now, some will say,

> I'm a pretty happy guy. I live in a high state of joy most of the time.

Notice the word "most." And understand that if there is anything in the world that you are still judging, still fearful of, still condemning, whether it be your monetary system, your government, your schools, your mass transit systems, garbage strikes— whatever it is, if you are judging it, you are blocking off the flow of joy that would transform the whole of your life.

I have said often to you: become wholly outrageous. And outrageousness requires ... joy. Joy! Has anybody dropped the bag off their shoulder underneath one of your lights at the intersection this week? [ref the previous gathering: Joy I]

[Laughter.]

Why not?

I didn't have the courage.

Beloved friend, when you can say to me, "I didn't have the bag..." Indeed.

What I am seeking to share with you is that the world you have dreamed into being — with all of its complexities, including the body — is really no big deal. It's quite harmless and holds no power over you. Each time you see something that seems to be a limitation, realize you are just looking at the boundary of your mind that you have chosen for yourself. Now, there is a great power in that because if you recognize the boundary of your mind but you know that what you really want is joy, you can choose to walk through that ring of fear, whatever it is. And just like stretching a muscle, the boundary expands. And as the boundary expands, more joy flows from the Mind of God through you. More creative ideas — and more responsibility.

Damn. I was hoping to get rid of that.

Do you see how the world would teach you to fantasize about winning a lottery so that you could be irresponsible? Isn't that true? So you won't have any "worries." *Worries are only the refusal to assume responsibility.* And yet, paradoxically when you join with me in being willing to assume responsibility for the atonement for the whole of creation — whew, now there is an eighty-hour-a-week job — paradoxically, your joy becomes full and you rest in what is eternal.

For when you have expanded the boundaries of your mind to allow joy to be the fountain in which you swim always, and when that deep part of the mind within you that is the Mind of Christ says,

> *All of creation is arising within me. This is my doing. Therefore, I'm going to heal it and I'm going to correct it and I assume responsibility for the whole of the world*

Joy II

Without jumping ahead to how you are going to take care of that—then the Father pours forth into you the power and the wisdom and the Light and the life to achieve your goal of healing the whole of creation and completing the atonement. First things first.

This temple, the body, is the means whereby it is given unto you to extend love; and love can only radiate from a mind that is wholly joyous. Now, you all know that when you are in the presence of somebody that is not wholly joyous, you are not quite as attracted to them. Isn't that true?

The body deserves your love. Not because it's your home but because it is your tool. And when you abide with only loving thoughts, you will find that such things as diet, all of those habits that you have, begin to naturally correct themselves. As you come to love the body by resting in the joy that is within you, you will indeed find miracles, for you will be attracted to new ways of being in and with the body itself. And that's a very important step, not one to be rationalized away by saying,

> *Well, all I need to do is zap myself with a little Light and nothing really hurts it.*

Are you sure?

If you are not sure, be honest with yourself and take steps to correct what you are putting into it. The body, this thing that starts here [pointing to head] and ends at your toes, is like a transmitter and receiver. As you choose to tune it up, it becomes capable of radiating higher frequencies of joy. As you choose the frequency of joy, the desire to tune up the tool naturally grows.

That's Step One. And Step Two is to realize that no one is

responsible for your thoughts save you. No one can change them. No one can heal them. No one is responsible for causing them but you. At first that seems to be a bit of a bummer because it means indeed accepting total responsibility, complete responsibility without an excuse, without claiming victimhood. And yet, claiming that responsibility is what empowers you. It empowers you to be willing, finally, to be able to choose to be wholly joyous.

And as you begin to tune into that frequency and you get a little bit of a shockwave going,

> *Whew, that was nice. Should I try it again? Oh, why not,*

and you open up and you say,

> *Father, I'm ready. Just pour it down through me.*

> *I dare You to overwhelm me.*

He'll try. He loves to try to do that. And then next the little shockwave goes,

> *Whoops. Well, that was nice, too, and I didn't even need another body to get it. I didn't need to go to the movies. I didn't need to win the lottery. What caused it?*

> *My God, I did. No causative factor outside my desire, my willingness, to feel joy.*

And the more and more and more that you tune to that frequency, you will find that your Father's cup overflows and never stops flowing.

Joy II

And every moment can become more joyful than the one before, and who cares what the circumstances are. As you tune into that frequency, the life that you have been living will begin to shift and change. Just remember that you are like a painter who takes a look at the color and says,

> *That's not quite right. I'm going to erase it.*

And a new color will come, and with that new color might be new friends, might be a new career. You might find yourself getting up at 3am for prayer and meditation. You might find a desire to discipline yourself just a little bit more.

> *Oh, God. Jeshua is talking about responsibility and discipline tonight. I knew I should have gone to the movies.*

[Laughter.]

Responsibility is what makes your joy full! Please remember that. Responsibility for the whole of creation is what will make your joy full.

Discipline? The terrible art of loving yourself. You have a statement regarding the improper use of some substances that seem to change the biochemistry of the body: drugs. The statement is "Just say no." Discipline is the art of loving yourself, truly loving yourself, and saying "no" when you can tell that to say "yes" will be to compromise your frequency of joy. Sounds simple, doesn't it? Rest assured, if you practice that simple little test of never saying "yes" to something that compromises your frequency of joy, you will be in for a surprise because what will be revealed to you is how many times in each day you do compromise your joy, know you that which is called "the rat-race?"

Know you that which feels like conflict? Like you keep trying to get out of it but your feet keep getting stuck more in it? It comes because, to some degree, you compromise your joy and then the soul within you becomes sad. And when you become sad, your frequency drops and you find yourself butting the head against the wall because you yet believe that that wall keeps you safe somehow. It stops you from growing. It stops you from becoming more. It stops you from stepping into the arenas you thought you could never perform well in. The brick wall is your limitation and it keeps you in hell, pure and simple. It keeps you from . . . Heaven. It keeps you from . . . the power to effectively deal, with complete responsibility.

Joy. For those of you that were with us last week, do you remember what that felt like last week? Joy. Did you practice evoking that in yourself in the week that followed? Or did you only think of it as a memory and go,

Well, that was nice. I hope we can do that again.

Ah. Hmm. Do you see how that pattern in the mind is the very pattern that must become disciplined? If you truly loved yourself, your desire to drink in joy would become constant and primary, and you simply would not tolerate in yourself any willingness to make any other choice, no matter what. Talk about an addictive drug. Don't say "no" to it, say "yes" . . . say "yes."

I want you so badly to come to where I am. I want you so badly to give up your dreams of suffering and pain and lack. I want you so much to realize the Love the Father has for you, that is poured forth and shaken down around you so thoroughly that you can't even comprehend it. The mind could never

Joy II

comprehend the Love of God—but the heart can become an open valve through which it can flow.

Your life is worthy of reconstruction if that is what you desire. And I say this unto you, and those of you that have perhaps studied my *Course in Miracles*, rest assured that if you are truly getting it, if the atonement is beginning to stir within you, you are going to eventually have to come to face the fact that peace isn't just mental gymnastics. The healing of the mind must necessarily affect the healing of how you are in the world, that changes how you are in the world; it must. And if that is occurring within you, certain things that you may have constructed in your life are going to start to feel like a prison to you.

Now, what happens is that the mind says,

Well, it's reality so I'll conform myself to it,

instead of letting your joy and your peace and your love burst the walls of it, so that you can grow into something higher, more radiant; so that more and more Light can be entrusted to you to flow through you.

In short, what I am talking about here is, don't fool yourself. Don't rationalize it away. Face it head on and admit it. If there is some aspect of your life that is not working, get straight with yourself. Nobody is doing it but you. And all around you is the power to effect change, because the power is within you.

What is one of the simplest ways of knowing whether or not you are allowing yourself to flow with joy, your heart's desires—not the ego's desires—the heart's desires?

If you feel frustration or limitation in any aspect of your life, it means that there is something yet within your perceptions that you have been fearful of turning to look at head on. And until you do so, you will never heal it. Never.

The same limitation will be made manifest to you in another thousand lifetimes. That's just the way it is.

Of course, the mind says,

Who thought up this game? That doesn't sound like fun to me. Can't there be another way out?

No, *you* created the game. You are the Milton Bradleys of creation. Life is one great big Monopoly game. You designed it. You bought and constructed the house in which you live, and that house is your mind. And its foundation is the amount of joy you are willing to open yourself up to and the degree to which you are willing to let that joy pour forth through your life to burst out through the limitations that you might experience — until your joy so far outshines the world that finally the perception is healed. The light goes on and you realize,

Wait a minute. This Monopoly game can't contain my Light.

And you will put away every last trace of need to try to conform yourself to the physical world And then you will come to where I am and abide in the unlimitedness given unto you in the very moment that our Holy Father thought you into being, as a perfect image of Himself.

Become unlimited. Choose to become powerful and it will look differently to everybody.

It doesn't mean that you are all going to become billionaires

Joy II

and run for President on the Independent Party ticket. But it does mean that you'll get straight with yourself and realize that there is some friction causing unhappiness in your life. Then you know there is a limit there, a limitation. You will turn and face it head on and declare that you are no longer willing to tolerate it because it does not befit the holy Son of God.

Honesty begets responsibility. The choice of responsibility begets discipline, and discipline begets the return to joy. And joy completes the atonement in you. Indeed.

So I hope that in this brief hour so far I have perhaps been able to shed light on a few things, to give you a few thoughts to chew upon.

I mean what I said when I said that my way is easy and without effort. The willingness to live an unlimited life filled with power and grace and beauty and creativity and effectiveness, the willingness to learn, to change whatever habits of perception and thought and behavior you are carrying that are limiting you — the choice to live that kind of life really doesn't require any effort.

What requires effort is the resistance to that life because it is a resistance to the overwhelming river of joy that longs to pour forth through you, to rebirth you. Being in the world is what takes effort. The mind has simply gotten it confused.

So, cut loose and go for it. Cut loose and be willing to use each day to face your limitations head on — to love them, to embrace them and to transcend them. And you will know when you have transcended them because they won't emerge any longer; a simple law of creation.

And remember, it's a law written on a card resting on a

Monopoly board that you created in your office and that you have sold to yourself— you've made up all the rules. Even the rules of mastery, and the mind has conveniently laid them aside.

I call you this evening to join with me in, shall we say, a bit of a new direction in our time together. I call you to join with me in learning how to express the mastery that you are. All that has transpired and all that we've done to this point is to shake things up a bit and find out who really wants to get on with it.

While I extend my love to everyone, I cannot force myself on any mind and I cannot give what gifts I would bring to anybody who chooses not to put them into action. And if you happen to have some friends who love to talk about unlimitedness and mastery, ask them if they are really ready for it.

For what we are going to begin in this evening is, if you will, a progressive experience of bringing mastery into manifestation. But it will require your diligence and your complete commitment.

It will require that you support one another and love one another. It will require that you set aside the whole of the world wherever you happen to be and choose joy.

So, right now, in your own way go inside your own heart. Let the body relax and just breathe into the heart, and when you are ready, ask yourself with complete honesty,

Am I really willing to take the curriculum, now?

And if as you seek to answer that question you see fears come

Joy II

up, you see questions come up that say,

> *Well, if I could only look ahead I might be able to make a decision,* rest assured that part of you really isn't quite ready.

And that's okay.

The atonement requires finders and not seekers. The healing of mankind requires finders and not seekers. It requires masters.

Not those who say, Well, gee, I'd like to master it all, but, gosh, I have so many other things to do. Those other things are there because you have resisted your own mastery to some degree and in some way.

To borrow a phrase that recently came into the mind of my beloved brother: *When you are willing to learn what you know you don't yet know, mastery is only a blink away.*

Interesting thought, don't you think?

And take it another step further: when you are willing to learn what you couldn't even possibly learn that you don't know . . . that is called willingness.

Now in your language that sounds a little funny, but the same thing was posed to me by the one who was my father. He put his hand on my shoulder and said.

> *Son, you've picked an interesting one. Quite a drama that you*

scripted.

And I looked at him and said,

What are you talking about?

And he said,

> *Oh, I think you'll discover what I'm talking about.*
> *All in good time.*

And in his own way he asked me the same question,

> *Are you willing to admit that there just might be something that you don't know and you don't even know that you don't know it? Are you willing to learn?*

And something in me, God only knows what, said,

Yes I am.

And that made all the difference in my own life and the completion of the atonement within me. And I like to think it's made some difference in the world. Just as your choice will make all the difference in the completion of your own atonement and, therefore, will also make a difference in the world. Hmm. Well, that was fun. How are you all doing?

Fine. Great.

Has any of this made a bit of sense?

Yes.

Look around you for a moment . . . fellow travelers, desirous of

Joy II

mastering the only curriculum that needs to be learned. There are many ways to approach it, but until you accept that- to learn that curriculum *must mean that the structure of your life around you becomes wholly and radically changed*—and that will mean something different to each of you even now—you really haven't quite yet been willing to learn the curriculum, no matter how many texts you've read. No matter how many verses you've memorized.

No matter how many prayers you've said. Some part of you has not quite been willing to become vulnerable. And yes, I would tell the Pope the same thing. Hmm.

Jeshua, how do you make yourself vulnerable?
How do you make yourself vulnerable?

Choosing joy?

But remember, Firewalker, it's not just thought. It is a feeling of power that literally wells up, vibrates the cells of the body so you can't contain it. It's not quite the same thing as what you experience as ecstatic happiness that seems to take you to a crescendo and then you're burned out afterward. That's not quite what I am talking about. This joy is a frequency that you can feel vibrating, and it can become constant and you can learn to master it so that you walk around, albeit a few inches off the ground, and you'll find that you will be able to function even in that frequency. Certain things begin to emerge within that frequency. Your ability, for instance, to be in this world and yet be totally with me, in total communication with me or any master you want to be, becomes available—no separation between you and myself whatsoever. The ability to tune in to see how your friends are doing on the other side of the planet and to know what they are doing—all becomes very natural.

Where to go, who to talk to; it all becomes an effortless flow.

Joy is like a fire and a frequency that burns off all of the cobwebs, gets rid of all of the static, clarifies the Mind of Christ. And if you don't feel it down to the cells of your body, you don't know yet what it is.

Does that help a little bit?

It helps... So at first the idea comes to the mind, "I choose joy" or "I choose to come from Love." But the body isn't healing yet, or whatever is going on is a heaviness. My mind will actually makes that statement, "I and my Father are one." Then, what's the next step after the statement is made? The desire is there but the body is feeling heavy, whatever the reason.

What is the reason?

The only thing I can think of is because I don't want it. For some reason I don't want it and I'm blocking it. I am scared of it at some level.

And that's what I was talking about earlier. That fear gets projected outside of yourself. You become fragmented, thinking the thing you fear is something outside of you. The fear is what is within you.

The next step beyond the words—and I've given you many, many cues—is to become outrageous; play and sing and dance. Get a new motion going in the body. Get a little crazy. Do things you've never done before. Interrupt the patterns of the mind. Ask the Holy Father to overwhelm you. It is fine and well and good to begin by saying,

I and my Father are one. Isn't that a great thought? But I'm

Joy II

depressed.

Now the next stage, Firewalker, is to learn to find ways to evoke joy even in the body. You know some ways, but I am talking about some others here in which you truly begin to create a frequency, and we are going to do a little bit of that in a few moments. But it must be felt. It must get to the point where you can turn the frequency on, no matter what.

Know you that which is Reiki or the hands-on healing? It's just a dimension of letting some rays of joy enter the field of another's mind. They think it's entering their body. It just enters the mind. The body follows suit.

You've already allowed it to enter the field of the mind, but you are keeping the trapdoor closed if it doesn't pour forth into the cells of the body. Eventually, no matter what, you can turn it on and you won't turn it off.

That's the next stage. And there is indeed, as you well know, a part of you that's a little reluctant to be overwhelmed with joy. A part of you yet carries the sadness that you unwittingly yet identify with. Not as much as in the past. It's lessening, but it's there. And so, when you speak joyous words,

I and my Father are one. I choose love and not fear,

it's almost like you tune into it up here [pointing to head] but there is a heaviness down here [pointing to heart] and there seems to be a gap between the two. What we are talking about now is really being willing to close that gap. To erase what is down here that blocks that downward descent of joy. Indeed.

So, Firewalker, are you ready to give it a shot?

Ready to go for it.

Fine. Come here. [The man comes in front of Jeshua.] Why did you get out of your chair so slowly?

I have a sore back.

Ah. Now, what I want you to do is clap your hands three times as loudly as you can. [He claps.]

Get into it.

Now, pick what an old friend of mine would call a goddess. Pick a goddess.

Now, dance. Get into it. Let's go.

I'm not a dancer. Yes, you are. That's a perception. [Addressing the others] Clap for them. Let's go. Come on.

[The group claps, and the two dance in the front of the room.] Shout your joy, Firewalker. I don't hear you. Shout your joy. Joy! Joy! Joy! Yes. Yes. [Clapping, dancing and shouting continue.]

Okay, all right. Now, thank your goddess.

Thank you, goddess.

You are welcome.
Now Firewalker, how did that feel?

A little spooky at first. A little fear came up. "Am I doing it

Joy II

right?"

Ah.

And then I got more response from people I felt saying "yes" with me in joy. It felt better and more at one with the group.
In other words, you felt safer.

I felt safer, yes. That's a good way to put it.

Yes, it is a good way to put it. Now, listen. When I first asked you to dance, what did you say?

In my mind? I don't know.
Give him a moment here.

What?

I am asking them to give you a moment so that you can just rest and ask yourself to look back to that moment, and what statement did you make?

To myself I said, "No", or something like that. Some block came up. An embarrassment or something.

What did he say?

"I am not a dancer."

You said, "I am not a dancer."

Did I say that?

Oh my goodness where did that come from! That is what you

said.

I didn't even know I said that.

Now, this is very, very, very important, and once again this man, Firewalker, has earned his nickname. Firewalker, do you see how I created a set of circumstances that evoked an old perception that expressed itself for this moment in the statement, "I am not a dancer?" What the Son decrees is. You see, I pulled a little bit of a fast one on you. You didn't know what was coming so you couldn't prepare, and the Truth came up: the perception you hold, "I am not a dancer."

Now, dancing isn't just a god and a goddess shaking their bags of dust around. Dancing is what life requires, you see. When you say, "I am not a dancer," it doesn't have anything to do with how you move your feet and all of that. Nobody is holding a placard with the little numbers up on them. Besides, God has a placard and He always gives you a ten. Do you see what I am saying here?

I do.

It means that that perception, that's the sadness inside. For you, Firewalker, have carried that belief, "I am not a dancer." And you are a dancer. You just proved it. I thought he did rather well.

Yes. [Clapping.]

Indeed. Now, the dancing goddess. Did you enjoy it?
I fell a little self-conscious at first, but I got over it.

Exactly. Could you feel how his energy state changed? That is,

Joy II

as *he* began to get into it, you also began to get into it.

Yes, it helped me.

Ah, there's the key. Firewalker, you just extended love. You chose to begin to set aside a perception that said, "I am not a dancer," and yes, it required the support of those who love you to give you the safety to begin to relearn a different perception of yourself, and as you extended that out, your frequency raised and it affected the frequency of the goddess. That's how love is extended, and that is what brings healing to the world. Do you see?

Yes.

Firewalker, are you willing to become a dancer?
Very much so.

Ah. It wasn't so bad, was it? Now, I know some of you are going,

> *Boy, I'm glad he didn't pick on me.*

[Laughter.]

When you can't wait to get picked on, the end of the journey comes much more quickly.

What I want to give unto you — now I'm not necessarily done for the evening here, but I want to give unto you what you might call a bit of homework.

Contemplate what just took place with Firewalker, and allow yourself freedom, total safety, imagine that this group of friends is with you all week long. Imagine yourself to rest in that safety just like Firewalker did, and let yourself take a look within at the ways in your own life at which you might be making the same statement to yourself, the ways in any given day in which you refuse to be a dancer: the things that seem to evoke fear, that depress you and conform you and close your Light down. Allow yourself just to look at them. Not to make a judgment, that's not what it's about. The Holy Son of God is far beyond judgment. But just look at it, and then choose one of those ways—and you'll find more than just one that will pop up.

Within the next weeks' time create a situation that seems to evoke that, and make a different choice. Find a way to become a dancer in that circumstance. It doesn't mean that you have to necessarily stand at a street corner and dance—although that's a good one. Become creative at looking at your life. It may be the way in which you try to communicate to your spouse. It may be the way in which you refuse to take care of yourself. And find a way to dance, a way that evokes the feeling of,

Yes, this is rather nice. I'm loving myself.

Because that is what Firewalker really just did. He loved himself enough to dance. He said,

The heck with the perception that seems to block me. I am going to dance.

And the day will come, you see, when Firewalker dances all the time and he won't really care if we are all around to support him in safety. He'll dance no matter what the world says. And that is mastery and freedom.

So, fair enough? Do you understand the assignment? Does it

Joy II

make sense to everyone?

Yes.

Indeed. So, Firewalker?

Yes?

Thank you.

Thank you for all your love and your teaching and your support.

Teaching and love and support are totally meaningless unless someone receives it.

It is received.
Thank you, I know. Indeed.

Ah. So, you see, we are going to be having some assignments as we go down the path. Some will seem to challenge you as you've never been challenged before—but not until you are ready for them. That's all you need to do this week: become willing to look at the ways in your own life that you are refusing to dance and find a way to make a different choice.

It could be as simple as how you feel when you walk in the door of your place of employment. You might choose to skip through the door, kiss your little time card, smile at the supervisor and say,

What an incredible day.

It may be something that simple, but you begin to interrupt what has become a chronic and unwitting and unaware pattern in the mind, because that unaware pattern is what has been telling you that the world out there is really real. And it's not. It's an illusion—it's all done with mirrors.

[Personal dialogue here – excluded in this transcript.]

So. I indeed love you, and in you is the worthiness of the holy Son of God to choose anew, to choose empowerment, to choose awakening—to find the small and little ways, that perhaps seem big, in which you are yet blocking that Light from flowing through your life. Will it feel like dying? Oh, yes. Thank God for that. Death is the most incredibly beautiful creation you have ever come up with. The death of the ego. The death of the small self. The death of all illusion. Oh, my God, what a beautiful and glorious sight. So go ahead and die a little this week that the joy in you might become full and the life in you might shine forth, and that life and that Light will be the means by which the atonement is completed on Earth as it is in Heaven.

Be at peace in all things, and know . . . it's not serious. Sing, laugh, dance, play. Indeed.

Peace be unto you.

Amen.

The End

WayofMasteryBooks.com
Book Catalog

All New releases will be announced on the website,
as well as access to Kindle/ eReader versions and special
audio offerings

IN BOOKSTORES

The Way *of* Heart

The Christ Mind Trilogy
Volume I

The Way of the Heart is the first of *The Christ Mind Trilogy* teachings, the core, formal, lessons of *The Way of Mastery* Pathway.

The lessons here are ones that Jeshua Himself was given in His lifetime, and subjects include the nature and meaning of reality, the power of forgiveness, purified desire as alignment to the Will of God, the four "Keys to the Kingdom," and much more.

The Way of the Heart teachings and experiential learnings provides the firm and essential foundation for all of that which follows in *The Christ Mind Trilogy*. It is a key aspect of Jeshua's Pathway of Enlightenment, and His Promise to us to help us awaken from the illusion that we have ever been separate from God, and to remember the deepest Truth of who we are: Christ.

ISBN 978-1-941489-41-3
Available in Paperback, Hardcover, Kindle, eReader & Audiobook

The Way *of* Transformation
The Christ Mind Trilogy
Volume II

The *Way of Transformation* is the second of The *Christ Mind Trilogy* teachings, or the 'Way of' Lessons. These were originally recorded as live channelings of Jeshua, and later transcribed. Together, the trilogy forms an in-depth three year Course in *The Way of Mastery* devoted to healing the illusions that bind us beyond mere 're-training' of the mind. It is meant to be read and studied only after the student has completed *The Way of the Heart* text and lessons.

Hear what Jeshua says of it:

"The Way of Transformation absolutely requires that you be committed to living differently. For is not transformation a change from the status quo? How can you experience transformation if you do not use time to think and be differently? Crying out to me will not do it. Reading a thousand holy books will not do it. One thing, and one thing only, will bring you into the transformation that you have sought — the willingness to abide where you are, differently."

The *Way of Transformation* teachings and experiential learnings provide the firm and critical foundation for *The Way of Knowing*, the final part of *The Christ Mind Trilogy*.

ISBN 978-1-941489-42-0
Available in Paperback, Hardcover, Kindle, eReader & Audiobook

IN BOOKSTORES

The Way *of* Knowing
The Christ Mind Trilogy
Volume III

The Way of Knowing is the third and final teaching of *The Christ Mind Trilogy*, a Course originally recorded as live channelings of Jeshua over a three year period, and foundational to the larger Way of Mastery Pathway. It is meant to be read and studied only after the student has completed *The Way of the Heart* and *The Way of Transformation* texts and lessons. In Jeshua's own words:

"In *The Way of Knowing*, the *final surrender* is entered — that surrender which is beyond the comprehension of all the languages and theologies of your world, beyond all that can be spoken or uttered, yet not what can be *known, felt, realized, and lived!*"

Here, He unequivocally tells us that what we consider as 'knowledge' is a pale substitute for the mystical transfiguration the Christ Path is truly devoted to:

"Knowledge is a knowing by being that which is known."

Following the completion of the *Christ Mind Trilogy*, Jeshua begins the astounding restoration of His original Aramaic Teachings, notably the Lords Prayer and Beatitudes, along with a one year online Course for the maturing student called *Jewels of the Christ Mind*.

ISBN 978-1-941489-43-7
Available in Paperback, Hardcover, Kindle, eReader & Audiobook

IN BOOKSTORES

The Jeshua Letters
A Remarkable Encounter with Christ

In July 1987, Jesus (Jeshua) appeared out of a field of light, fully formed, to his chosen channel and scribe Jayem. Over a period of nearly two years Jeshua appeared many times and gave 'dictation', which Jayem recorded, and which became the earliest parts of *The Way of Mastery Pathway*. Eventually Jeshua asked that these be published, and they, along with Jayem's personal reflections on how all this unfolded, make up *The Jeshua Letters*.

The Jeshua Letters is the start of an astounding body of work given by Jeshua which restore the essential truths of His original teachings, previously 'lost in translation' in their passage from Aramaic to English. Jeshua's 'Letters' are simple, profound and practical. His voice is certain but always gentle; inviting, never demanding. To read them is know beyond doubt - to know palpably - that Truth is being expressed.

ISBN 978-1-941489-45-1 • *Available in Paperback, Hardcover, Kindle, eReader*

IN BOOKSTORES

The Way of the Servant

The Way of the Servant is the second text dictated by Jeshua and scribed by Jayem in *The Way of Mastery Pathway*, following The Jeshua Letters.

Jeshua oftens speaks of "beginning at the end", and here He does so, showing us nothing less than how the Pathway flowers as the highest pinnacle of Consciousness (fully realized Christ Mind) that can be known in this world: *true servantship*, devoted to the realization of Humanity's highest evolution or, the 'coming of heaven to earth'.

Short, succinct, of extraordinary mystical depth, countless Pathway students find that immersing in *Way of the Servant* every year reveals depths and brings illuminations they were incapable of truly comprehending before!

ISBN 978-1-941489-44-4 • *Available in Paperback, Hardcover, Kindle, eReader*

IN BOOKSTORES

The Early Years
Volume I
Now, We Begin

The Early Years (volumes I & II) are transcriptions of gatherings recorded live as Jeshua taught us all. The wisdom, guidance, and sheer brilliance of them is astounding; there is so much in these pages, dear reader, that will help you grow in understanding, support you to truly heal into peace, and more!

Volume one includes the talks below:
- Awakening
- Choose to See
- Death Earth Changes
- Decide to be Christ
- Grace as Reality
- Healing
- Heaven on Earth
- Ignorance is Bliss
- Joy I
- Joy II

ISBN 978-1-941489-46-8 • *Available in Paperback, Hardcover, Kindle, eReader*

IN BOOKSTORES

The Early Years
Volume II
Now, We Begin

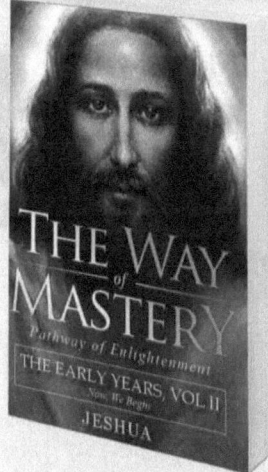

The Early Years (volumes I & II) are transcriptions of gatherings recorded live as Jeshua taught us all. The wisdom, guidance, and sheer brilliance of them is astounding; there is so much in these pages, dear reader, that will help you grow in understanding, support you to truly heal into peace, and more!

Volume two includes the talks below:
- Mastering Communication
- The Blessing of Forgiveness
- The Divine Feminine
- The Holy Instant
- The Holy Spirit
- The Light that You are
- Walk with Me
- Love Heals All Things
- The Meaning of Ascension
- Teach Only Love
- The Heart of Freedom
- The Master of Time

ISBN 978-1-941489-47-5 • *Available in Paperback, Hardcover, Kindle, eReader*

COMING SOON

Darshan

Over a period of 3 years, originally in live group video recordings, Jayem offered for the first time an in depth immersion into each lesson of The Way of Mastery Christ Mind Trilogy. He reveals the rich beauty and practical wisdom of the Teachings and shares transforming insights into their timeless Lessons, garnered from his own studentship of them for over some 25 years.

This is a remarkable and vast treasure trove of material, and we anticipate 6-8 volumes as we transcribe over 178 hours of audio into written form.

COMING SOON

The Later Years

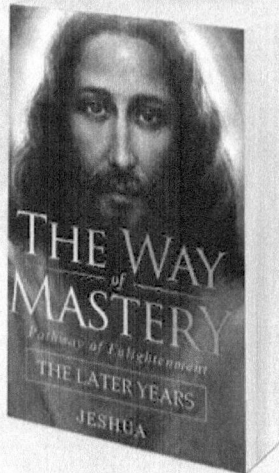

While Jeshua guided Jayem deeply into the Aramaic Teachings and their application to the students transformation, He ceased public channelings. Then, in 2010 He abruptly stated it was to begin again at a Pathway gathering in England, where He announced the 'Turning of the Ages'.

Also, gathered here, are some of the promised messages from other Teachers of the Lineage, notably Mary Magdalene and Elijah.

COMING SOON

The Living Practices
The Alchemy of Living from The True Heart

Well beyond the *Christ Mind Trilogy*, Jeshua –over a several year period – revealed the profound methods of healing the roots of Separation while cultivating the ground of mystical consciousness, and restored His original teachings utilized by the Essenes, as given in the Beatitudes and Lords Prayer. Principally, these are LovesBreath and Radical Inquiry. Here, find a rich and practical treasure trove of genuine transformative practices meant to also be utterly practical in our daily lives.

COMING SOON

The Christ Mind Trilogy
Spanish Edition

T he Christ Mind Trilogy in 3 volumes will be published in Spanish and we are anticipating a 4th quarter release date. Keep an eye out at WayofMasteryBooks.Com for updated release dates on all our upcoming additions.

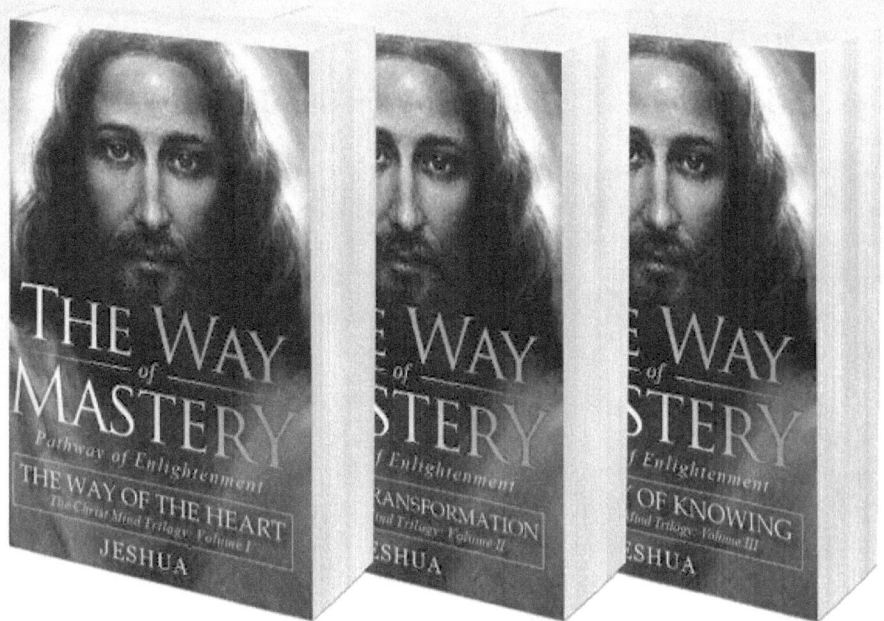

COMPLIMENTARY READING

The Essene Gospel of Peace

For the first time the complete 4 books of the Essene Gospel of Peace are available in one volume.

- The Essene Gospel of Peace
- The Unknown Book of the Essenes
- Lost Scrolls of the Essene Brotherhood
- The Teachings of the Elect.

The Essene Gospel of Peace were found in the Vatican Library and translated by Edmond Bordeaux Szekely

Edmond Bordeaux Szekely, grandson of Alexandre Szekely, eminent poet and Unitarian Bishop of Cluj, is a descendant of Csoma de Koros, Transylvanian traveler and philologist who, over 150 years ago, compiled the first grammar of the Tibetan language, the first English-Tibetan dictionary, and wrote his unsurpassed work, Asiatic Researches. He was also Librarian to the Royal Asiatic Society in India. Dr. Bordeaux earned his Ph. D. degree from the University of Paris, and other degrees from the Universities of Vienna and Leipzig. He also held professorships of Philosophy and Experimental Psychology at the University of Cluj. A well-known philologist in Sanscrit, Aramaic, Greek and Latin, Dr. Bordeaux spoke ten modern languages.

In 1928, he founded the International Biogenic Society with Nobel Prize-winning author, Romain Rolland. His most important translations, in addition to selected texts from the Dead Sea Scrolls and the Essene Gospel of Peace over a million copies in 26 languages are selected texts from the Zend Avesta and from pre Columbian codices of ancient Mexico. His last works on the Essene Way of Biogenic Living have attracted worldwide interest. He is the author of more than 80 books published in many countries on philosophy and ancient cultures.

ISBN 978-1-941489-40-6 • *308 pages, Paperback*

www.ingramcontent.com/pod-product-compliance
Lightning Source LLC
Chambersburg PA
CBHW020048170426
43199CB00009B/207